With John Barrymore, 1925

With Mother and Daddy
on the farm, 1914

First recital

Movie star

☆

My Story:

an Autobiography

☆

My Story:
an Autobiography

by Mary Astor

1959

Doubleday & Company, Inc., Garden City, New York

I want especially to thank
Frank Carothers for his labors
on my behalf in organizing
and editing the original manuscript
of this autobiographical analysis.

Library of Congress Catalog Card Number 59–6265

For my mother and father
with love
because I understand them now

☆

My Story:
an Autobiography

Prologue

People have often said to me, "You haven't changed a bit!" They meant it as a compliment, but I could hear it only as an accusation, a statement of brutal fact.

And I have thought bitterly, "You are so right!" For I knew that if I had not changed I had not grown. To be a perennial child, an ethereal Peter Pan playing with pirates and Indians throughout all eternity, can be a lovely thing in the never-never land of fantasy, but it is an unhappy thing in life. The child is born so that he may become a man. It is his destiny to grow—to learn, to understand, to assume responsibilities. Growth can be painful, I know; but I have found that a stunted and retarded growth can be a pain beyond belief.

My father often used to rebuke me by saying, "You're almost nine years old" (and then "ten," and then "eleven," and "twelve") "and you haven't learned a thing!" Well, here I was, *fifty* years old, and I still hadn't learned a thing! My father's rebuke had always seemed to imply a promise that years, the very accumulation of years, would bring experience and understanding. So, at

whatever age I was, I wished I were older. At seventeen I longed
to be twenty-five. At twenty I wanted to be a woman of the world
of thirty. At thirty I read that the French thought a woman did
not reach a full maturity of beauty and attractiveness until she
was forty. Finally, at forty-five, I decided that the whole thing was
a pack of lies. Where was the "serenity" that the years were to
bring? Where was "the cooling of passion's blood?" I realized that
I, who leaned on so many people and things, had been leaning
even on the abstraction of time.

I was still refusing to grow up, to face the oppressive fact that
I should long since have become a responsible, mature adult. I
continued to seek people and things I could lean on, to escape
the need for making my own decisions and assuming responsibility for my own acts. One event above all others should have
brought me to a full realization of my responsibility and dignity
as an individual, but even in that I failed. My conversion to the
Catholic Church was almost purely emotional. I felt, instinctively, that I had finally found something substantial to lean on,
never realizing that it is the Church above all else that demands
a stern and courageous individuality. So my conversion did not
turn out to be the conventional "conversion story" where the
sinner is baptized and lives happily ever after. I leaned, and I
fell. It is true, the Church would repeatedly pick me up and dust
me off after each fall. She would dry my tears and heal my wounds
and comfort me. Then she would gently say, "Go! Walk alone,
with God." But I couldn't walk alone.

So I went on, blindly and childishly, never learning from my
past mistakes. I have always found the world surprisingly com-
passionate about mistakes. People may laugh a little, but it is a
good-natured laugh that says, "All right, that was a bad one. But
come on now—let's go on about our business." And that, I
suppose, is simply because everyone makes mistakes and most
people learn to profit from them.

But years alone will not bring maturity. Maturity can come
only with a normal pattern of learning and true growth. I had
never been permitted to grow. Too early I became a very valuable

piece of property to my parents, closely guarded, closely watched. I was not permitted to make decisions, therefore I could not learn *how* to make decisions. I was not permitted to make mistakes, for mistakes could be too costly to my parents. I was *told* that the stove was hot and that I should burn myself if I touched it. I achieved none of the growth that would have come from making my own small mistakes—making them and learning not to make them again, learning from the small mistake to see the larger and avoid it. No imprisonment could have been more thorough and more stultifying. The nun cloistered in a convent is trained in character, brought to growth toward sanctity. The closely guarded young girl of European countries is trained for womanhood and marriage. For me there was no goal—except tomorrow's movie job. I escaped—the desperate flight of a child into an unmapped and unknown adult world. And I rushed headlong into nothing but trouble!

And I was still a child, saying over and over, "I want, I want, I want." The child's "I want" can never be satisfied. The adult's "I need" can be. I did not know the difference.

The New York television show was over. The long, tedious days of rehearsal—the aching feet and shortened tempers—the mounting tension—the countless changes of costume—the unending effort to hang onto a kernel of sanity, to keep from screaming at the drone of the director's voice over the talk-back, and at the constant movement and confusion of the big dusty stage hot with lights but drafty and chilly off the sets—the maddening demand for concentration, in all that bedlam, about positions (to the very inch) to be remembered so well they could almost be forgotten so there would be room for "acting"—and above all in this piercing tautness the desperate need to appear pleasant and energetic and enthusiastic and excited—this had all led to the one precious moment: the second that the red light went off on the last camera of the last scene, and the floor manager with his lopsided earphone waved the script as the blessed signal of "released."

A few more moments of quiet, while the sponsors had their

say and the credits were unrolled and the show theme crashed to a finale, and then all hell broke loose. I was being kissed and hugged. Everybody was congratulating everybody on "a great show." The booth opened to disgorge heads of the studio and sponsors and wives, and finally the weary director and his aides. I felt a warm content to see his forefinger and thumb curled in a sign of "okay" and a look on his face that showed he meant it. That was what I had worked for. Not the money—that was something nice and necessary that happened—but for the director's approval. I had been a good girl; I had done what he expected me to do, and he wouldn't scold me.

From my window seat in the big airliner I watched one of the great sights of the world—New York from the air at night. Below it was clear, but up here the clouds tore themselves to shreds around the plane, then with a little lurch we would be greyed out for a moment, emerging to look over the edge at the city again, like looking over the edge of a mountain into a great lighted valley. For a while I was lost in this glowing beauty, but I could not for long forget that those gently mist-shrouded lights masked dark and noisy canyons, dirty streets, faces strained with dissatisfaction and impatience. I fought against the persistent memory of the pain of being alone and uncertain on those streets among those faces.

A sound from the seat in front of me brought me back to the semi-darkness of the plane. A woman was crying, her face pressed against the window to get a last hungry glimpse of the disappearing city. She didn't want to leave; she'd said good-by to someone. My own eyes smarted a bit, but in self-pity rather than in sympathy. "Dear lady," I thought, "you should be happy. You have someone to leave, someone to be separated from. The person *exists*. That is a pleasant kind of pain compared with mine."

But I wasn't ready quite yet to acknowledge the presence of my pain. It would have to wait for a little while—a little while and then I would be ready for it. I walked up forward, where the stewardess was breaking out the liquor cabinet. We discussed altitudes and day flights and night flights and the TV show of mine, which she had seen, and then she asked me what she could bring me to drink. I hesitated, as though deciding whether I even wanted a drink, and then said casually, "Scotch and water, I guess." I had a pint of scotch in my toilet case, and I did not intend to mix my drinks.

My drinks. The show was over; the stern discipline could end. And I was out of sight of the prying eyes that watch and exaggerate: "You know, she was *loaded!*" after a third drink or a slurred phrase. I still felt tense down to my toenails; my shoulders and neck ached from the tension, from the week of unmerciful pressure, and from the mask I dared not remove.

I settled back with the drink and a book, but I gave up on the book almost at once. The pages blurred; the show crowded everything else from my mind. "I wonder if Paula moved 'up' on me intentionally—but she's too good a comedian not to know I had the feed line—poor George, hating to throw the champagne in my face—almost missed, too—oh, forget it, forget it, the show's over—at least it puts the bank balance over a thousand again— now you're just another actor out of work—you can forget about working for a while—I wish I *could* forget it—I dread getting a call, and I dread not getting one—oh, forget it, *forget it!*"

I slipped the pint of Johnny Walker into my handbag. The man in the seat across from me brought out a bottle and asked the stewardess to bring him ice and a glass. Why couldn't I do that? Why couldn't I keep it simple? Why did I have to sneak into the ladies' room with a hidden bottle and use a Lily cup and luke-warm water? Skip the answer to that one. Why did I do lots of things? Skip that too.

The lav was brightly lighted, clean and shiny with chrome. I downed my drink and chased it with tap water. I looked into the mirror, checking the focus of my eyes. Okay, but my arms and legs felt a little cottony. Better than the wired-up feeling though. I poured another—a larger—shot into the Lily cup. Somehow I always had to see how much; never could take it straight from the bottle.

I began my "am I or am I not" argument. How could I drink

so much and not be an alcoholic? But how could I be an alcoholic and yet stop drinking whenever I had to memorize a part, or
when I couldn't have liquor on my breath within two days of a
show? Like now—how could I be an alcoholic when I knew for
dead certain (a) I would make no trouble on the plane and (b) I
would get off the plane in the morning quite sober. And what
about the times when something just plain hurt too much, and
I would be all alone in my four walls, and then I really drank, and
then it meant trouble and doctors and . . .

Back in my seat I put my head against the cool window. Far
below, clusters of lights formed intricate patterns. I wondered
about patterns. What was the pattern of drinking? Why were
some things so unbearably painful for me that I had to drink myself into oblivion? I wondered if a psychiatrist could tell me. I
wished *somebody* would, somebody who wouldn't just fasten a
fishy eye on me and say, "Why don't you behave yourself?"

Item in the *Hollywood Reporter:* "Mary Astor is going to a
head shrinker—and about time, too. She has her pals worried."
Ha! What pals? No—have to rewrite that one.

I should have some "pals," I suppose. I suppose. Easy enough
—just pick up a phone. And get—who? People who know too much
about me? People who don't know anything about me? Have people to my place? *That* place? What was it Wes Rogers said when
he came up once? "This place makes me feel you are trying to
make me feel sorry for you." Funny thing—I never have asked
anyone up since then. But I like it. There's a heavenly view of the
city, and a pine tree that shushes—yes, I know, and feet that tramp,
tramp, tramp over my head, and a shower where I bump my
elbows, and hideous furniture. But I can turn out the lights and
watch television, or go to bed and read and watch my lovely Siamese Missy stretch herself to her graceful feline perfection. . . .

Thinking of that furred lesson in relaxation made me stretch
a bit, too, and I began to slip into sleep. The freewheeling of my
thinking slowed down, and then fastened, pin-pointed, on my
special pain. It drove everything else out, and the refrain ham-

mered at me: "I'm lonely . . . I'm lonely . . . I'm lonely—alone
—alone—alone. . . ."

I wakened painfully. My legs and arms were cramped. I felt
too low and depressed even to formulate a thought. It was still
dark; I tried to look at my watch, but my glasses had walked off
someplace. I bumbled up the aisle to the lavatory.

The drink made me feel queasy for an instant. I snapped the
cap firmly back on the bottle. "That's *it* for tonight." I bathed
my face and tried to see in the mirror—but no glasses, no face.
Faceless.

I pulled the curtain away from the window as I slid back into
my seat and a symphony in black and silver shone up at me.
Moonlight—the Rockies—snow—bluish silver white. I stared for
a while at the dark shimmering beauty, and my teeth ground
tight, and my nails dug into my palms, and I felt desperately the
need to share beauty like this.

Los Angeles was overcast; visibility five miles, clear to 1500. In
my mind I was doing "stick and rudder—right together," alone,
in a little blue Stinson. I put the flaps down and began to ease
the stick back—steady on the rudder—back, back more—and the
wheels smacked the earth with a resounding kiss and a sharp
squeal of delight. My heart began beating rapidly in hopeful
anticipation that a beloved face might be searching for mine at
the barrier, and then a bear hug, and words toppling about:
"You look wonderful—the show was great—I've missed you—
where are your baggage checks?—here, let me take that—I'll do
that for you. . . ."

I gave the taxi driver the address and said, "Stop at a liquor
store someplace first," and I damned my imagination for tortur-
ing me.

The morning was new with the first tempered excitement of
getting back to the security of familiar surroundings. Missy
stalked into the bedroom to greet me, her tail held high like a
banner, her blue eyes cool and distant. My landlady and her sister
made all the nice welcoming noises—they said that they *loved* the
show and that I looked "cute." Me cute! They asked me if I had

seen any plays while I was in New York, and I told them I had
been lucky enough to get a matinee single for *My Fair Lady* and
that even the opening curtain had made me proud to be in show
business. "What's it about?" they asked. "Who's in it?" "Well,"
I said, and I felt too weary to explain. Civilians! I went back
down to my rooms muttering, "The rains in Spain stay mainly in
the plains."

The day leveled off into a solitary dullness—dullness of weather,
dullness of mood. Even the stack of mail was dull—bills, ads, a
book from the Thomas More Book Club. Good, but too heavy-
going for just now. The phone rang; it was my daughter. They
hadn't liked the show much; there were some pretty bad shots of
me; the baby had a cold; my son was fine; her husband was upset
about something to do with his job; they just don't appreciate
him. See you soon.

At the market I caught a three-quarter glimpse of myself in the
mirror as I walked toward the meat crib. My grey slacks bagged
a little at the knees. I bulged at the waistline. My eyes looked back
at me arrogantly, defensively. Suddenly I caught a glimpse of a
woman just behind me, an unmistakable look of recognition on
her face, and I braced myself.

"You *are* Mary Astor, aren't you?"

I made myself smile pleasantly.

"Well, I want to tell you what a loved person you are in our
family. My husband and I used to hold hands and watch you in
the movies, and now it's so good to see you, right in our own
home, on television. Keep up the good work." And she was gone.

I poked blindly among the packages of meats. Me, loved!

It was dark when I got home. The wind was blowing the rain
in little gusts. I pulled the curtains in my bedroom and tiny
living room and lighted the lamps. The warm glow softened the
hard outlines of the furniture, and the room became mellow and
cozy. "At least," I thought, "I know my lighting." It was a good
night for TV. "Climax"—and I had done two shows for them, and
the theme music and Bill's voice would be pleasantly friendly
and familiar. "Lux"—earlier in the year I had done a TV version

of the Bette Davis film *The Star*, and before that a number of other shows for "Lux Radio." There was another half-hour drama that I knew Jack Smight had directed—I'd done one with him last March in New York. It was going to be a good evening.

I got into a terry-cloth robe, built a drink, and curled up on the couch. For a few moments I relaxed in the comfort of a warm contentment; then that insistent awareness that I was alone forced its way into my mind. I went over to break out some more ice cubes.

"I don't care what you say," I announced, "those Actors Studio kids really do have something. Oh, I know, they are irritating when it *shows*."

No one disagreed with me.

"Frankenheimer's camera work is swell. A little slow on his cuts though."

No answer.

I went over to the window and pulled the curtain back. The city lights melted into the mist. The pain exploded inside me. Its very sharpness made me laugh a little. "*I'm so damned lonely*." I knew I could relieve the pain; there were at least three people who would have been over in a minute if I called them. And there were dozens of others, people whose image of Mary Astor was that of a very busy woman, with many friends and obligations and no free evenings. Well, I wanted none of them. But I couldn't even decide why I didn't.

The evening passed. "Lux" was not a good show. "Lux" was a very bad show. "Mike shadows all over the place," I muttered. I got up to turn off the set and banged my knee on the coffee table. "Stinks!" I growled. I poured another drink. "And all that green-room stuff at the end. Why don't they use the time to tell the story? What story? Maybe it should all be green-room time."

I decided against sitting down on the couch again. I might fall asleep there and catch cold. I took my drink and set it very carefully on the table beside the bed. I missed the kneeler on my *prie-dieu* and banged my knee again—on the floor.

". . . to thank Thee for all the favors which Thou hast bestowed upon me this day. . . . Remember, O most gracious Virgin . . . despise not my petitions, but mercifully hear and . . ."

O my mother, *answer* me.

Within a few weeks I would realize, with relief, that I actually was sick and that a sick person can get well. But at the moment I was bewildered, very weary, and angrily impatient with myself because I could see no solution for my problems. I felt as though I were desperately trying to climb hand over hand up a slippery rope, with no end in sight, but with a horrible certainty that to give up would bring inevitable disaster. Thanks to this kind of grim courage, I was not in very bad shape materially. I had come a long way in four years, from a time when no one would have been surprised if I had gone into complete collapse. I was working—enough. I had a car and a comfortable place to live. I clung to my religion because I realized, while God in His justice permitted me to let myself down, He had never failed me. And that was enough for me, for I knew that if I kept trying I would somehow find strength and help and understanding. Somehow I would come to understand, and I remembered hearing somewhere that anything can be stood if it is understood.

A few days later I was called to do a "Matinee" TV show; then there was a call for a picture at Metro. My only pleasure at the Metro job was that it would help the dwindling bank account. I hated the idea of working there; it had been six years since I had set foot on the lot, and it was charged with unhappy emotions and associations. I thought it was simply because I "hated" to make movies. But I hated everything, including myself—especially myself. Drinking helped for a few hours at a time, but alcohol will soothe and relax for only a while. Then it will turn and viciously exaggerate the moods of the drinker. And this drinker's moods were not the kind that could safely be exaggerated.

The engagement at Metro was a short one—mercifully short, because my discipline was torture. The "Matinee" TV show had been much easier on me. From the instant you go into a TV show, every minute is filled, right down to the last red light. Rehearsals are long hours of intensive work, but they leave no time for brooding or self-pity. Pictures are much harder emotionally because the long hours of waiting between scenes provide too much time for boredom and brooding.

The assistant director dismissed me and thanked me. I made my farewells, got into my street clothes, and drove home. I was too tired to eat or go to the market—until I discovered only two cans of beer in the icebox. At once I decided I ought to have a steak. I got back into the car and drove down the hill to the market. Of course, I would have to get some more beer, too; it would go well with the steak. But perhaps I needed something stronger—vodka and tonic would be wonderful. No work tomorrow—or tomorrow—or tomorrow. . . .

Back home I fixed my drink. It was deliciously relaxing, just what I had needed. I would take my shower, have dinner, and go to bed. I would play it smart—stop with one drink.

While I was in the shower, scrubbing off the body make-up from my arms and legs, I leaned over to scrub my left leg and bumped my right elbow sharply against the wall. My temper shot up. I scrubbed the other leg and bumped my head. As I ducked from the pain I got my hair wet. In a fury I shut off the faucets; the hot one went first, and I was doused with icy cold water. A wave of angry self-pity swept over me. "Can't even afford a place with a decent bathroom. How many movies does it take to buy a bathtub?"

Missy worked an inquisitive paw at the crack in the door and, as it swung open a bit, slipped in to inquire what all the yapping was about. I laughed, and felt a bit of the strain sink away. I picked her up and hugged her. "Oh, Missy, what would I ever do without you!" That was all. I was off again, off into my misery of loneliness.

And I was off into another drinking cycle. Round and round, for over a week. Not quite remembering what the last TV show of the evening had been. Heavy sleep. Waking late to jitters and disgust and self-reproach. Getting through the day somehow, straightening up my rooms, sitting on the steps outside my door to avoid conversation with the landlady. Trying to read, trying to think, trying to pray. Trying to figure things out. Drinking more vodka. Trying to make a fifth last a few days, but it's all gone in one night. Buying just a pint at a time, every other day. Every day. What did I see on TV last night? What am I *doing?* Why can't I just quit? I don't need help. I don't want anyone to come near me.

It was an impulse, one afternoon, that sent me down the hill to Blessed Sacrament Church. I knew only one of the priests there personally, and I didn't know him very well, but it didn't matter. I was going to talk to somebody; I was going to get help. But there were no priests at the rectory. They were all busy over in the church hearing confessions.

"Can't I do *anything* right?" I thought. "Why did I have to pick a Saturday?"

At the same time, I felt a tired sense of relief. I didn't want anyone. I had tried. Now I could go off and die quietly.

But I couldn't force myself back to my rooms and the vodka and the emptiness and the futility and the final, complete defeat. I went on to another church, where I had gone for a time, and asked to see Monsignor Devlin, whom I had known fairly well. I knew that with him I could keep it simple, I wouldn't have to bother him with all the details of my troubles.

Monsignor was in. Yes, I could see him. Well, this was it.

I told Monsignor that I had a "drinking problem" and had decided I needed psychiatric help. But I had to be sure my help came from the right man; I couldn't afford to take any chances, and I knew there were too many fakes in this town, too many who catered to money and whims.

Monsignor reached for a slip of paper and jotted something down on it. "Go see this man," he said. "He is professor and chairman of the department of psychology at Loyola University. I understand they think a good deal of him over there. You'll be able to trust anyone he recommends."

By the time I got home, the emotion of my impulse had spent itself. "Now why did I do that?" I asked myself. I didn't want to see anyone, and now I was committed to action. I would at least have to see this man, or Monsignor would find out I hadn't—and then what would he think! I looked at the slip of paper again. It was a foreign-sounding name—"Reverend Peter Ciklic, Ph.D." —and worst of all, the address was at some parish rectory clear down in Manhattan Beach. I hadn't driven that far in ages. Rats! Maybe I'd better call Monsignor and tell him——

But instead I phoned the Manhattan Beach rectory and made the appointment with a pleasantly accented voice. Father Peter Ciklic would be glad to see me Sunday afternoon.

Sunday afternoon I had a good case of stage fright. Because of the long drive I resolved that I was *not* going to take a drink, but as I bathed and dressed the nervous sweat poured off me and my hands shook so that I could hardly get my lipstick on. After all, I hadn't had a drink since the night before—surely one ounce wouldn't hurt me. I measured out the ounce carefully and drank it. Nothing. Oh, break the appointment! Who cares? One more shot, this time a little more than an ounce. Then I set the bottle firmly aside, put on my coat, and walked out to the car.

The drive was endless, and the Sunday beach traffic set my nerves on edge. I got a little lost and was a few minutes late. By the time I arrived at the rectory and sat waiting in the little "parlor," my drinks had worn off and I was shaking. And then Father Ciklic came in—a tall, fine-looking man with a quick flash of a warming smile.

He made me comfortable and easy at once, with his half-humorous apology for not knowing who I was. The war years, his studies in Europe had given him little time for the movies. I liked this. He would have no preconceived notions, none of the curiosity people sometimes had shown toward me. I was just another human being in need of counsel and advice.

I took the plunge. "I drink too much, Father. I don't really enjoy it. I can't explain—I suppose I take it like an anaesthetic for a pain I can't quite describe."

He said something about group therapy.

"Yes, Father, I've tried that, but I had too many reservations, I didn't get anything out of it. I honestly don't think the 'one drink' idea applies to me. When I had to look well, Father, or memorize lines, I wouldn't drink. I could discipline myself. If I had enough reason, enough——" I couldn't think of a word.

"Motivation?" he suggested. "You know, Miss Astor, drinking is a symptom——" He paused.

I fumbled ahead. "Father, I know now I can't do this alone." And I told him how I had gone to Monsignor Devlin, and how Monsignor had sent me here. I asked him if he could suggest a reliable psychiatrist, one I could trust. I was emphatic about that. I had been brought to the edge of insanity by one smooth-tongued sham.

Father sat there for a moment. His face was quite expressionless; the light reflected from his glasses, and I could not see his eyes. My hands were clenched tightly in my lap. The silence seemed endless.

Finally he said simply, "Perhaps we could work together. You could come to me a few times, and we would find out if we liked each other. Maybe I could help you. There are some I have been able to help."

My jaw dropped a little. I had never heard of a priest as a practicing psychologist, and besides, I knew Father must be very busy with his work at the university. But what wonderful luck! How safe I would be! Why, it would be like an open confessional! This was unbelievable luck! "Grab it!" I told myself. "Grab it!"

I heard myself say something about its being a fine idea.

"Good!" he said. "Next Saturday at one-thirty in my office at Loyola."

So it was arranged, and our meetings began.

To eliminate any possible physical sources of trouble, Father asked me to have a complete medical examination. The doctor reported that I was perfectly normal, in better physical shape "than I had any right to be."

So we settled down to finding out why life meant nothing to me. For a while we just talked, like two people who have just met and want to get acquainted. Then Father found out that

I liked to write, but that I had never done anything about it because I didn't think I could.

One afternoon he made a suggestion. "Mary," he said, "you would help me very much, and it would save a great deal of time, if you would sit down and write the story of your life. Write every day for a few hours, just as you remember it. Write fully. No one is looking over your shoulder."

It was hard to do. I clubbed my memory, and sometimes during an entire afternoon of sitting at my desk I would have only a couple of pages. Then things seemed to clamor to be remembered, odd things, forgotten things. And I lived through them all over again. There was much that was beautiful, pleasant, amusing. But sometimes I put my head down on the keys and cried, lost in bitterness and pain.

Saturday was the highlight of the week. I usually arrived on the campus a little early, sitting in my car, daydreaming and watching a stray sea gull floating over the green of the lawn. Then the deep sound of a single note from the tall clock tower would announce the half-hour and I would go into Father's office with the pages I had written during the week. Together, hour after hour, we would discuss them—finding the answers to the whys— why I am like this—why did I do that?

Gradually the tangled threads began to form a pattern, and I began to see and understand things that I had never been able to see or understand before. And the months passed.

Father saw something more. But what he saw, I didn't like— not at all.

It was fall again. Temperatures dropped on the Atlantic coast, and in the West, Los Angeles emerged from her veil of smog and began her own brilliant season. I was full of plans for another trip to New York and an excellent TV script. I had decided to stay over long enough to see some friends and some shows, then a leisurely trip back by train, stopping in Chicago to renew other friendships. There would be no hurry, I could rest and read, and look at the country.

Father listened to my enthusiasm with a smile and then said,

"It has been a great joy to work with you, Mary; you were most wonderful and co-operative." I heard the past tense in his words and was reduced to an inanity: "You mean——?" "Yes, Mary, I think we have almost finished our work together."

I realized how full, how busy my life had become. I had taken the summer course in psychology at the university, I would be taking a credit course in February, I was buying a new home, shopping for furniture; and I had met a whole group of new friends. No longer was Saturday the *only* day of the week.

"What do you mean—finished. Don't you want to see me any more?" He laughed, "No, Mary, I'm not trying to get rid of you. You can always call on me and return to me any time you feel the need."

He relighted his pipe and blew a fragrant cloud.

"We have talked many, many hours. We have brought out and discussed the deepest conflicts of your life—you have talked without fear of punishment or censure. You have 'worked through' your problems and have achieved a more effective personality adjustment, so that you really don't need me any more."

I said, "Do you think, Father—is it possible that I can—walk alone?"

"Yes, Mary, now you can walk alone—with God's help. You have accomplished great self-knowledge; with self-insight you will continue to grow, to achieve more self-acceptance and maturity. And with maturity you are more competent to cope with the problems of everyday life."

I was free. Free of the cocoon. The confining mass of self-centered thinking—infantile, emotional, ineffective solutions of problems that had bound me deeper and deeper in loneliness and misery.

Father reached into his files and drew out a formidable stack of paper. "This belongs to you," he said, "you wrote it for me as a biographical sketch, an auto-analysis, and it helped us greatly in our work together; but I feel that by now you know much more about yourself than when this was written. I believe you have learned that in order to keep what you have—your security, your confidence, your serenity—you must, in a sense, give yourself away. You have found great release of tension in admitting and talking about your helplessness and defeat to me—one person. You are more fully aware of your dependence on God. You have discovered as part of your program of living that you have begun to be of help to others. I feel you should take this material you have written and make a book out of it."

My mind took a sickening plunge back into time. I remembered the horrible humiliation of having my words appear in print. The dreary story of the diary rose up before me, and I shook my head miserably.

Father knew me well enough to know that at this moment I was close to hating him. I had felt so safe, writing these things just for him, talking with him about them. And now he was suggesting that I publicly flaunt my wounds and my hurts.

But this man was not an expert psychologist for nothing. He took another tack, parallel to mine:

"You have been in the headlines often enough, Mary. People who have loved you have read only the superficial, the sensational things, the worst part of your life. I know that they have been bewildered by the contradiction of what you represent on the screen and television and the image of one who seems to have so much and yet periodically afforded shocking material for the press. You have, in a way, offended real friends, and I feel you owe them an explanation."

Stiff words, but real and true. And by now I could "take it." ". . . to make amends . . ." Perhaps.

The shadows on the campus lawn grew long and deepened into blue. In the office there was only silence; friendly, comfortable.

A light breeze stirred the fragrant haze of tobacco and blew away the thoughtful mood. It was getting late. I rose and gave my hand to my good friend, matching the warmth of his smile. "I'll think about it, Father."

One

"This is for Lucile—she *asked* for it!" The dedication, with its ominous double meaning, was written on the flyleaf of one of the three black-covered ledger books my mother had used for her diary.

She had begun the diary soon after her marriage in 1904, and had kept it up at intervals throughout the remaining forty-one years of her life. Now she was dead; the three black-bound volumes were my only memento of her.

I have sometimes felt that the bitter memories of my early life were colored by my own desire to explain away my faults in terms of an unhappy childhood and unsympathetic and unloving parents. I know that you don't remember things the way they really were when you were a child. You remember them through the alembic of intervening experience. Your pictures are colored by what you have since learned, or you remember things the way you think they should have been. Perhaps in my memories I was simply trying to justify my own failures on the grounds that they were really the failures of my parents.

My mother's diary was written in gall. It told me, shockingly and painfully, that my bitter memories were not merely the inventions of self-justification, but that the truth was even bitterer than my memories of it.

It took me almost a month to decipher the handwriting and laboriously retype the diary so I could read it through from beginning to end. When I finished reading it I burned it, and I tried to forget it.

Much that was in it I already knew—my mother's love for my father, her pride in him, her quiet unhappiness at Daddy's gradually alienating her from the other members of her own family. But I was horrified by her attitude toward me. The diary was a shocking hymn of hate for me from the time I was born. There was an occasional note of pride about "our baby," but mostly I was just a disappointment from the beginning. I was "planned," but I was supposed to be a boy. I was a husky ten-pounder, and "tore" her "to pieces." I "interfered with" their "happiness." I was a nuisance. My eyes were infected, and I nearly went blind. I was jaundiced—"yellow as a Chinaman"—and unable to eat certain foods. And I was a girl.

Mother suffered from Daddy's attentions to me, and from his cruelties to me—his spanking me for crying when I was six weeks old, spanking me so hard he left the imprint of his hand on me. Their quarrels were always "about the baby." Their own mental and cultural inequalities, combined with poverty and hardships, made their life extremely difficult. But when their tempers clashed, it was over "the baby," "the kid."

My father, Otto Ludwig Wilhelm Langhanke, had come to America from Berlin in 1889, when he was eighteen. He came for the same reasons that so many immigrants came—because America was the land where the streets were paved with gold, the land where great dreams could become greater realities.

The early years of his struggle to achieve his dreams are the traditional story of the immigrant's fight for success. He had crossed the Atlantic in a small ship crammed with steerage passengers. After a stormy passage, made miserable by crowded quarters and seasickness, he arrived in New York with little money and some knowledge of the English language. But there were German friends in Lawrence, Kansas, so it was to Lawrence that he came, paying most of his remaining money for a slow, interminable ride across the country in a freight train.

With a characteristic stubbornness and perseverance, he was determined that his dreams should come true, and he was willing to work unceasingly to make them come true. Education was necessary, so he attended the university at Lawrence, living with his friends and working as a janitor before and after his classes. During the summers he clerked in a clothing store in nearby Topeka. For fifteen years he divided his time between the university in Lawrence and the store in Topeka, although long before the end of this period he had achieved a fragment of his dream— he had moved up to teaching German in the university and doing window decoration and display work in the store. It was in the store, in the summer of 1904, that he met the woman who was to be my mother.

Helen Vasconcells was the oldest of the six children of a Lyons, Kansas, farmer. Her farm background was as narrow and limited as my father's was broad and varied. She came of a good family and a fine name, de Vasconcellos. Her grandfather had been born in Lisbon and her father was very proud of his old-country ancestry. Her mother, of Scotch-Irish descent, was educated well above her station as a Kansas farmer's wife. Before her marriage she had taught in a young ladies' finishing school. She was gentle and sweet and very wise, but these qualities were not transmitted to her oldest daughter.

Helen had had a serious romance with a young man who was enthusiastically setting about to acquire recognition as the town drunk. When the engagement was broken, she wanted to escape from the town and everything associated with her erstwhile fiancé, so she came to Topeka and found a job as a ribbon clerk in the same store where Otto Langhanke was working on window displays.

Her romance with Otto was partly "love at first sight" and

partly a rebound from her broken engagement. The story of their meeting has been told me so often that I almost feel it happened to me. The first day Helen was working at her new job she became aware, with increasing interest, of Otto as he worked around the windows and displays. Late in the day she stopped one of the other clerks and asked, "Who is the handsome man with the accent—the man who decorates the windows?" The girl at once called him over and introduced him.

"This," she said, "is Otto Langhanke."

Her coy acknowledgment of the introduction was, "Why, that's almost as bad as Vasconcells."

Otto looked at her with evident interest and admiration. "But perhaps," he said, "you could get used to it?"

A month later they were married at Lyons, in Mother's home.

I know from Mother's diary that they loved each other deeply, that they were both excited by their romance. To her he was a man with a splendid dream of greatness, although his dreams were sometimes too remote for her to understand. Certainly she could not fully understand the man himself; he was too subtle and his thoughts were too complex for her farm-insulated mind to cope with. Their love had to surmount many obstacles—obstacles of intellect, temperament, and background. The cliché "made for each other" could never have been applied to them.

My father's appearance and bearing shouted his unshakable self-assurance and his strong, unbending will—his stubborn confidence in his own abilities, his own judgment, his own prejudices. He was short, about five feet eight, but strongly and solidly built. His every movement was definite and positive, as though he well knew his rights, and heaven help anyone who infringed upon them. His complexion was fair, his hair light brown (although he was balding rapidly even at the time he was married), his teeth a brilliant white and straight and even. His hazel eyes looked at you with a sharp, accusing expression, as though he were expecting an insult and were well prepared to retaliate. But his mouth was his most expressive feature. In its set firmness it revealed all his sternness and determination, and yet managed to convey an oppressive suggestion of bewildered bitterness. He had a quick, analytical mind and a fertile imagination, but he was almost totally lacking in a sense of humor. Almost nothing struck him as "funny"; he could rarely get the point of a story, but once having got it, he would repeat the story until it was threadbare.

With his brilliance, his imagination, and his perseverance, he should have had the elements of greatness, or at least of success. But success always eluded him, his dream dissolved away, his great projects all turned to dust. He trusted too much in his own abilities, his own judgment; with his strong will and stubbornness, he could not accept advice or admit flaws in his own plans. As long as I lived with my parents I knew my father only as a frustrated and embittered man.

Mother was his opposite in almost every way. She was tiny— a bare five feet one. She was small-boned, tough, and wiry. It is hard for me to describe her, because most of the time I thought she was rather absurd. I know she was not; many people admired and respected her. I think that the absurdity I sensed resulted from her futile efforts to conform to the strange man she had married.

She had black hair and black eyes, an olive skin. Her late girlhood pictures show a very pretty young woman, but ever since I can remember she was worn by care and hardship. Her good features were obscured, and her worst ones intensified—especially her teeth. She was slightly buck-toothed, and her laughter was usually covered by an embarrassed hand. But she loved to laugh, and her black eyes would sometimes fill with tears of merriment. She had great energy and a remarkable talent for making people like her. And she loved people, she was interested in what they did, and she was always ready to help and give of herself.

Her responses to all experience were emotional rather than intellectual. She cried easily; she spontaneously screamed at anything that startled her. She talked well; she had a knack for the effective word and the right phrase, but she had no imagination. She had no depth, no real understanding. I often watched her when she and Daddy and I were listening to music—and there was a wonderful kind of harmony between us at those times; Mother would say all the things that we couldn't say, but she was visibly bored.

They were married in August. In September my father returned to the university at Lawrence. The income was barely enough to keep the two of them alive, so the following year, when an offer came from the high school at Quincy, Illinois, my father took it.

I was born in Blessing Hospital and brought to my first home, a shabby little flat over a saloon in Quincy, May 1906. I was their only child.

Naturally, my memories of those earliest years are confused and vague. I remember the tension that was everywhere throughout the house when my father was home. When he came in the door, the very atmosphere seemed to close in. Mother was constantly fearful that I would do or say something that "would make Daddy cross." We adjusted all our activities to his moods. If he was in a good humor, we could laugh, partly with relief, but quietly and cautiously, for his mood could change in a moment. A careless word, a loud noise, even a gesture could anger him; and then he would shout his fury and bang his fist on the table and stride out of the room, slamming the door violently behind him. And Mother would be in tears, helplessly wringing her hands.

I escaped to the security of the dusty floor under the bed. I learned very soon when I was "in the way," and I found it pleasanter to be alone. When I was punished I was often shut in a dark closet to think over my faults, or to be frightened out of them. But I enjoyed the dark and the quiet, and I would soon be asleep.

My father loved us, but he felt no need to express his affection. And he expected us to assume, without question, that we would order our every activity according to his interests or even his whims—although he would not have called them that. He ruled his little family with an iron hand. The possibility of our dissatisfaction or disaffection could never have occurred to him.

When he did display affection he meted it out with great

formality and ceremony, on such special occasions as Christmas and birthdays. He liked the ceremony—the carefully decorated tree, the lighted candles, the music on the phonograph. But I always knew that even at these times I must not fall into an impulsive demonstration of affection. I could never rush up to him and fling my arms around him, or tease him. Without ever being told, I knew better.

I don't remember much about playmates. They were probably somewhat afraid of my father, of his sternness and bursts of temper, so they stayed away. And my father, I think, encouraged this isolation, feeling that I should be protected and insulated from some unnamed and unidentified harm. I vividly remember one afternoon when I was playing contentedly in my little "play yard," a small area fenced in with chicken wire and containing my sandbox, with the inevitable pail and spoon, and usually my collie dog. I decided to go into the house for some reason, but when I reached for the gate it was locked. I felt a sense of shock, an unbearable sense of imprisonment.

One other incident of these early years stands out sharply. Mother and I were visiting neighbors across the street, where there was a little girl I had played with on rare occasions. The two mothers were sewing, and we had been told to play quietly. I invented a rather sad little game: we were two sisters on a train, sitting side by side, and we were making up some very melodramatic dialogue.

"Dear Sister," I was saying, "you must not weep for your beloved husband. He is in heaven."

She was pretending to be very sorrowful, and crying. She put her head on my shoulder, and I gave her my handkerchief. Suddenly my mother appeared in the doorway. We were embarrassed and startled, and we both jumped.

To my mother our reaction was a sign of guilt. That night, after I had been prepared for bed, she stood me up on the toilet seat so that she could look directly into my eyes, and questioned me as though I were a criminal.

"What were you and Marjory doing so quietly?" she asked me

again and again, entirely unsatisfied with my fumbling explanation. "What were you and Marjory *doing?*" And finally, "Did you
—touch—each other?"

I had no notion of what she meant. And I cannot explain how
a six-year-old child can have a sudden comprehension of the idea
of evil, but I had it then.

The real memories of my childhood begin in the summer of 1913,
when I was seven years old, for it was then that we moved to the
farm. I don't know why we moved; I only know that for four
blessed years I had the freedom and the solitude and the beauty
that I had never had, and that I was never again to have in quite
the same exhilarating way.

We rented a great, ugly (but incomparably beautiful to me)
mid-Victorian mansion that sat in the middle of eight acres of
land. Eight of its twelve rooms were huge—twenty-five feet square,
with twelve-foot ceilings—and each had a marble fireplace—which
we never used. Four of these rooms downstairs and four upstairs,
split down the middle by a wide staircase with mahogany banis-
ters, formed the main square of the house.

We had furniture for only three rooms, so we lived in parts of
the house. Sometimes our bedroom was upstairs, and sometimes
downstairs. In it was a big double bed, where I slept with Mother,
and a studio couch, where Daddy slept. In the "sitting room" was
the Franklin stove, a center table, some chairs, and later an upright piano. We ate from the center table, which afterwards was
cleared for Daddy's writing. The kitchen was enormous, and we
often ate there, especially in the summer. One of the small back
rooms was filled with brooders for baby chicks, and later Daddy
converted one of the big upstairs rooms into a workshop where
he made "show cards." The other rooms were empty.

There was no peace in this house either, but always a frenetic
activity. Both my parents worked hard. They were worried,
irritable. Daddy's face was always set and grim. Mother was constantly biting her lips to keep the tears back.

They were trying to catch up with Daddy's dreams of greatness.

He was not satisfied with merely raising chickens. He had dreams of transforming the farm into a great "Edelweiss Poultry Farm," with all White Orpingtons. He paid fifty dollars for a male bird. He built, without help, an elaborate twelve-pen chicken house; he designed and built his own feeders; he experimented with and mixed his own "enriched" chicken mash—which, he complained bitterly, a feed company "stole, and never gave me a penny for it." He put a great deal of time and a little money into a mushroom-raising enterprise, which failed. He invested a little more of his painfully scarce money into a project for walnut groves, and that failed, too. He wrote a first-year German text and teacher's manual; the First World War broke out just as it was published, and the study of German was discontinued in almost all the high schools. And because of his pro-German sympathies he lost his teaching job as well; and poultry raising, which had been only a side line, became our only support.

My main concern was to escape this angry man, to plan my day so I would not be spanked for some trifle, or lectured scathingly. And because my parents were working so hard they often left me to myself. I was set free in a pair of overalls and sandals, with my collie at my heels, to roam the fields and the ravine with its beautiful old oaks and elms.

There was Cedar Creek, about a mile away, where I had some fine hideaways. On its large flat stones I could lie with my face close to the running water and lose myself in the illusion that I was moving and the water was standing still. I skipped stones, and watched the minnows, and loved the sounds of the water and the sparkling jewels of sunlight on the water.

In the woods at the top of the hill was a "fairy ring," one of those strange spots one finds in the midst of brush and brambles and vines and fallen leaves, with short grass and clean-swept as though it were tended by a careful gardener. In its quiet sunlight I lived the fairy stories I had read. I was Rapunzel, and the Sleeping Beauty. I dreamed of the tunnel I was permitted to descend to see the Brownies' treasure of gold. I even deigned to be one of Daddy's Valkyries and ride a great horse to Valhalla. And a Prince came to rescue me and carry me away to his castle.

From the limb of a pine tree Daddy hung a rope swing with a board seat. The limb was high, and the ground rolled away sharply below the tree, so that when I "pumped" I was excitingly high above the ground. I loved the swing, the feeling of remoteness from noise and trouble, the purple clover that covered the ground, the apple trees I could see in the distance. Not far from the swing was the dead stump of a peach tree, and I noticed one spring that every time I swung by it I was disturbing a pair of bluebirds. They became an exciting project—to bring them feathers and grass and the kinds of seed I knew they liked best, and then to get back in my swing and swing very gently. Even now I can remember when the little hen was finally sitting on her eggs; she had become quite confident, and I can still see the tiny head and the beady eyes moving back and forth like someone at a tennis match as I swung—oh, very high now!

And one day I found a "trophy." I was wandering around Mr. Thien's pond—a forbidden area, for the pond was full of water moccasins. I found a perfect snakeskin that had just been shed. I took it home and carefully placed it on the steps of the kitchen porch to dry it before I added it to my collection. The next day it was gone. I was crushed with the misery of my disappointment. I felt like crying, but I kept the tears back because I supposed that Daddy had taken it to punish me for going to the pond. Some days later I found it—in the lilac bush a few yards away—beautifully and skillfully woven into a thrush's nest. It gave me a wonderful feeling of joy to see how beautifully the skin had been used and to think that I had helped "make a nest."

I saw very little of other children. My father did not approve of the neighbors; they were ignorant, common. I was made to understand that we were somehow better than the families that lived around us. But periodically, early in the night, when I was supposed to be asleep, I overheard allusions to my "lonely childhood" and the repeated insistence that "it was not good for her." After every such discussion there would follow a period of visiting other farms to spend a day with Esther Summers, or Vida, or Jimmy Allen, or playing next door with the Brown boys. I did not especially enjoy those excursions; I was too used to being alone, to making my own games, and reveling in an unconscious enjoyment of the fields and the trees and the birds.

I had lived so close to nature that I instinctively, without ever asking, understood the courting and mating among animals. I had seen the strutting pigeon and I knew about the fresh cow. These were facts as interesting as the fact that bark grew on trees. I knew about my own birth, that Mother had "carried me in her womb," and how I had been born. This was all a part of the wondrous and curious marvels of nature—like the miracle of a lightning bug "lighting," and the way my throat tightened at the sudden sight of the crab apple trees in bloom, the aching pink cloud where the day before there had been only tight secret buds.

I couldn't communicate these things to other children; I didn't particularly care to. I couldn't even tell them to my mother or father—although I think I loved my father most when he was telling me how wonderful a blade of grass was, or about the design of the veins on the leaf, or about the snail and its shell. But somehow even then he destroyed the magic and the wonder with his matter-of-factness. I tried to master his schoolroom facts until I could rush back outside to my own discoveries.

My visits with other children seemed always to stir up some kind of trouble, either with their parents or mine. I remember that some little girl told me how she thought a cat had kittens. She was misinformed, and I told her so. I explained the process in detail, for I had seen it happen, and had had it explained to me. This was still early in the century. There were some furious, shocked telephone calls, and a friendship broken. And once more Mother told me that we were not quite like other people. Daddy thought it right that I should know certain things, but I would have to learn to keep them to myself.

More often, though, it was my parents who were displeased by my childhood friends. After one of my rare visits to another farm I was usually noisy and nervous. I would forget myself for a moment at the table, and my father would be angry. "Now where did the kid pick *that* up!" And at once he would answer his own question. "From those Brown kids, I suppose. Whenever she goes over there . . ." And there would follow a long monologue on the failings of the Brown children, the stupidity of their parents, and the ignorance of farmers in general and of my mother's family, who, of course, were unfortunately also farmers. And Mother and I would eat as unobtrusively as possible, our eyes on our plates, and at the close of the meal, after Daddy had stormed out, we would wordlessly do the dishes.

I preferred to spend my days alone, in the attic or in the fields or in the ravine or at the creek. But when the days began to shorten and the leaves were turning, I would be less relaxed. I had to spend more time in the house; I was more often under my father's eye, and inevitably the cause of his displeasure or anger. School was a respite from anxiety and tension. But even at school my home training could lead to embarrassments and conflicts. And the sense of superiority that had been instilled in me did not help make me popular among my classmates.

It was called "Highland School"—a typical Middle West farm schoolhouse, two rooms, white clapboard, a steeple with a bell that was large enough to sound an alarm a township away, but was used only to call about forty students to order. I started there in the second grade. My first year I had gone to the big grade school in town; it had had drinking fountains in the halls, playgrounds with swings and other equipment, and indoor bathroom facilities. Not being a very skilled diplomat at seven, I innocently but loudly wondered where the swings and teeter-totters were, and why did we have to use a *privy!* The other children interpreted this as contempt, and they resented it—and me—from the very first day of my life at Highland School.

My long auburn curls, carefully combed by my mother each morning before school, were another reason for my unpopularity. The rest of the girls wore the conventional skinned-back braided hairdo. This was another source of unhappiness for me; on the eve of any school "entertainment" all the girls came to class with their hair done up in glamorous rag curlers in happy anticipation of curls for the evening. I longed to have my hair done up, too. But for me there was none of the fun of preparation. Mother's skillful brush wound my hair around her fingers, and there were my curls, just like every day.

The very precise speech that Daddy had drilled into me set me further apart from the other children. "You talk funny," they would tease me.

I succeeded even in bringing the wrath of the teacher down on me. She was teaching us a little song one afternoon, singing, "The wind goes woo-woo in the chimbley." I raised my hand and waved it eagerly.

"Yes, Lucile," she said.

"It's not pronounced 'chimbley,' it's 'chimney,'" I proclaimed.

She told me that I was mistaken, but I insisted. After all, Daddy had told me so. I had to stay after school, but Daddy went to the school board and raised a storm about his child being taught by illiterates.

I didn't stand very high in the eyes of either my teacher or my classmates after that.

When I graduated into the "big room," which held the impressive fourth, fifth, sixth, and seventh grades, the work began to be more challenging and I felt more interest. I enjoyed history and reading and spelling, but arithmetic was a painful mystery. One day I was at the blackboard struggling with the puzzle of long division. I could do as I was told, and the problem would work out all right, but I couldn't understand *why*. Then I suddenly felt a most wonderful illumination. I saw why; it became dazzlingly clear. And to the teacher's amusement and the children's disgust, I stayed in all through recess working problem after problem, with the luminous joy of discovery.

I went home that night, happy that I could at last tell Daddy something that would make him proud of me—a goal that I would always strive for but never achieve.

"That's fine," he said, "but you should use an easier system." And he tried to teach me how to put some of the figures over the line, and some under the line, and I became more and more confused, until finally everything blanked out and I couldn't tell a six from a nine. Then there was another long and violent lecture on my stupidity, and the whole thing left me. I remained a C– student in arithmetic—and still am.

My last two years at Highland School are for the most part a happy memory. I enjoyed learning, and I did not feel too keenly the lack of close friends. And I delighted in the three-mile walk to and from school, through a little wooden turnstile into the dusty road, kicking the grasshoppers in the long grass, and the smell of burning leaves in the crisp air, and the great thunderstorms, and the heavy somnolent heat. But winter transformed the walk from a happy adventure into a dreaded ordeal. Bundled up, fastened down with gaiters and scarves and mittens, I floundered through the deep drifts of the interminable three miles to school. And then we sat around the little potbellied stove in the schoolroom to thaw out, our bodies too close together, steaming with odors that were not quite clean.

At home winter confined me more closely yet to the uncertain temper and inexorable demands of my father. And worst of all, there was the piano, with my father, whatever he was doing, relentlessly following each note, measuring, it seems to me now, the exact duration, intensity, and pitch of each tone. And in winter the piano was a constant threat. "Now that you can't go outside to play so much, maybe you could put in a little more practice?"

The piano had arrived when I was ten—to the day and moment, because Miss Lula Felt, head of the Quincy College of Music, and a lady whom Daddy considered his equal, had said that at ten my fingers would be strong enough to begin lessons. And it was planned, not just that I would learn to play the piano, but that I was to become a pianist—and there is quite a difference. Of course it was my father who loved the piano, and who had longed to become a pianist. He would often tell how he had been a boy soprano in the church that the Kaiser attended, and how he had been offered a scholarship to a school of music—a scholarship his father had forbidden him to accept, saying, "No son of mine will appear in public except in the pulpit."

Therefore I must become the "great musician" that he had longed to be. I can now deeply feel his exasperation with his ungrateful child, who "had the opportunity I would have given my life for." I know he had done janitor work in the basement of a church long ago so that he could have the privilege of playing the organ. And I saw him sit at the little piano and with work-gnarled hands try to struggle through Chopin's Fifth Nocturne. So he tried to force musical knowledge on me. I liked music, but not the way he did. My lessons went well enough, but the practice was an ordeal. Not the practice itself—what I hated was the constant criticism over the slightest mistake. My nerves jangled at the loud, sharp "No!" from another room if I missed the lift of a phrase. I sat on edge, waiting for the caustic "It sounds like a lumber wagon," or "*Can't* you get some life into it?"

Then there was the ordeal of the "evening concert for Daddy" that made me sweat with fright. These were the "pieces" that I had more or less completed. The Bach first, of course; then something like the Chaminade Scarf Dance. This went on until I was playing Beethoven, and the Chopin Nocturnes and Valses and Studies. The evening would begin with a beaming smile of anticipation, then a reasonable correction, then a "You'd better go over that again," and then biting exasperation—until I was aching and my nerves were jumping. Once a ruler was slammed flat on my fingers and I was lectured for crying. I cannot play the piano today.

How I longed for the freedom of the hot summer days, and the magic of my fairy ring, and the cool rush of the wind as I swung under the pine tree. But even those bright summer days brought their dark moments.

One tragedy that lay deep under the folds of memory occurred during my last spring on the farm. I have forgotten even the boy's name. I'll call him Ed. I was ten; he was about fifteen, a farm hand from the Thiens'. I was enchanted with him. I thought he was beautiful, and the things he did were beautiful—the way he could crack out a long whip and whistle to the cattle—all with such authority! He herded a few of Thien's milch cows on our clover, so that I had a chance to talk with him. He was friendly, and I soon learned that he was not so terribly superior. He seemed even less remote when I found he didn't even know about Bach fugues, or who Shakespeare was. That increased my own courage, but it didn't lessen the glamour about him. He was still older than I was, he was beautiful—and Daddy didn't like him. I wanted his approval, some definite token that he accepted me. One day I felt very brave.

"Wouldn't it be nice," I said, "for us to have a picnic together —I mean, maybe just take a watermelon and eat it under the trees somewhere?"

But he was a very realistic farm boy, and he found all the reasons why it would be impossible. He couldn't take time from work; the family would expect him for lunch; they would think it was "funny."

I felt his embarrassment, and with a casual self-possession and social sensitivity beyond my years I passed it off lightly. "Oh, sure, of course you couldn't," I said. "It was just an idea I had."

But his refusal rankled. I suffered from this slight, this rejection. In my mind I exacted horrible vengeance; perhaps I would even kill him! But for the time being I settled for the less drastic but still satisfying revenge of merely humiliating him.

A few days later I was riding Flora, the aged, sway-backed, one-eyed mare, up and down the sides of the ravine. Ed was plowing the Thiens' field that adjoined the topmost part of the hill of the ravine. The field was bounded by a barbed-wire fence. Ed was walking behind a plow and pair, plowing down the hill away from the fence and then up again and back. I met him at the barrier of the barbed wire and challenged him to a race; he was to plow the length of the field and back, and I was to ride Flora in the opposite direction, to our barn and back. We would see who could return to the wire first.

It was a simple trick, to ride down the hill out of his sight,

linger a few moments, and then return to the fence and be waiting
for him when he sweated up his side of the hill on the return
lap. Three times he pulled up his team, rubbed the sweat out
of his eyes, and exclaimed in exasperation that he just didn't
understand it. Then he whipped his team on to try again, harder.
I laughed at him for a dull clod not to see through me. The fourth
time, I stayed longer down in the ravine, to make the "race" closer.
Suddenly I heard a terrible scream of pain, then a fear-struck cry
for help. I became a frightened little girl again; I whipped Flora's
thin shanks and raced for the barn. As I got there and slid off
I saw Daddy running down the near side of the ravine. I hid in
the barn and listened to the distant sounds of emergency, the
shouting, the call of "Get a doctor, quick." I peeked out and saw
Daddy, his face very red, running back to the house. Then nothing
more.

That night at dinner, Mother and Daddy were very grave. They
talked little, and in hushed voices. But I heard enough to know
that Ed had somehow cut his throat on the barbed wire—"because
he was hurrying, trying to beat me," I thought. "I killed him."
I could never bring myself to ask what happened to him.

In spite of Ed's accident those four years on the farm were happy
ones. However, the First World War had affected us a great
deal. At school I was unpopular because I was not allowed to
buy Liberty stamps—and I was practically ostracized the day I
jumped up and down singsonging "The Germans'll win, the Germans'll win, the Germans'll win." Daddy had lost his job at the
high school because of his strong and voluble pro-German
sympathies. And one day Mother fainted at the telephone because her favorite young brother, my uncle Jerry, had joined the
Aviation Service in Canada.

In the fall of 1916, Daddy was reinstated in the high school—
they must have decided he was after all not a dangerous enemy
alien—and with his reinstatement my happy idyllic days on the
farm came to an end. We moved back into town.

The house on Kentucky Street must have been an architect's nightmare. It had no beauty by any standards. It was simply a brick box, without even the gingerbread ornamentation typical of its period. It was the ugliest house on the street—a street that on the whole had a certain quiet charm. The houses were all set back behind wide green lawns an equal distance from a street lined with maples and elms. Behind the houses was an alley lined with unsavory garbage cans, ashes, and trash. After the farm I hated it all.

The day before we left the farm I made a pilgrimage to all my loved places; I patted the fairy ring good-by; I put my arms as far as they would reach around each of the great oaks and kissed them with tears running down my cheeks. I crated my pigeons, hoping they would stay in the small loft of the shed on Kentucky Street, but even though I kept them shut up for a few weeks they flew away as soon as I let them out, and never returned. Daddy's dog got sick and died. We kept my collie chained up, but he was miserable until we relented and let him run loose. A few months later, as I was coming home from school, he bounded across the street to meet me and was run over by a truck.

My attitude toward my father had grown into a kind of fearful respect; I wanted to please him, but I despaired of ever succeeding. It was easiest just to keep out of his way, to avoid rousing his temper.

Sitting at the piano one afternoon practicing some very dull Czerny, I lapsed back into dreams of the happy days at the farm, an existence that was much more real than the life I was living now. I stopped playing and laid my arms on the keys. In a very few minutes I heard Daddy's footsteps coming down the stairs from his study. Ordinarily I would have sat up and begun practicing busily, but my mood was too strong.

For once my father decided not to be unkind. When he walked into the room he saw at once that something was troubling me. He began talking gently about my increasing lack of interest in the piano—or in *anything*. I remember his words now.

"Don't you want to *be* somebody?" he said.

"Daddy," I said, "I *am* somebody, I am myself."

"Well, what do you want to do then?"

I honestly thought he wanted to know, and I felt happy and eager to tell him.

"I just want to grow up, and go to high school and maybe Gem City Business College. I want to work a little, and then get married and have children."

The heavens and earth opened in wrath; fire and brimstone rained down on my head. I was lectured as I had never been lectured before; I was shaken with a violence and fury that I had never seen in my father in even his worst moods. He shoved me back onto the piano bench and pounded the top of the piano to give emphasis to his words. He pounded so hard he hurt his knuckles—I saw with pleasure. I was too stunned to hear what he was saying, but I know he used the phrases "hoi polloi," "no ambition," "lazy," "good-for-nothing," and "after all we are sacrificing." And then Mother was standing in the doorway wringing her hands and crying and saying, "Daddy, don't hurt her, don't hurt her!" And he turned on her, shouting, "You keep out of this!"

It was the end of any possible understanding between my father and me. He was too strong for me; his will was too inflexible. Hereafter "Daddy, thy will be done."

I don't know how consciously I gave up forever any idea of establishing any real communication with my father, but I know I never again attempted it. I felt a kind of embarrassment that I had revealed myself, and that I had revealed myself as being made of pretty inferior stuff, according to his standards. I became more obedient. I decided to go along with him; it was safer.

The years on the farm had given me a simplicity and naturalness that contrasted sharply with the "airs" and affectations of the town girls. The boys at school liked this unaffected directness; a group of them trailed behind me each afternoon after school, vying to carry my books and indulging in the usual boyish horseplay to attract my attention. One boy even tried to impress me by whispering that he had stolen some money from his aunt to buy me a box of chocolates. I accepted all this as a matter of course; it built up my self-confidence, I enjoyed it, and I became less sensitive to Daddy's moods and tempers.

At home the Great Idea was being born—slowly, quietly, with little to indicate that it would ultimately determine the destiny of each one of us. The Great Idea was born out of the rapid flourishing of motion pictures. For motion pictures were becoming important. D. W. Griffith's *Birth of a Nation* had swept the country. Mother and Daddy took me to see it; and for days I floated on a purple cloud, identifying myself with the tragic character played by Mae Marsh. We were awed by this strange new amusement. Religiously we went to the local theatre every Friday. The family conversation developed a new dimension; we took these moving pictures seriously, and carefully analyzed the work of the actors and actresses. We dwelt on the merits of Olga Petrova and Clara Kimball Young. We dismissed little Mary Pickford as insipid—she had no depth. In rapt admiration we watched the great Griffith pictures, with Barthelmess and Lillian Gish.

And the Great Idea was born. My father decided I should become an actress, and my father had never been wrong.

My mother and father discussed the possibilities backwards and forwards, up and down. Daddy sent off letters to directors and producers. In my passive acceptance of all my father's decisions, I saw no reason to question this one. In fact, the idea of being a movie actress might not be bad at all.

I grasped the Great Idea with growing enthusiasm. I became an avid movie fan. I had my own bedroom now—a small room at the rear of the house with a sharply sloping ceiling. Ceiling and walls were plastered with photographs cut out of movie magazines. No longer did I dream of the farm with its brook and trees and flowers; now I dreamed of being an actress, clothed in satins and ermine, and draped in orchids.

Daddy was somewhat more serious.

"Lucile," he assured me, "one day you will be a second Duse."

I had no idea of who Duse was, but I had long before learned my lesson. I agreed thoroughly.

Next door lived Marian, a little girl who became my first really close friend. She is the only child I knew during the years in Quincy whom I still write to, even though our correspondence may be confined to cards at birthdays and Christmas, and a rare note in between. She was a very sweet little dark-eyed girl, sensitive and understanding, sympathetic to my moods and enthusiasms. And "even though she was a Catholic" (as my father put it), my parents regarded her as an acceptable playmate. I gratefully accepted her understanding, her sympathy, and her friendship. I identified myself with her; she was my "twin." It was a blessed relief finally to be able to share my troubles and my joys with someone who understood them, who would not dismiss them with a casual disinterest or a snort of contempt.

Like most of the girls of our age, we succumbed to the coupon-clipping fad, sending in to magazines for samples of perfume or face creams, or entering contests for winning bicycles. Together we collected a magnificent assortment of unusable samples. And together we read the movie magazines avidly, and became experts on who was who in the movies.

In the strange and inscrutable working of Providence it was our childish game of mailing coupons that led me to a career as an actress.

Three publications of those years were devoted to the movies: *Shadowland, Motion Picture Magazine,* and a third whose name I do not remember. All three were edited by Eugene V. Brewster. As one of his promotion devices he ran a contest, a "Beauty Contest," to find "beauty in our land" for the movies. Anyone could enter. All you had to do was send a photograph and a short biography to the office of the Brewster Publications. Each month eight contestants were chosen, and their pictures and biographies published in *Motion Picture Magazine.* At the end of the year four finalists would be selected for screen tests; the winner was to be given a studio contract.

With the same attitude I had in sending for a sample of soap I entered the "contest." I scrawled a short account of my life—the minimum and conventional biographical information—and sent it in with a small "cabinet portrait" of myself. I didn't even tell my parents about it. It was just another contest. I wouldn't win it any more than I had won the bicycle.

To my pleased amazement, almost the very next issue of the magazine carried my picture. I can see it clearly, down in the left corner of a page with the pictures of seven other young ladies. And the exciting caption THIS MONTH'S FAME AND FORTUNE WINNERS.

I was pleased and flattered—but the bicycle contests had instilled in me a kind of caution. Daddy, however, erupted into energetic plans and strategems. This was Opportunity, not only knocking, but holding the door wide open! Look at those other girls; they couldn't hold a candle to Lucile! I was as good as in the movies.

I don't remember the details of what followed. With Daddy, to plan was to act. Almost at once our furniture was sold. We didn't have enough money to get as far as New York, but we had enough for our fare to Chicago, where there was a branch office of Brewster Publications. We would be there, and we would be ready.

The tremendous upheaval, Daddy's energy and activity wore Mother and me to a dull, uncomprehending fatigue. But not for a moment could there be a question of opposing Daddy's excitement and determination and certainty. Marian and I exchanged vows of lifelong friendship. I told my gym teacher we were moving to Chicago.

"Why?" she asked.

"I'm going to be a movie actress."

She looked at me for a moment, and then said quietly, "Oh, you are?" I felt her understanding—that it was an imprudent move, that the odds were long, and that disappointment and heartbreak loomed ahead.

We arrived in Chicago. Until we could find a place of our own we stayed with an Irish family in a wretched flat on the South Side. I recall it very vaguely, like a dream—the smoky, dirty city; the big dark flat with shadowy, unidentified people; Daddy out walking the streets looking for a place for us to live.

We moved into a small but clean and decent apartment in a court on East Forty-seventh Street, on the South Side. It had a living room with a wall bed, a small bedroom, and a kitchen. We were to live there for the next three years, for I did not win the contest.

And times became really rough. Daddy tried to get some substitute teaching; he would have had to take an examination to qualify as a regular teacher, and he felt that the examination would be a waste of his time. Soon we would be going to New York for next year's contest; we would be "on the spot" so "nobody would get a chance to play any favorites." To pay the rent and buy food he finally had to put all his time into making his "show cards," which he had made as a side line for some years—cards used in window displays in stores, advertising "Spring Clearance," or "Special Price, $2.98." He did fine lettering and airbrush work. Mother would take his samples and peddle them from store to store to get quantity orders. We ate, at least.

I was finishing out my sixth year in a public school nearby. It was a dreary and unhappy time; these were tough kids and tough teachers, city-bred, and I was miserable.

Mother is the real star of the Chicago years. She made friends and found work while Daddy lived in his dream and answered "sucker ads"—like the one that offered, for a small fee, to get a test with a famous film director. The "small fee" was sent, but there was never any test.

Meanwhile Mother somehow got a position teaching English literature and a drama class in a very exclusive private school, the Kenwood-Loring School for Girls. In exchange for her teaching I was accepted as a pupil without having to pay tuition. She had "made a deal," and a good one. I loved the school. It was a converted old mansion; the atmosphere was informal; the classes were small. I felt I was learning again.

I was fascinated by a science class, where we did wonderful things like finding how iron filings behaved with a magnet, how to make a simple doorbell, what makes lightning bugs "light." The girls loved Mother, and I was proud of her because she made her class so interesting. She worked hard at it, and the reading she gave us was chosen with a sure sense of the tastes and interests of our age group. It was just right—Hawthorne and Whittier and Longfellow. We had a wonderful time weeping for the tragic love of Evangeline . . . "This is the forest primeval. The murmuring pines and the hemlocks . . ."

Mother had also made friends with a Bertha Iles, who had a good dramatic school on Michigan Boulevard, and I found myself enrolled in her Saturday afternoon class. It was fun. She was a big, attractive, merry woman, with a great gift of contagious laughter. And she was good. She got us up on a little stage and made us act. She taught us how to stand and walk, how to carry a train, how to handle a fan—many little things I have remembered and used. She was practical, too. She used her group for charities and benefits and the many fund-raising activities that were going on during the war. We had a sort of juvenile stock company, and we put on shows at Ravinia Park, at Municipal Pier, and at Fullerton Hall, and we put on a pageant at the new Soldier Field.

One time I was called on for a recitation in a hospital auditorium, at an entertainment for returned soldiers. I was unprepared, except for an excerpt from *As You Like It*. I knew it was a poor choice, but there was nothing else. I was jittery and sweating with nervousness. A little barrette that held my hair back kept slipping, and, as they say nowadays in acting schools, I "used it." I pulled the barrette from my hair, tossed it to an imaginary maid in the wings, and said, "Take this for me please." I shook my hair loose, as though that were the way I wanted it, and announced what I would do. I found the magic of authority. They listened, and they loved it. And I knew I was *good*.

In the evenings Mother was also working with various "War Camp" community groups, directing little plays for the entertainment of soldiers. One or two nights she was ill; the groups happened to be within an easy streetcar ride away, so I took them for her. I was only thirteen, but I knew the play and I knew what she wanted, and I had no hesitation or shyness about taking over. I remember arranging a bit of stage "business"—going up on the stage and showing a girl how to do what I wanted. I had the feeling of how it should be done and how to convey the idea to the actors. Afterwards Mother reported their expressions of enthusiasm, and someone's complimentary "She's tougher than you are, Mrs. L." That had also felt "good" and "right."

I was maturing during these years, developing into womanhood. The process was painful, physically and emotionally. Moods alternated with erratic rapidity; at one moment I would be giggling hysterically, and at the next I would withdraw into a pensive melancholy. Daddy was annoyed; he complained that I was always "either sour or silly." Mother, of course, felt a greater sympathy and understanding. "How do you feel now?" she asked. "Do you feel that you are a woman?" I told her that it had made no difference that way. I knew I was changing emotionally, but I said nothing. I had never felt free to discuss these things with either of my parents.

I developed secret "crushes." One of them was a wounded boy at Cottage Grove Hospital, where I was a "cigarettes and coffee girl"—part of the volunteer war work that Mother and I did. The boy had been in vaudeville, and I used the fact that "I was going to be an actress" as an excuse to talk more to him than to the others. He had sparkling brown eyes and a mustache that I thought was the most becoming thing I had ever seen. I remember the lovely weakness I would feel when his wheel chair was rolled into the group room. Of course I never told him, or anyone else, how I felt.

Later the "crush" was transferred to my young uncle Jerry, who was now a captain in the American Aviation Service, and had recently been with Eddie Rickenbacker. He visited us on one of his leaves, and he was beautiful in his uniform with his Sam

Browne belt and his highly polished boots. One afternoon he kissed me gently and said, "You're so sweet, Lucile." And I thought I would faint.

I did not feel any "rightness" or "wrongness" in these attachments; they were simply very personal emotions, preciously my own. I was not surprised by them, and they caused me no worry. I just enjoyed them. I did not associate them with any moral law, for I had been taught nothing about a moral law. I knew nothing but the laws of society, as they were defined and interpreted by Daddy. He was the high priest, the infallible judge of right and wrong. It was possible that society could be mistaken; it was not possible that Daddy could be. I instinctively accepted his judgments, implied or expressed, as my only standards. These standards were about to undergo a frightful shock.

It was Halloween, and the shop windows were streaked with the usual soap drawings and scribblings.

At the dinner table I casually and quite innocently inquired about the meaning of a well-known four-letter word I had seen written in large letters on a grocery-store window. Mother and Daddy passed the matter off lightly. I gathered that they didn't know either, and I thought no more about it.

Mother went out to one of her War Camp groups for the evening, and Daddy and I were left alone. I set about my regular evening practice at the piano, and Daddy sat reading the paper. After a few moments Daddy put his paper down and said, "Lucile, I want to talk to you."

"Oh, what now!" I thought, and I swiveled around on the piano stool so I could listen with the proper respectful attention.

"Do you remember that story we all used to laugh about so much on the farm?" he asked. "The one the Smiths told us?"

"Yes, I remember," I said. "I thought it was funny."

He didn't say anything for a moment; then, "Do you know what it meant?"

I didn't, so he proceeded to try to explain it to me—one of the hackneyed traveling salesman-farmer's daughter stories. I suppose my father thought he was being very clever, starting a serious subject in a light and humorous vein. But I was frozen. He soon saw I had no idea what he was talking about, so he began again, with a more detailed explanation. In his own mind he was being merely objective and matter-of-fact perhaps; but in ignoring all the aura of emotion and sympathy and love he achieved only a shattering brutality and coarseness. He tried to keep his explanation in a light mood, but that only made it seem grosser. I was in a state of absolute shock. I dimly heard him say, "So if you ever start to have those feelings about a boy you just come and tell me." It was simply a definition of a four-letter word.

Somehow I made my excuses and went to bed in the little back bedroom. I can't explain the depths I was in, the revulsion and disgust and terror that my father's "objective" explanation had wrought in me. Yes, I had known about these things on the farm, where they were a part of the wonders and mysteries of nature; but now, in applying them to human beings, my father had stripped away all the wonder and mystery; he had even stripped away the humanity.

Usually Daddy's instructions, lectures, and pontifications were listened to with half an ear, an attentive face, and a wandering mind. They were dismissed except for a kernel of information which I could store away as another clue toward living in peace with him. But now I had learned that human beings were animals, and nightmares filled my sleep. Vaguely I heard my mother crying during the night after she came home—sobbing during their low conversation. In the morning her eyes were red. She gave me a searching, bitterly sad look and said, "Well, now you know." No amplification, no softening, no explanation of the possibility that what had been told me was about an "act of love." It had nothing to do with love; to be human was vile, we were even constructed so that we would do vile things.

It may have been coincidence, but I think not—my breasts stopped developing and my menses became monthly crippling periods of pain.

Shyness became part of my personality. Physical contact of any kind was avoided. My growing emotions were repressed completely. During the following four years there were several one-sided "romances." Always with older men, since I had no association with other adolescents. I enjoyed a "romantic" feeling of wanting to "be in love" but my ideal was still the knight in shining armor who would never touch me. Because my ideal was not reality, I got even with reality by being a somewhat vicious little tease. As soon as there was any response, it was the end. I was as cold as ice.

I graduated from grammar school, the Kenwood-Loring School for Girls, in 1919. Daddy decided he would take over my high school instruction, and he sent for the Horace Mann correspondence course, so my courses could be accredited. All I remember about that final year in Chicago was that I fell while I was roller skating, and I broke my nose. It bled violently, and the pain was agonizing, but not a word of sympathy did I get. My father kept saying, "It may ruin her career!" But it didn't. It improved the shape of my nose.

My father had always looked on Chicago as only a halfway point. When we left Quincy, our money would take us only this far. The "Fame and Fortune" contest was a yearly event, and Daddy always felt that if we could be "on the spot," in New York, I would win the contest. Each year he entered a picture of me, and each year the picture appeared on the "honor roll," but never on the winning ticket.

In June 1920 he had saved enough money to take us the rest of the way. So on we went; on to New York; on to "Fame and Fortune."

☆

Two

We arrived in New York with three hundred dollars and hope. During the coming weeks both would be stretched to fearful thinness.

In the confusion and noise of Grand Central Station, bedraggled after the long trip from Chicago, we must have looked like weary immigrants, bird cage, tied-up bundles, and all. It was late at night. Mother and I slept on the station benches while Daddy went scouting for a place where we could spend the night.

He came back brimming over with satisfaction. With his invincible enthusiasm for the "grand," he proudly announced he had found a place "just off Fifth Avenue." That, of course, was supposed to suggest elegance. It was off Fifth Avenue all right— west a few doors on about Thirty-third Street. It was little better than a flophouse. Mother and I slept on the bed, and Daddy slept on the floor. We were kept awake most of the night, or what was left of it, by bedbugs and a fire alarm.

I shall never forget the next day. We walked, and walked, and walked. Daddy, in his vigor and enthusiasm, loved every minute of it. It never entered his mind that Mother and I were not as strong as he. We pushed on, through the Park, over to Amsterdam Avenue, until we began longing for even the vermin-infested room where we had spent the night. Finally, at about 110th Street, we found an apartment for rent and took it on the spot. We had a living room and two bedrooms to ourselves; the kitchen and bathroom we shared with a woman who worked during the day, and with another woman and her young "daughter"—who I later learned visited the male occupants of the apartment house for a fee.

As I remember, I was dazed and confused by the rapid changes and the frantic activity of these weeks. I don't think that I especially shared either my parents' enthusiasm or their hope. I did what I was told without thinking too much about it. I was interested in the newness of an unfamiliar city; I studied the maps and knew a good deal about its physical features, but nothing about its character. It seemed cleaner than Chicago—the air was from the sea—and the people seemed kinder. But I wanted time to think about what was happening, to try to remember who I was and what I was. So I preferred to sit on the fire escape of the apartment, where I could feel safe and quietly content. A little sun came into the court for a while during the afternoon, and I would brush my hair, and watch the cats fighting, and wonder at the long lines of clothes hung in the areaway, and listen with curiosity to the strange speech: "Fa cryin' out loud, Jimmy, ya comin' in 'r aincha!"

I was only dimly aware of my father's unceasing activity, his telephone calls and letters, his tremendous perseverance. He was still hot on the trail of the contest; he was convinced that the "Fame and Fortune" road would lead us to wealth and happiness. Finally, through sheer tenacity, he achieved an interview with Eugene Brewster; and with the air of a conqueror he returned home one day with an invitation to bring me to Mr. Brewster's estate in Roslyn to make a screen test with some of the other contestants. This was what we had waited and worked for. This was why we had sold our furniture and left Quincy, why we had suffered through three years of poverty and thwarted hope in Chicago. The pressure was crushing. By the time we arrived at Roslyn, I was tongue-tied and awkward. My mind was thick with uncertainty and confusion. My reticence exasperated Mother and Daddy. Daddy gripped my arm so hard it hurt, and he whispered angrily, "You have to be more *forward*, Lucile. Don't just stand around like a bump on a log!"

Someone led me into the house and up the stairs, and into a bedroom swarming with beautiful girls, all prettily dressed. The blur of chatter bewildered me. A man was helping with make-up, going from one girl to another with a bit of advice. He saw me standing there, frightened and uncertain, and he walked over to me. "Let me make you up," he said rather brusquely. He looked at me with the odd impersonal look of a painter, neither approving or disapproving, but seeing only form and color and light. It made me feel more comfortable, and I didn't feel called on to make the small talk that was always difficult for me.

Soon after he had finished, we were all called down to the garden. There, threatening but yet impressive, was the first movie camera I had ever seen, and some reflectors. Mr. Brewster was standing beside the camera. Each of us in turn had to walk in front of the camera, look up at Mr. Brewster and hold out our arms and say, "Darling, I love you, I want you!" Maybe Mr. Brewster enjoyed it; he was so unattractive that it was probably the only way he could get a pretty girl to say that sort of thing to him. But I didn't enjoy it. I was awful. The reflectors hurt my eyes, and I squinted. I walked awkwardly, and my arms felt as though they were made of wood. The road to "Fame and Fortune"? For me this was strictly a detour.

While I was waiting my turn to walk in front of the camera I saw the man who had made me up deep in conversation with Mother and Daddy. I watched him for a moment, and I liked his serious air, the sensitive face, and the eyes that seemed to look through and beyond the things and people in front of him. His name, I learned later that afternoon, was Charles Albin; he was then one of the foremost photographers in New York—not a society photographer, but a true artist who was developing new methods and lighting and effects in photography, treating it, he explained, as "painting in light." When I walked over to them later, Daddy was saying that we couldn't afford that kind of photography, and Mr. Albin explained that he wanted some sittings for his own pleasure. He felt I had a "Madonna quality" that he would like to try to capture.

Our friendship with "Allie" became a lasting and a valuable one, and it led directly to my next chance.

I like to think back on his big studio loft at Sixty-sixth Street and Columbus Avenue. I loved the atmosphere of its quiet and even strangely relaxed intensity, and I loved the work with Albin. He used only daylight and screens, and the pace was slow and restful. Mother would sit quietly sewing while we worked.

I was thrilled to find there in the studio some pictures that he had done of Lillian Gish, my idol! I was even more thrilled to learn that he knew her well, and that he would arrange for us to meet her! This was the first real, heart-thumping excitement that I had felt in my quest for an acting career. I was not just meeting my first movie star; that would have been interesting, but not a cause for the breathless anticipation I felt. I was going to meet Lillian Gish!

We met her. My first reaction was a momentary astonishment that here was merely a flesh-and-blood woman, simply dressed, with no make-up—and not even a sign of an ermine cloak. And the next moment I was utterly captivated by this sweet, lovely woman, completely unaffected and genuine. Best of all, she shared Allie's enthusiasm over my possibilities, and—she would arrange for me to have a test at Griffith's studio!

I had been happy and excited at the thought of meeting Lillian Gish; I can't describe my happiness at the thought of a test in the studio of the great D. W. Griffith. I had seen and loved all of his work; he was the great producer of his time, and the people who worked with him were the great stars of their time—some of them the great stars of all time.

We went out to the studio at Mamaroneck. We caught a brief

glimpse of the fabulous D.W., but it was Lillian who met us, and greeted us warmly, and helped me make up, talking and explaining and calming my jitters. She showed me how to apply mascara to my eyelashes, and how to blend the grease paint, and then she helped me put on one of her own dresses, one that she had worn in *True Heart Susie*, to wear for the test.

The sets of *Way Down East* were still standing in the studio. The picture had been out for some time, and I had seen it. It was wonderful to touch the furniture, the doorknobs, to admire the realistic detail, even to the worn risers on the staircase. Griffith was the first "realist"—he was not satisfied with slap-dash "flats," with walls that swayed if someone touched them.

The test was long and difficult. Lillian sat in a camp chair beside the camera, suggesting shots, suggesting angles and lighting and movements. She had me recite a few lines of poetry. It took hours, but they were exciting, rapturous hours.

Now there was indeed jubilation among the Langhankes. My father was triumphant. Of course I would get a contract. We were in! We stayed in the apartment, hardly daring to leave for a moment lest the telephone should ring while we were gone. We waited for days. The days became weeks, and our exultation gradually wore away into a bitter disappointment.

We had lost out. No one knew why, but we had lost out. Albin asked Lillian, but she couldn't, or wouldn't, tell him. Inquiries at the studio met only evasive, non-committal replies. It remained a mystery.

Three or four years later we saw Lillian at the Savoy-Plaza, and she took the blame herself. "Mr. Griffith is peculiar," she told us. "He likes to make his own discoveries, and I think I pushed you too hard." But a few years ago I saw her, and she told me the truth. Mr. Griffith had taken one look at Daddy, and that had been enough. "The man is a walking cash register," he had told Lillian. "I would never have any freedom to develop the girl; the 'old man' will always be an interfering nuisance." Of course D.W. was right; in about ten years the Motion Picture Producers Association would tell Daddy the same thing, and they would state it flatly: I would simply not get any more work if he continued to represent me. He was just too much trouble; every item of a contract became an argument. They could not tolerate his arrogance.

This was my first professional disappointment, and it was a great, a crushing disappointment. There were to be many more, and more serious ones; but this one I wept over quietly into my pillow at night. But a few days later, when I could think about it more calmly, I told myself firmly that if I had been what Mr. Griffith wanted he would have signed me up. I wasn't, so he didn't. And if he didn't want me, I didn't want him.

We had been in New York several weeks now, and there was still no job. Money was getting desperately low. Daddy and I began to "make the rounds." It was a weary time. I sat on every bench in every casting office in New York. No one was interested. The folder of pictures Albin had taken got some attention, but I was always either "too young" or "too tall," or "lacking experience." And the money got lower and lower, and we began to live on coffee and cereals and bread.

It was September, but it seemed that a lifetime had passed since that night in June when we straggled into Grand Central Station. Daddy finally decided that he ought to try to get some work, anything to earn the money for rent and food. He had written an adaptation of Sudermann's *Elga*, and he thought there might be a chance of doing translations from the German for movie scripts. He got an appointment with Harry Durant, the head of the writing department at Famous Players-Lasky, to discuss the possibility. Mr. Durant wasn't interested, but he was interested in the folder of Albin pictures that Daddy had carried with him "just in case."

Things suddenly began to happen very fast. In a kind of "montage" I remember meeting Mr. Durant and being taken in to meet Jesse Lasky, a man named Walter Wanger, and a lady called Louella Parsons. There was a frantic hour of shopping on Forty-second Street to find me some shoes with low heels: the best we could do was a pair of "Ground-Grippers," hideous heavy oxfords that looked terrible with a taffeta dress. I was painfully ashamed of them, especially in Mr. Lasky's office, when I had to "stand up and walk over there . . . Now turn around . . ."

When objects and ideas again emerged out of the chaos, it had happened. Almost before we could comprehend it, I had a six-month contract at sixty dollars a week. And a few days later I had a new name, supplied by the publicity department. Lucile Langhanke, the little girl from Quincy, had become Mary Astor, actress under contract to Famous Players-Lasky.

The first sixty dollars came, and we could eat again. We celebrated. Daddy went out and bought a steak and a large bag of oranges and some phonograph records.

I was not to begin working in a picture right away. Mr. Lasky planned to develop me into a new "star," and that would demand a great deal of necessary and valuable groundwork. They sent me to see my first plays: William Gillette in J. M. Barrie's *Dear Brutus*, and then Ruth Chatterton in *Mary Rose*. And they wanted me to get used to the atmosphere of the studios, so Mother and I went as observers out to Astoria, Long Island, where the new Famous Players-Lasky studios had recently been opened. It was fascinating. This, of course, was in the days of the silent movies, and as many as three to six companies were all shooting on the same stage at the same time. Ethel Clayton would be working on a set on one part of the stage; Rudolph Valentino and Bebe Daniels on another. I couldn't talk to them, but I could see them. For a "movie fan" this was paradise. And I was still a "movie fan"; I could not realize that I would ever become a part of this strange world.

The thrill of seeing the people I had known so well on the screen soon died. On one of our first days at the Long Island Studios, a vision in tulle and satin, twinkling with diamonds, swept by us, leaving in her wake a delicious, if mildly overpowering, aroma of gardenias. Mother's eyes popped, and she grabbed me and gasped, "Do you know who *that* was?" "Sure," I said, "it was Mae Murray. And I can't see why they say her lips are 'bee-stung.' She has a pretty mouth, but she puts too much goo on it." Mother was visibly annoyed by my irreverence.

I was impatient to get to work, to begin "acting." Finally I was assigned to a "bit" part in *Sentimental Tommy*, which they were making from the J. M. Barrie book. I had read and loved the book and its sequel, *Tommy and Grizel*; and I was delighted at the chance to be a part of the picture. Gareth Hughes was playing the part of Tommy and May McAvoy was Grizel. My "bit" was simply a double-exposure "dream figure" that appeared beside Tommy while he was dreaming, sitting on a garden bench. The still taken from the scene was reproduced and used on all the twenty-four sheets advertising the picture—but the scene itself ended in the limbo of the cutting-room floor.

More weeks of inactivity followed, and then I went to work on a one-reel propaganda picture called *Bullets or Ballots*. It was directed by two men who were on the writing staff at Famous, Frank Tuttle and Monty Woolley (without the beard), but it didn't come off very well. The studio heads looked at it and conferred briefly. They had no difficulty in arriving at their decision. The picture was shelved.

The six months ended, and with them my contract. I was out of work, and my six months with Lasky had come to nothing. I had not a thing to show from it. A scene cut from a picture and a shelved one-reeler are not much of a recommendation.

Money was low again. When we had it, my father spent it. And now we didn't have it. Once more we trudged from casting office to casting office. Or we sat gloomily around the apartment —a bigger and nicer apartment now. In looking back to this period I discover that it is hard to find "me." I merge impersonally into the concerted activity of the family. Mother and Daddy and I lived so intimately, so closely, with such singleness of purpose, that there could not have been five minutes out of the day when one did not know what the others were doing. I was impersonally caught up in the pursuit of whatever it was that we were chasing. There was little quarreling or scolding.

Albin was an always reliable source of reassurance and confidence. It was Albin who got me my next picture—and this was the picture that marked the real beginning of my career. It involved no famous producers, no big-name studio, none of the turmoil and hopeful expectation that had accompanied my earlier attempts. Albin knew an artist who was trying an experiment in diffusion photography. This artist—Léjaron Hiller his name was —planned a series of two-reel pictures on the background of famous paintings and how the artists came to paint them. The first was to be King Cophetua and the Beggar Maid, of Burne-Jones. I resembled the girl in the painting very closely, auburn hair and all. I made a screen test and got the job.

We worked three weeks on it, in the studio and on location. I had very little "acting" to do. I was cast as a simple farm girl who was used by the painter to pose for his masterpiece—it was practically type casting!

The picture was a resounding success; the critics described it as a "little gem." And it put my name in lights on a theatre marquee. That part of it I didn't know about at first; it was a surprise that Mother and Daddy carefully staged for me. The picture first played at the Rivoli Theater. The subway exit was just around the corner, and as we came up the steps and walked around to the theatre, there it was, my name in lights! MARY ASTOR in THE BEGGAR MAID.

Mother always told the story that I almost fainted, and they had to carry me into the theatre. I did no such thing. I was just pleased and gratified. But I never contradicted her; hers was the better story.

I was on my way now. I had had my name in lights, and that would make it easier to get more jobs. There was no reason why I shouldn't keep going up. Apparently I was intelligent; I could at least do what I was told, and that passed for acting. I photographed as an extremely beautiful young lady. And nothing in my personal life could distract me from my work. In fact, I had no personal life. There was no school, no beaux, no parties, no friends of my own age. There was just Mother and Daddy and the people in the studios. And I was chaperoned ever more and

more closely. I was given no chance to "get off by myself"; even
if I got up to go to the ladies' room, Mother would say, "Wait,
Lucile, I'll go with you." Or if I talked a little longer than usual
to any one person, Mother would walk up and cheerfully barge
into the conversation.

At home the high school work had been dropped. There was
not enough time to do everything, and I had been getting nowhere with it anyway. Algebra or geometry as taught by my father was an impossibility for me. I simply sat there. It wouldn't
penetrate. Except when I was working on a picture I was expected
to put in six hours a day practicing the piano—three two-hour
periods. And as soon as we could afford it, Daddy took me to
Carnegie Hall, to Charles Stuart, for vocal lessons twice a week;
Mother took me to Denishawn for dancing lessons three times a
week. Singing was difficult; Daddy sat in the corner during lessons, and I constantly felt his unspoken criticism. But dancing
was different. I was taking the lessons because Daddy decided I
should get rid of my adolescent awkwardness, but it turned out
to be the first thing that I *had* to do that I *wanted* to do. Ruth
St. Denis and Ted Shawn were fine teachers. They made you feel
a love and enthusiasm for dancing. I don't know whether I was
any good or not, but I didn't care. I liked it. I liked the drill work
at the bar, the stretching and pulling that made my muscles ache,
with a *good* ache. I liked the group work, the working in unison;
I felt an exhilarating outlet for all my built-up aggressions. I still
like to remember the deep breathing and the "toned-up" feeling,
and I like to recall the pungent odor of the banana oil that was
used in gilding the ballet shoes. Even today I can be perfectly
content being a spectator at a concert, or even in the theatre, but
when I see a fine team of dancers I ache to be up there with them.

For a while my film work did not progress beyond the two-
reelers. During the summer after *The Beggar Maid*, I made three
of them on location in Augusta, Maine. They weren't very pro-
found—thrillers, Canadian mounties, and that sort of thing. But
it was a beautiful summer; most of the work was in pine woods
and around little lakes. And of course the leading man and I

persuaded ourselves that we had fallen in love. There was nothing we could do about it though. Either Mother or Daddy sat between us in the car going to and from location, and if we wanted to "go for a walk" they decided it was a fine idea—they'd like a little walk, too. Behind their backs I looked at him with properly gauged expressions of tragic frustration, and it was all very romantic—and completely safe.

After making six two-reelers I finally got into a feature picture, *John Smith*, for Selznick Brothers, with a great but waning star of this period, Eugene O'Brien. He and Norma Talmadge had done many memorable love stories together; I had seen all of them, and again I felt a glow of pleasure at being there on the set with him and working with him. Not that I did a great deal of work in that picture; my part was small, and most of the time I sat and watched, chewing on my fingernails meditatively until they bled, or pulling at my eyelashes, which, being heavily laden with mascara, were irritating. And as I sat I perpetually heard the sound of Mother's coquettish "company voice" chattering easily. There must have been a certain amount of jealousy on her part. The men around the sets liked her; she could keep up a conversational patter with them, and they looked on her as a "good sport." But I think she would have liked to do what I was doing. I was in front of the camera, and she would always be behind it. So she compensated with her joking and talking, and her mild flirtations. I sat there, expressionless, listening, and enduring the constant references to me, and the talk about the hopes for me and the plans for me.

Work became steady. Several of the films I did I have almost forgotten, but I remember doing one important one—as Richard Barthelmess' leading lady in Hergesheimer's *The Bright Shawl*. We were working at the Fifty-sixth Street Studio, on the upper level of a stage. On the lower level Alice Brady was making one of her famous comedies. Visiting other sets was a common practice, and now I found myself meeting and talking to players I had only looked at before—Bebe Daniels, Valentino, Ethel Clayton, Elsie Ferguson. But Miss Ferguson had a special sign on her set which read: "Please do not speak to Miss Ferguson unless she speaks to you."

Still I had no feeling of belonging to this strange new world, or being a part of it. It was too unbelievably different from the world I had grown up in; it still seemed remote, even inaccessible. Some of this alien feeling was washed away when I did *Second Fiddle* with the Film Guild group. They were not hardened manufacturers of movies; they were young, well educated, enthusiastic, and withal a bit snobbish and full of high-sounding theories about the moving pictures as an art form. Before I worked with them, no one had tried to make me feel I "belonged"; they did. They brought me into the group; they made me feel important. I began to open up, to join in conversations, and finally I even tried to make jokes. When suddenly I found I was beginning to be teased I hastily withdrew back into my shell; it was then that one of them (Osgood Perkins—Tony Perkins' father) had the perception and kindness to give me the world-shaking news that people just didn't tease a person they dislike. Then the world was all right again, and once more I could feel comfortable. My conversation became more certain, I began to read the things that they were reading—they were worshipers at the F. Scott Fitzgerald shrine; some of them had been his classmates—and to join in the sophisticated discussions of manners and ideas and personalities. I was growing rapidly, filling out emotionally and intellectually.

But every night I had to go back to my prison, to the constant watchfulness, the petty corrections and dictatorial advice, and listen to Daddy expound wisely and scathingly on "all their superficial nonsense."

In April 1923, I signed a new contract with Famous Players, far different from the first one I signed with them. This contract was for one year, and called for five hundred dollars a week. Daddy blossomed happily in such prosperity. He bought expensive though somewhat too youthful suits and carried a malacca cane. And he bought a co-operative apartment in Jackson Heights, Long Island. We ordered all new furniture; there was even to be a baby grand in the living room. And I had a bedroom done in my favorite colors (then!), orchid and green.

I had to wait almost a year before I could use the room. The family was still surging with the excitement and prosperity of the new contract when Famous announced they were going to send me to the West Coast for a picture. This called for a solemn family council, with Daddy doing all the discussing and making all the decisions. He decided he would stay in New York to look after the work on the new apartment and Mother would accompany me to Hollywood. I concealed a palpitating excitement; to have shown any pleasure at his decision would have been the worst possible tactical error. But the thought of the excitement and glamour of Hollywood *without* his constant watchfulness and nagging criticism stirred me to an enthusiasm that was hard to disguise.

Mother and I arrived in Hollywood on April 19, 1923, just two weeks before my seventeenth birthday. It's hard to describe the calm, hard kind of excitement that I felt, and felt very intensely. The very name "Hollywood" seemed to bring me closer to the fact that I was a real live "movie actress." The work in New York, the first rungs of the climb to success, the lessening of money worries—all these were fine, but nothing could bring the golden haze of glamour that was Hollywood. Here were all the buildings and places I had seen in the movie magazines. I devoured it.

We walked up and down Hollywood Boulevard, though this was a little disappointing after the brilliance and rush of Broadway; it was a little drab—until a great shining car would streak in and out of traffic with the initials "T.M." blazing from every possible space in leather set with brilliants. And we checked in at the Hollywood Hotel, "popular rendezvous for the younger set," the movie magazines had assured me. I inspected with interest the building where I would work, the Famous Players-Lasky Studio—a green frame building set behind a row of pepper trees. And I rode in complete disbelief down Sunset Boulevard, "the address of the stars," with its houses that were monstrosities of architecture, but reeking with money, and I looked down the side streets at the houses that were smaller imitations of their grandeur, complete with red tile roofs and Moorish wrought-iron work at their windows.

Ralph Faulkner, with whom I had made one of the "painting" two-reelers (*Hope*) in New York, had come to Hollywood to try his luck, and he had bought a fairly smooth-running but very unglamorous Model T Ford. He drove Mother and me through the beautiful hills, with the Model T wheezing like an old woman, and I loved the smell of the manzanita and the eucalyptus. We drove to the beach down Wilshire Boulevard—just a two-lane tarmac road west of La Brea, and none too safe to travel at night—and there was the beautiful Pacific Ocean, and Castle Rock, where we went swimming and made a bonfire for weiner roasts. They blasted the top of the rock off to make way for a highway a number of years ago and changed the shape of some pleasant memories.

Mother and I decided to give up our rooms at the Hollywood Hotel; the expense, with the added burden of maintaining the apartment and Daddy in New York, was too great a strain on our budget. We moved to a comfortable but rather dreary apartment, the Hillview. And I went to work.

Famous had brought me out to do a picture called *To the Ladies*, but when I arrived at the studio they switched me to the ingénue in a picture directed by William DeMille. I don't even remember the name; it wasn't a very good picture, and I was more interested in the new and unfamiliar sights, the strange antics of those unpredictable Hollywood people.

Instead of just the one picture I made two—the second as insignificant as the first. And then an astonishing and wonderful thing happened. It changed all our plans, and Daddy closed the apartment in New York and came out here, and we rented a larger furnished apartment at the Hillview. The cause of the turmoil and activity was the biggest thing that had happened to me yet. John Barrymore had asked for me to play the lead opposite him in the picture he was to make for Warner Brothers—*Beau Brummel.*

Famous Players had negotiated a loan-out deal at a substantial profit to themselves; Warner's was paying eleven hundred dollars for me. This, of course, was a cause of great anguish to my father. He stomped around a few offices about it, but there was nothing that could be done. It was a quite customary procedure. The financial side of it did not bother me in the least. I knew I was to work with the greatest actor of our times; that was well worth all the disappointments and boredom and hard work I had been through.

I was already signed for the role, but there was a preliminary test to be made to see how we looked together and for us to get acquainted. I shall never forget that afternoon. Mother said my feet never touched the sidewalk all the way home afterwards. She was inclined to say things like that, but this time I think it was true.

We were both in costume of sorts, just enough to indicate the period, and as we were standing in for lighting my awe for this great man made me confused and awkward. Mr. Barrymore broke through my shyness by talking about everything under the sun but the picture; he made me laugh about something, and he gradually and skillfully made me feel that I was his contemporary as an actor and as a person. He told me he had seen a picture of me in a magazine while he was on a train coming out from New York, and the caption had appealed to him: "On the brink of womanhood." I told him I was seventeen, and he said, just a little sadly, "It seems so long ago that I was seventeen. I'm *forty* now."

"*That's* not so old," I said, and we were great friends.

I know that on that afternoon we fell in love, and I am sure he was even more startled than I.

Three

The romance flourished, quietly and unobtrusively, under the unseeing eyes of everyone, including my parents. In the filming of the many romantic, delicate love scenes of *Beau Brummel* we could stand in each other's arms, Jack in his romantic red and blue hussar uniform and white wig, I in the beautiful Empire style dresses, while the camera and lights were being set. We whispered softly, or just stood there, quietly loving the closeness; and no one was the wiser. Between scenes, Jack had the prop man place two camp chairs together just off the set, and we sat side by side.

When Jack was shooting a scene without me, I followed his every movement and word. To sit there and watch him was for me a perfect joy; but absorbed though I was in my love, I found that to watch him was also a lesson in acting. I was impressed by the keenness of his analysis and interpretation of character. He was the first actor I ever heard speak of a character in the third person. Instead of saying "*I* will do this," or "*I* will make my entrance when a certain event occurs," Jack would say, "I don't think the guy would do that. I think he's so mad he wouldn't even bow to the king." He was thinking of the character as a real being, with an intrinsic character that would cause him to re-act in ways quite different from the way he, as John Barrymore, would react.

To me everything he did was perfect, but I am sure that even an impartial judge would have been impressed by his unassuming friendliness among the other players and workers. He was the first star I knew who behaved like a human being around the set, with-out a hint of affectation or condescension. He called the workmen by their first names, and often became engrossed in long conversa-tions with them. But he always preserved a sense of dignity; you could never quite forget that he was John Barrymore. There was a story about a man who did forget it and called, "Hey, Jack!" Mr. Barrymore fixed a glinting eye on him and replied icily, "Why so formal? Just call me kid."

And sometimes his unpredictable behavior and language would cause Mother to engage me quickly in conversation. Jack and Wil-lard Louis, who was playing the part of George III, had become great friends; when they played a scene together they would em-bellish the dialogue with the most colorful obscenities. The peo-ple on the set thought it was hilarious; Mother was distressed— and she would hurry me out of earshot. I understand that after the picture was released the studio received a mountain of mail from deaf people who could read lips.

Our romance could not be confined to the hours we were on the set. Jack at once cultivated the friendship of my awed parents. He would come to dinner at the little apartment and praise Mother's cooking. He knew more about Germany than Daddy did, so he talked Germany with him by the hour. He used all his charm on them, and he had more of it than any other man I have ever known.

He immediately saw and understood my parents' attitudes to-ward me, and he saw that I would have to break away from their selfish and smothering domination before I could achieve any real growth as a person or as an actress. And now their constant presence, their control of every moment of my life, became a new source of irritation. We desperately wanted to be alone, away from their incessant talk and their intrusion into all we said or did.

Jack discussed my career with Daddy with great candidness. "She just doesn't know what it's all about," he concluded, "but I think she can learn, and I want to help her." In this, he told me, he was being absolutely truthful. He talked about Margaret Carrington, Walter Huston's sister; she was a truly great dramatic coach, he said, and he gave her credit for the fullness of his own development as an actor. At the time, he was working with her on his *Hamlet*, which was to open in New York in about two months. He thought he could help me with some of her methods, and if my parents agreed, he would work with me.

Of course they agreed, they were almost incoherent with pleasure and gratification at the thought that John Barrymore would work with their daughter. So on afternoons when we were not working on the picture, Mother and Daddy sat in the dining room, reading and whispering, while in the living room Jack talked to me. He talked about fundamentals of breathing and of diction, and gave me exercises in both. He explained to me about "authority" and "vitality." One afternoon I asked him to show me what he meant by one of these terms; he stood up quite simply and began the great soliloquy:

> Now I am alone.
> O, what a rogue and peasant slave am I!
> Is it not monstrous that this player here,
> But in a fiction, in a dream of passion,
> Could force so his soul to his own conceit . . .

The tawdry little living room vibrated with magnificence.

He finally told Mother and Daddy that he must work alone with me. "I feel she's too self-conscious. She's too afraid of what *you* are thinking, instead of listening to me." This was true, but it was only a part of the truth. They hesitated. He knew what they were thinking, and he beat them to the point. "Don't be ridiculous!" he said. "This is a *kid!*"

Every Sunday for the rest of the summer he sent his car for Mother and me, and we rode to his suite at the Beverly Hills Hotel. There Mother sat on the veranda and sewed. And we were alone.

In looking back I do not find it easy to discuss or explain my love for Jack. I know, first of all, that the overwise and cynical will dismiss it as just another case of the naïve and inexperienced girl blinded and made giddy by the wiles of a man of the world, an accomplished roué. If it had been that simple it would be a great deal easier to talk about. But it wasn't. I know Jack loved me. I know it as surely as I know the fact of my own existence. Fifteen years afterwards he was talking to me about it, telling me how surprised he had been to find himself beginning to love me that first day on the *Beau Brummel* set. Even then, fifteen years later, he didn't dismiss it lightly. "It's a good thing I wasn't free to marry," he said then. "And it's a good thing I couldn't get you away from your family. I would have married you, and you would have had a miserable life."

Or, if you wanted casually to brush the whole thing away, you could say I had fallen in love with the glamour of a name, or the vibrant Barrymore charm. Perhaps, but I think it was more than that, much more. I know that he gave me a love, wholehearted and undemanding, such as I had never before known. I had certainly not found it in my family. And I know that I suddenly found myself loved and wanted and needed. I grasped at that love with unthinking and unquestioning violence, as a starving man will grasp for food. I didn't ponder over it; I didn't analyze it. I just gathered it to me greedily and thankfully.

Not for a moment was I concerned with the violation of moral laws or the breaking of a commandment. The only moral law I knew was the law proclaimed by my father, and it had been many years now since I had had any faith in his laws. So I felt no guilt. I knew our love must be concealed, but I did not conceal it because I was ashamed of it. It had to be concealed from my parents, because to me it was something indescribably precious, and I knew they would destroy it. Somehow, despite all I could have done, they would have destroyed it. They would not then have tolerated anything that might weaken their influence. So I had to be extremely cautious not to let it make any difference in my relationship with them. And it had to be concealed from society because society could not know about it without my parents knowing.

I know that Jack never told anyone about us; he protected me completely. In Gene Fowler's book about him, *Good Night, Sweet Prince*, there is a noticeable gap in his personal life during these years. Only the stage triumph of *Hamlet* is mentioned. His personal life is not resumed until his meeting with Dolores Costello. And I know that Fowler was very close to him, so I know Jack did not talk about it even to him. It was many years before I could bring myself to talk about it to anyone but my closest friends. It is only now that, for the first time, I can force myself to focus all my attention on it, to try to recall all its details.

Our romance moved slowly, over a period of some months. Jack was much like a young boy in love courting his sweetheart—not bashfully, for that would have been totally unlike him, but gently and tenderly. He knew from my behavior that I had received some strong shock, that I was repelled even by a kiss, and he respected my feelings, willing to wait until I outgrew them.

He gave me love, affection, humor and, above all, beauty. He always had flowers in his rooms, and inevitably a bowl of tuberoses in the window. He encouraged me to think out and talk about ideas—often some rather abstract ideas. To help feed my growing mind he gave me books on philosophy, art, music, drama, poetry. He collected rare books, and he showed me beautiful samples of the art of printing; he picked up an ordinary-looking volume, flexed the front edges of the pages, and showed me the beautiful fore-edge painting—which I had never heard of before. He taught me about manners, consideration for others. Social conduct, he explained, was not designed to "impress" people; but by considerate behavior "we acknowledge their existence, which

everyone needs to be assured of." He stretched my mind in all
directions.

With all this he never lost sight of his promise to deepen my
knowledge and understanding of the theatre. We worked on
scenes from Shakespeare; we were Richard and Anne, Hamlet and
Ophelia. He worked hard on my speech; it was heavy with Mid-
western *r*'s, and he drilled me tirelessly on words like "purple"
and "world." He was demanding, intolerant of careless or slip-
shod work, but he was at the same time patient and loving.

He seldom drank around me. His language, since he was John
Barrymore, was often strong, but it was never filthy.

He was extremely considerate and tactful with my parents. He
did many thoughtful things: a beautiful dinner at the Biltmore,
with caviar and special coffee brewed at the tables, expanded
Daddy to beaming delight. When the four of us were together, he
talked over my head to them, listening to Daddy's views on everything. Sometimes I would see his nostrils go white and thin, and
his mouth tighten with the restraint he forced on himself. When
we were alone, he blasted them in his own colorful language,
which I wish I could remember more clearly. "Your father would
make an excellent butler," he would say, or "They talk about you
as though you were a trained seal instead of an artist."

He warned me vehemently that I could never grow as long as
they dominated me. "Mark me well," he said, "you can never
develop your potentialities as an actress until you develop as an
individual. Until you break away from their domination, they'll
stifle you. They'll just make a meal ticket out of you. And you're
the only one who can do anything about it. I can't do it for you,
although I hope I can at least instill some dissatisfaction in you.
But you're the only one who can make the decision that you're
going to stand on your own feet, to walk without leaning on other
people."

Beau Brummel came to a close, and Jack went back to New York
and opened in *Hamlet*—which made theatrical history. I don't remember whether I made another picture then; my mind and heart

were too full of him. I remember only the ineffable joy I felt when I learned that we too were to return to New York. I would be near him, with him, once more.

Then we were back in New York, at the apartment in Jackson Heights. The day we arrived, Jack had the apartment opened, and it was overflowing with flowers, baskets and bowls of roses and chrysanthemums. And there in the window, a bowl of tuberoses. I knew he meant them just for me.

I saw him every day, except matinee days. Daddy and I drove to the Ambassador (we had a rented car and a chauffeur) every day at one, and he called for me at six. For several months we led an almost domestic life. Jack had an elaborate suite on almost the top floor of the hotel in the beautiful rooms that we called "our house." He kept it as a permanent residence, and had many of his own things in it: elaborate chandeliers from Venice, shelves and shelves of books, a great Steinway concert grand piano, exquisite rugs and lamps and bits of sculpture and fine paintings. Driving over the Queensboro Bridge in the morning, I would search out the building, and locate "our windows," and my heart would fill to bursting.

Of course the subject of marriage came up. Jack had been separated from his wife for two years; she was in Paris with their child. But I shied fearfully away from talk of marriage. I knew he loved me, but I was afraid of so irrevocable a decision as marriage would be. I wanted things to stay just as they were. I was afraid of Daddy, and I was afraid of breaking away from his domination. I had become accustomed to the protection from responsibility, from the need for making decisions. There was an unhealthy feeling of comfort in this spineless, will-less existence. So I told myself that I was not really adequate for this great man. I convinced myself that all these half-truths justified my attitude. I avoided the real truth, that I could not accept the burden of thinking and acting like a responsible adult.

And then separation loomed bleakly in front of us. Jack was to take *Hamlet* on a short tour of the principal Eastern cities: Philadelphia, Boston, Washington, and some others. We didn't tell my family exactly when he was going, for they would have been there smothering us both with their good-bys and we wanted to be alone. As the time grew near, we clung to each other and wept. He begged me to be faithful. "You have become wise at deception," he told me. "Don't use it against me. I need your fidelity; I need to know that there is someone in the world who can be faithful."

The elevator was at the end of a long hall. I stood miserably at the door of the apartment; he kept turning around, or looking back over his shoulder, until he reached the elevator. There he waited a few moments until the elevator came. Then the doors closed behind him and he was gone.

The separation was to last longer than we knew. By the time he returned to New York, I was in Hollywood; and then he took *Hamlet* to London. My loneliness was a constant torment. There was no one I could talk to, and we couldn't even write to each other. My mail was not private; all letters were opened and read before they were given to me, and any letter I wrote had to be read before it was mailed. I couldn't write secretly, for I was not allowed out of the house alone, not even to go to the corner mailbox.

To protest against this situation would have caused suspicion, and it would also have been received by my father as a personal affront. Daddy could transform my simplest desire or need into a monstrous and preposterous passion that must be curbed. If I said, "Why can't I close my bedroom door, just so I can read and think quietly?" he would counter with a self-righteous resentment. "What are you doing that you don't want us to know about?" he would say. "Or maybe your own mother and father disturb you. Perhaps we should just pack up and move out. Maybe you'd rather we just moved off the face of the earth." I had become wearily accustomed to this from my childhood, but now that I had met Jack, and had savored a bit of independence, and had grown up a good deal, this repression was intolerable.

I languished in moodiness and melancholy, in my longing for Jack. After Mother and Daddy had gone to bed, I would sit in the embrasure of my window, my knees hugged up to my chin, and look out at the stars and wish we were like the lovers in *Peter Ibbetson,* who by "dreaming true" could find each other while they slept and travel all over the world together. I found a sad comfort in thinking about it; Jack had done the play, and had given me the book to read, and to think of it seemed to bring him closer.

I was low and spiritless; I ate little, and felt weak and dull. In my apathy I don't think I had the strength to "stand up to" my father, as I probably should have done. And if I had stood up to him I wouldn't have known how to follow through. If I had walked out of the house I would have had to come whimpering back, to bear his reproaches and insults. I had nowhere to go; I had nothing to escape to. I could not have made "a life of my own" because I wouldn't have known how. And even though I was almost eighteen I knew nothing of the ways of business; I couldn't even make out a check. If Mother and Daddy were discussing some problem of business relating to my work they never asked for my opinion. If I intruded a question, Daddy would look at me as if he hadn't realized that I was in the room, and he would dismiss me with "Never mind! You wouldn't understand."

We received telegrams and brief letters from Jack, written to all of us but containing a few code words and signs we had agreed on before he left. They meant as much to me as an impassioned love letter. And always he would end it with "and love to the dear Goopher." That was the absurd name he had invented to sound casually affectionate and offhand. He had schooled himself sternly to use only this name, so he would never give us away by accidentally calling me something more intensely and personally affectionate.

Just as the tour of *Hamlet* was drawing to a close, I was called out of New York to work in an adaptation of Booth Tarkington's *Magnolia,* renamed, as only the movies can rename things, *The Fighting Coward.* We had first to go on location at Natchez, Mississippi, to do the exterior scenes; then we would go to Hollywood to do the interiors. I remember something of that new, strange part of the country, the hanging moss, the beautiful mansions. The company was entertained at one of the great homes, and I remember marveling at the beautiful candelabra in the halls and rooms, actually lighted with candles. I wore hoop skirts and side curls for the picture—but I can't recall anything more about it. For me the music had stopped; I was living only for it to begin again, and meanwhile I was trying to hear again in my mind the music that I had already heard.

I had just made friends with a young actress in the company, and it was to her that I first confided my love for Jack. I could no longer keep it to myself; I was bursting with the pain of it, and I had to talk about it with someone. It was lucky that I did. Jack sent me a cablegram, and he must have been very drunk when he wrote it. He sent some hundred words of the most impassioned language that could be sent over the wires. I was desperate. Mother had been out shopping, so she didn't yet know about it. But the desk clerk at the hotel would tell her that a wire had come, and then it would be all over. I took my problem to my new friend and she solved it. She hurried down to the telegraph station and typed out an innocuous message on one of their forms; then she brought it to me, and I slipped it into the envelope. When Mother came in, I casually told her that a wire had come from Jack, and handed it to her. It seemed to me to have been a very narrow escape.

We finished our work in Natchez, and went on to Hollywood, where my father joined us. We rented a small house, bought a secondhand Dodge sedan, and hired a chauffeur, since none of us could drive. Then we went back to New York for another picture. Then back to Hollywood again. It is all a hazy jumble in my mind. The entire year of 1924 is an almost total blank. I know only that I was waiting for the time when Jack and I could be together again. Nothing else mattered.

One thing did matter a little, but only because Jack had wanted me to do it. He had profited from his work with Margaret Carrington; he thought she was wonderful, and he wanted me to work with her. During the summer, after we had returned from

New York, I went up to Santa Barbara to see her. She agreed to take me, though I sensed her feeling that I was only one of Jack's "passing fancies," and that she was doing him a favor without any real interest on her part. So almost every Sunday afternoon the rest of the summer we drove up to her beautiful estate, Villa Riposo. She was married to a very wealthy man, and had an elaborately beautiful house with magnificent gardens and a little studio in the form of a small Greek temple. I was ill at ease in all this grandeur. Several people always came in for luncheon, served by a number of maids; the array of silver baffled me, and the conversation I didn't understand at all.

She was nice to me; she introduced me as "Jack's little protégée." But she frightened me a little. She was a big-bosomed, Wagnerian soprano kind of woman (she had had something of a career in singing, I believe), with great vitality; and her brilliantly blue, penetrating eyes disconcerted me. We would work for an hour or so in the afternoon. Much of what she tried to teach me was over my head, but she did help me to lighten my speaking voice, which was rather low and on one key; she kept pushing it up so it had more variety and vitality. After the lesson I would walk in the gardens until Mother and Daddy picked me up at five.

The only picture of that year that I especially remember was *Enticement*. Ian Keith and Clive Brook were in it. I remember it because Jack and I saw it together, later, in New York, and he was annoyed that I should play in such "trash." And I remember it because it was a physically grueling picture to make; we had a long location trip to Banff, Alberta. The hotel at Lake Louise had recently burned down, so the company had to live at a hotel in Banff. Every morning we had to get up at four-thirty, drive in the snow to the lake, and then get into dog sleds for the long trek up the switchback to the glacier. Mother (Yes, she was there. She was always there.) complained that it was just too much for her; she started remaining behind at the hotel, and for the first time in my life I found myself unchaperoned during the filming of a picture. I took advantage of my brief freedom to try my first cigarettes.

I must have been making a good deal of money by then, for it was in the early months of 1925 that Daddy bought the home on Temple Hill Drive. He bought the house from a pleasant, congenial couple, the Hotcheners, who became our close friends. They were Theosophists. Mrs. Hotchener called herself "Helios"; she was an enthusiastic student of East Indian philosophy—she had studied with Blavatska, and was an associate of Annie Besant. She was considered very "advanced." But she was a warm, cheerful person, without any suggestion of "hocus-pocus" or phoniness. Her husband, Henry, was a sincere and devoted man, with a good business sense; he managed the financial affairs of their extensive real estate holdings. They had built several homes on a winding street leading up into the hills, and had named it Temple Hill. The houses were all unhappily Moorish in design, each with a "lotus flower" cupola, quantities of stained glass, and many East Indian archways.

Our house was ornate and "showy." Downstairs there was a large living room which joined through an archway with a music room and a small conservatory; a dining room, kitchen, and maid's quarters. Upstairs were three large bedrooms and two baths. I liked it. I was pleased that I was to have a bathroom all to myself and that my room had a small balcony that looked up into the hills.

When we acquired the house we also acquired a maid, a gardener, a Pierce-Arrow limousine, and a chauffeur. And we acquired friends. The Hotcheners lived next door, and became very close to all of us. Mother met and found common interests with a Dr. Glasgow (a woman osteopath) and Mrs. Thomas Ince. I found a girl friend, a little older than I was, in Menifee Johnstone. She immediately became a close confidante; I could talk over all my problems with her, and especially I could talk about Jack.

Making friends was not easy. Daddy was strongly anti-social; he regarded any attachment we might form outside of the family as a threat to his authority and control. At any rate, he seemed completely satisfied by his own small universe—his home, his wife and daughter, his books and music. He professed incredulous amazement that we should not be fully satisfied by the same small universe. "Why do you have to have people around? What's the matter with your own family?" was his inevitable reply to the suggestion that we "have someone over."

Hard work can be a great comforter; and I now found myself caught up in an especially difficult task, with less time and energy to spend brooding about Jack. Piano lessons and practice and singing lessons and practice ate away great lumps of time, and I was making another rigorous picture, *Don Q, Son of Zorro*, with Douglas Fairbanks. I had looked forward to meeting this man who was something of a legend around Hollywood, but I found the man himself to be less exciting than the legends. For one thing, I was put out by his attitude toward me. He was nice to me, in the way a sophisticated man about town would be nice to a small and reasonably well-behaved child. I felt that I merited more attention than that! He was interesting—shorter and slighter than his now more familiar son, with the same breathy voice, but without the British quality that Doug, Jr., has acquired. He seemed to be awkward, and almost embarrassed in his love scenes, but he flung himself into his athletic scenes with a wholehearted gusto. He was a perfectionist in them. Every athletic skill that he used as a "gimmick" in his pictures (in *Don Q* it was the bull whip) he studied from experts and practiced unceasingly. While I was making up in my dressing room on the Goldwyn lot I could hear the repeated swishshshsh—SMACK of the whip.

He had Snowy Baker as his trainer, and he acquired the skill in an amazingly short time. He could soon do all the tricks with the bull whip, and he was boyishly proud of his accomplishment. Snowy was hired to wield the whip for the close-ups of shots like the one where a cigarette is detached from a surprised face, but Doug would always say, "Let me try, Snowy. Then if I can't, you do the next take."

Feeling an impulse to show off one day, and wanting to please my "star," I refused a "double" for a scene in which Doug was supposed to teasingly crack the whip and let it slither around the girl's shoulders when she was not aware of his presence—a strictly

Fairbanksian method of saying "BOO!" I had a great deal of confidence in him after watching him perform many tricks for many months. I knew that the most frightening part was the sharp CRACK, and that the CRACK came *before* the whip began to circle around an object, firmly but not painfully.

Of course Mother objected, and there were conferences, and I insisted that I was not afraid; and Doug beamed and reminded us that it would be much more effective if we could get the whole sequence in one shot. Finally it was left up to me, and I said I wanted to do it. So I did. Two takes went uneventfully: the leather slid harmlessly around my shoulders, I was properly startled, and Doug leaped to untangle me. But Doug wanted "just one more"; it had to be perfect. And Doug miscalculated. After all, the whip was twenty feet long, and I don't see how he ever *did* calculate. But this third time I heard the crack, and knew it was too close to my head, and then I felt a sharp burning pain as the whip lashed around my neck. Doug was incoherent in his remorse; doctors were fetched; there was a chaos of noise and confusion. Donald Crisp, the director who was also acting in the picture, suffered the same accident at Snowy Baker's hands a few days later, and the edict went out, "From now on we stick to dummies."

But when my film work and my music permitted it, I would think about Jack, and be miserable. I have a little line-a-day diary that I began a short while before I started work on *Don Q*. Its first entry is dated March 7, 1925. It reads, "Cable from J.B. Says he'll be back the middle of May. Haven't seen him since December 1923." The entry is cautious and restrained. It had to be. The whole book was open to inspection at any time; it is very cryptic, filled with code words and symbols that no longer have any meaning for me. But I haven't forgotten my transport of joy when that "cable from J.B." arrived.

I slipped back into lethargy. I didn't feel well; I had colds and headaches. I read a good deal in the evenings while Daddy worked on his "books," or on plans for improving the house—trees, rosebushes, a driveway, and an ornamental iron fence that completely surrounded the property. "All you need now," my friend Menifee Johnstone said, "is a sentry pacing on the roof."

The close surveillance had not let up. I was chaperoned everywhere. Mother accompanied me at all times to the studio when I was working. If I went anywhere else, when one of my parents could not go, Parker, the chauffeur, delivered me and picked me up. No one could come to the house and take me anywhere—to the movies or to the beach or just for a drive. I could go to the beauty parlor alone, or to Menifee's. That was the extent of my freedom.

A luxurious house and furnishings had done nothing to improve the family atmosphere. Mealtimes were especially oppressive. Daddy always found something to discuss, even if it was only the question of why I should eat the food that was placed before me. I had no appetite; the food tasted like cotton and sand, but to quiet that strident voice I choked food down, sometimes sweating with the will it took to keep from throwing it up again. Even so, I could never succeed in quieting my father. When the subject of why I should eat had been worn thin, he would only switch to an explanation of why I should something else. There was no avoiding it.

I did not protest. Largely from the habit that had been ingrained in me, I sat there passively, trying not to hear what he was saying. If any of our friends dared to suggest that I might be allowed a little more freedom, Daddy would flare dangerously and demolish them with an effective though not very original "You attend to your business, and I'll attend to mine."

I think I had become too lazy mentally to rebel, too afraid of the consequences, too weak morally to face the changes that rebellion would bring. It was easier to continue my submissive existence in my lonely ivory tower. I doubt that I even realized I held the whip hand. I earned the money. All I had to do was to say, "Things are going to be changed around here or I won't work." But it was easier to escape into the solitude of my room— I was permitted to close the door now—and read, or work a little at learning to write on the typewriter. I even tried my hand at writing a short story. Or I just sat on the balcony and dreamed at the moon, living in the time when my love would return to me.

Even that I did not face realistically. This was a man who loved me, who would marry me, if only I grew up. It never occurred to me that he would inevitably tire of my infantile failure to face up to reality, to assume mature responsibility. I dreamed that we would simply go on as we always had. That he would not be satisfied with clandestine afternoons in a hotel suite, that he would despise the continued deceit, that he would scorn the pretense of friendship for my parents—no thought of this ever entered my head.

A cable came announcing he would be in New York on the fifth of May. I was scheduled to make a picture in New York; we were leaving on the eighth of May. I suddenly regained my health and spirits. The tempo of life picked up. I was excited; there was much to be done, and I enjoyed it all. I bought new clothes. I fretted over the possibility of retakes for *Don Q.* I posed for publicity stills. And finally the time came.

The Hollywood quality of the trip across the country provided enough diversion to take my mind off Jack for at least part of the time. On the great day of departure an impressive crowd of friends and publicity people gathered at the station to see me off. We had a drawing room, filled with flowers. There were great quantities of orchids. "Just like a movie actress," said I. A brief layover had been arranged for Kansas City, and all of Mother's family were there to greet us and visit with us. My grandfather, aunts and uncles and cousins whom I hardly knew were there. Mother was glowing with the happiness of seeing her family again. Daddy was politely condescending, but he clearly felt his superiority. "These people," his expression seemed to say, "are only farmers."

In New York the apartment was filled with flowers, just as it had been before. I was almost wild with excitement, but I had well learned to control my face and my actions. Jack was expected for dinner; when the time drew near, nothing could prevent me from watching for him from the window. I saw his cab pull up, and I watched him get out. Mother and Daddy were in the kitchen. I slipped out of the apartment and went down on the elevator to meet him. We fell into each other's arms with shouts of laughter and joy. For a few deliriously happy moments we were alone in the universe. Nothing else existed. But we couldn't linger. We went back up the elevator, and by the time we entered the living room we had tempered our excitement to a proper degree. We were, after all, both professional actors!

There was much to talk about; each of us had a year and a half of our activities to describe, so the evening was not too unbearable for us. Jack told about his great season in London, his ill-health from "too damned much drinking," and the long vacation salmon fishing in Norway. He told us of his plans for his next picture for Warner's—he was reading several scripts, and he wanted me for the picture. And we in our turn had all the news of our new home and my progress in moving pictures and the mounting salary I was getting.

But the following day at the Ambassador we picked up our life together where we had left it seventeen months before. I had wanted nothing to change, and nothing had changed. It was just as I had dreamed of it during that lonely year and a half. No one had ever told me that you can't make time stand still; and if anyone had told me now, I would have jibed happily at him and pointed triumphantly at us, in joyful refutation of his stodgy cynicism.

Jack told me of plans he did not think it wise to tell the family yet. He was to do *Richard III* in London next season and he wanted me to play Lady Anne. "So we must work hard," he said. "You will learn the part, and I will help you become the actress you should be."

Very carefully, a few nights later, he brought up the subject of my doing a play with him in London. Daddy was very cool toward the idea. Even if First National would give me a leave of absence (which they would have done), "we couldn't afford it." The difference between movie money and theatre money was too great. "It wouldn't be practical."

I think now that this was the critical moment. I think Jack sat there waiting for me to assert myself, to show that I had a mind and a will. I could have said, "But this is the opportunity of a lifetime, if I am really to be an actress. What if we do have to give up the limousine and the servants—and Daddy's membership at the Athletic Club, and his daily game of billiards? I want to be an actress, not a machine. I'm going to go to London, and I'm going to play Lady Anne." But I didn't say anything.

The next day at the hotel Jack said to me, "You haven't changed a bit. Nothing has changed." I was happy to think that I had made time stand still, but he got rather drunk that afternoon.

In my line-a-day diary there was space for a short memorandum at the end of each month. At the end of May, I wrote, "J.B. has come and gone. He wants me for his first picture, but I will be busy. Plans are now to make his second one in September. The next three months will be just *work*." And so it was.

Like a sleepwalker, I went through two pictures. I was weighed down with the disappointment of the lost chance to work on Jack's first picture of his contract, *Moby Dick*, and biting my nails in fear I might not be permitted to work in the second, which was to be *Don Juan*. When Dick Barthelmess wanted me for a picture in September, I held my breath. I knew I would have nothing to say about it; these decisions were made by my father, and I was afraid even to voice too strong an opinion for fear I should reveal my feelings about Jack. But both Mother and Daddy decided that the picture with Barrymore would be the better choice (besides, they wanted to be back in California, too), and once more I could breathe freely.

On June 11, I started work on something called *The Pace That Thrills*, with Ben Lyon. For me it was too slow a pace, and there were no thrills. According to my diary, the picture was "slow to start." It was "hot on the set." There were days when we "couldn't work. Too cloudy for exterior ball park." September seemed a long way off.

On days off I kept up my piano and vocal lessons, posed for magazine covers and fashions, and occasionally went to the theatre or to concerts. I filled my evening with reading, reading books that Jack had given me: *The Master of Ballantrae, The Way of All Flesh, The White Company*. And I wrote many long letters to Menifee—and managed to find a way of writing to Jack. On the top of the desk, where Mother could, and did, look over my shoulder, I was writing a harmless newsy letter to a friend of mine. Underneath it was the letter I was also writing to Jack. As soon as her back was turned, I would take it out and continue with it. Then I sealed and addressed it, and enclosed it in the letter to my friend, who would post it in Hollywood. Of course I could not receive an answer, but always in a few days a telegram would come from Jack, containing some detail about the picture, and that would mean he had received it.

The days dragged on. It was hot, and I was tired. The diary records the drudgery and the boredom. July 11: "Worked hard all day in the broiling sun. It was awful. Am too tired at night even to read." July 18: "Finished *The Pace That Thrills*. At last! Dick Barthelmess wants me for his next picture starting in Sept. Nothing doing." August 17: "Began working on *The Scarlet Saint*. Hectic melodrama, but good training, I suppose." September 4: "Cloudy again. Worked inside till 7:30. Made three changes of costume. Very tired—oh so damn tired—26 scenes."

And on September 26 there is an entry that seems to me now to ring false: "Such a home-coming! All the dear ones to greet us. The Hotcheners, Menifee, and Jack. Jack met us at the train —everything just as I had planned."

Well, I was back in Hollywood, and I was with Jack, but everything was *not* "just as I had planned." One of the reasons why I was "tired" and "impatient" was that I had heard rumors, from Menifee as well as from the papers, that Jack was being seen a great deal with his lovely leading lady, Dolores Costello, who was doing *Moby Dick* (later retitled *The Sea Beast*) with him, and when we saw Jack I had a distinct feeling that his pleasure in seeing us was slightly forced.

My uneasiness grew. There were all the signs and hints that are so dear to the writers of second-rate movie scripts. Several times when Jack was coming over for dinner he telephoned to say "something had come up" and he couldn't make it. Or he would have someone else call and announce that he had been "detained." I began to be frightened.

At a dinner party celebrating Daddy's birthday, October 2, I found something to comfort myself with. It was empty comfort, but I liked to think about it. We had a very pleasant dinner with Jack and the Hotcheners, and after dinner Helios told us a fascinating story. She had "seen" us in a previous life! I was a reincarnation of Sarah Siddons (Helios swore that she had never heard of her), and Jack had been my brother, John Kemble. She went into many other details, but that was the core of it. And the story of Bridey Murphy is tame compared to the tale told by Helios! Jack's curious mind was captivated by the idea, so much so that he started studying the occult, and even took up Yoga. But I was satisfied to dream of the possibility that in another life I had been Jack's sister.

It was also in October that Jack decided he ought to get away from the noise and pressures of the town for a few days, so he and Mother and Daddy and I drove up to Lake Arrowhead. It was cloudy and blustery when we arrived, but we took a long walk around the lake. Jack wanted to talk to me; there was no chance of our meeting at his rooms in the Ambassador Hotel out here because he had a bungalow, and everybody's comings and goings were too easily observed. We couldn't risk it. So we tried to get off by ourselves, where we could talk. We walked rapidly to get ahead of Mother and Daddy, but they walked fast enough to keep close behind us. We increased our pace, and they increased theirs. Finally Jack shuddered and said, "It's like a nightmare."

We never did get a chance to talk, and according to my diary, we left sooner than we had planned: "Stayed all night at the lodge, got back home about 2:00. Took a nap. I always feel happier when I wake up."

Then there follow days of simply "Lovely talk with Helios. Jack phoned." And then there were fittings and tests for *Don Juan*, and days of visiting the set after the picture began but before I actually started work. And then all my hopes and dreams died, and I wanted to die with them.

I visited the set of *Don Juan*, and there was another visitor— Dolores Costello. And I saw, with a sick and aching heart, the two camp chairs, placed just off the set, as they had been for *Beau Brummel*, only now Jack and Dolores were sitting in them, talking and laughing. And then I knew.

I was tired and sick when I got home. I had been worried and nervous for some days, and had been neglecting my vocal practice. That afternoon I skipped it altogether. I wanted to scream rather than sing. Daddy met me on the staircase, and with the dangerous whiteness about his mouth he said sternly and, I thought, a bit pompously, "Lucile, I want you to explain why you are not on schedule with your vocalizing."

I pushed by him and snapped, "I don't feel like singing."

He grasped my shoulders and punctuated his words by shaking me. "You—are—going—to do—as you—are told!"

But finally I had had enough. My own temper flared to meet his. I jerked myself free and slapped his hands down, and I did scream. "You keep your hands off me—forever. I'm nineteen years old, and I won't take any more of this shoving around and being slapped when you're mad. And when I feel like singing again I'll sing!"

At first he couldn't believe what had happened; he just couldn't comprehend it. When he finally did he went into a sort of shock. For hours he sulked at his desk, with his head on his arms, and he would speak neither to Mother nor to me. Mother and I went next door to ask advice of Helios. She was an excellent diplomat, and she came over and talked to Daddy. She told me that she had been waiting for this to happen; she had been sure that it would have to sooner or later. Anyway, Daddy re-established communication with reality long enough to decide he had a "touch of lumbago," and to move to the upstairs balcony, where he sat with a shawl over his head and around his shoulders.

The next day there were some very cool "discussions," in which

I did my share of the discussing; and finally there was an agreement. I contended that I was embarrassed to have Mother in constant attendance on me at the studio, so it was decided she would hereafter remain home. I was to have a maid, I was to be allowed to go where I wanted to go, and I was to have a small allowance for pin money. I was then earning about twenty-five hundred dollars a week. My allowance was to be five dollars.

Don Juan was a long and difficult picture; it went all the way through December. It was hard on me physically. In the torture scenes I was bent backwards over a wheel and tied to it, so securely tied that it took too long to untie me after every scene. In hopes of getting a sign of approval from Jack I tried to be cheerful and "brave" as I stayed in that agonizing posture for hours. I got nothing but a stiff neck and a back that was sore for a week. And the night work was additionally tiring. We were not then protected by regulations of the Screen Actors Guild; we often worked until we had finished an episode, even though it took until four or five in the morning. And we had to be back on the set at nine.

I couldn't "get through" to Jack at all. And even though I must have known, I could not bring myself to admit that it was all over. Hopefully I told him of the changes that had been made at home. He said, "Well, that's some progress," and started talking about something else. He was drinking steadily; he often showed up on the set with a hang-over, or he was "delayed" and came in late, or he didn't come in at all.

And I slept. My diary shows many entries like "Slept this afternoon—I am so tired." "Slept two hours this afternoon." I remember that I would go to bed early at night, and Mother could hardly awaken me in the mornings.

Each year a publicity group in Hollywood called the "Wampas" —a name formed from the initials of the press organization —selected twelve of the most promising "Baby Stars"—the "Wampas Babies." There were always many group photographs and publicity stunts, and each year the climax was the formal presentation of the "Wampas Babies" to the public at one of the big theatres. In 1925, I was one of the twelve Wampas Babies; the group also included Joan Crawford—and Dolores Costello. I asked Jack if he intended to go to the formal presentation, to be held that year at the El Capitan Theatre. He said, "Don't be silly. You know I couldn't bear it."

Backstage, the night of the presentation, was a flurry of happy excitement. We were all gowned magnificently, proud of our beauty and our grandeur. And then an usher bustled up to me, carrying a huge basket of roses, and asked where Miss Costello's dressing room was. "They're from Mr. Barrymore," he confided to me. A chill knifed through me, and I thought no one could possibly feel more miserable than I felt then. But I soon discovered that one could. As we were presented, I came on stage— and saw Jack sitting in the second row with Dolores's mother and sister.

So all I had to comfort myself with was the cheerless thought that in "another life" we had been brother and sister, we had belonged to each other. Of course it was no comfort. I couldn't believe such a thing for a moment. But at that time I wanted to believe it with all my heart.

Work went on. By the middle of January I was playing in *High Steppers*, of which I remember nothing. In the diary the only entries are "Worked today" or "Did not work today." Fatigue was becoming chronic. I was crying a great deal at night after I went to bed. And Daddy didn't help. He blamed the Hotcheners for my outburst of independence, and he was fuming and complaining constantly that he was "getting fed up with their meddling and interfering." And he decided Menifee was another "bad outside influence," and he banished her.

We saw the preview of *Don Juan*. It was beautiful, but too slow in places. It needed some changes in the ending. And we saw the opening of *The Sea Beast*, a gala affair in the full tradition of Hollywood premières. "Jack made a charming speech. We saw him for a minute to speak to in the car," my diary reports. It says nothing of the agonies I underwent watching Jack and Dolores on the screen.

I started another picture, *The Wise Guy,* with Betty Compson and James Kirkwood, and in the middle of it I was called for retakes on *Don Juan.* We finished *The Wise Guy,* and then there were some more retakes for *Don Juan.* The work on *Don Juan* was torment; working with Jack made me feel brittle and dry. I marshaled all my defenses and tried to be very offhand and casual with him.

But in May we had to go on location. We had a whole afternoon's work with Jack and me on a white horse—I had just been rescued from the castle of the Borgias, or something. All afternoon we sat there together. It was agony to be so close to him again. Sitting there in his arms, it was like my own fairy tale dreams of the girl and her Prince who came riding out of the night. The dream must come true! During the long hours I gathered all my nerve and courage, and then I asked him. I don't remember what I said, but I remember his answer. Rather sadly he said, "Dear Goopher, I'm just a son of a bitch."

Four

I had wanted it drawn, diagrammed, and signed before I could be convinced. Now I was convinced. And this final, flat knowledge brought with it a strange sense of relief. Now, at least, I knew, after eight long months of the torment of not being sure, and before that the long year and a half of waiting. I felt relief, and the beginning of bitterness. I looked for something, someone, to blame; and since I could never have thought to blame myself, I blamed his drinking, I blamed my parents for their failure to give me freedom, and finally I blamed him. I decided he was—what he said he was.

And in my bitterness I felt an angry impatience with everything around me. I was bored, short-tempered, rebellious. For me it was a dangerous mood. Even my diary, always so cautious and circumspect, flares up. The entry for May 5 complains, "How thoroughly sick and bored I am over all these futile family discussions about nothing at all. We seem to be like tinder ready to flame up at any moment."

On May 20 another such discussion took place, in full family conclave. I sat on the piano bench in the living room watching the clock tick off two solid hours while Daddy droned endlessly on. Mother was lying on the couch with a cold compress on her head, but her discomfort did not discourage him in the least. On he went, tearing me into small shreds—telling me how lazy I had become, criticizing my failure to follow his advice and counsel, outlining my faults in maddening detail. And a very strange thing happened. Without intending it, without even realizing what I was doing, I hypnotized myself. I remember looking down at the pattern on the rug, silently listening to the drone of my father's voice without hearing what he was saying; my eyes followed the pattern around and around and around to the rhythm of his voice, which became fainter and fainter. The next thing I knew I was on the couch, and they were distractedly trying to revive me. Mother, for a change, was scolding Daddy in heated anger; and he seemed genuinely concerned that he had put so much strain on me that I had fainted.

I was touched by his obvious remorse; and when he said rather affectionately, "You'd better run on up to bed now," a conciliating reply was on my tongue. And there it stayed, for he immediately added, "But you *will* try to do what Daddy has told you, won't you." This was the last straw. Wearily I muttered, "I'll try," and went up to my room.

I paused in front of my mirror and looked at the strained face that stared back at me. "Mary," I said to the face, "I'll bet a week's salary that he won't let it alone. And if he doesn't, that'll be all. If he says one more word to me tonight, I'm getting out." Almost at once I heard him call from the foot of the stairs. "Oh, baby—ah, just one more thing." A moment later he came into the room to deliver a fifteen-minute peroration.

I went to bed. For about two hours I lay there, waiting and listening, until I was certain that they were both sound asleep. I dressed and packed a few things in a small case; then I stopped to think how I could leave the house. I didn't dare go down the stairs; both their doors were open, and I knew that Mother at least would be sure to awaken. The only thing left was the balcony, which was risky, but I had to get out. It had a melodramatic quality that fit well with my present mood. Taking the cord from my robe, I tied one end to the small cypress that had grown just a little higher than the railing of the balcony. I grasped the case and the cord, and swung out. The tree bent to lower me easily to the ground, and I walked away from the house.

It was about two o'clock in the morning, and the darkness and silence together with the realization of what I had just done filled me with fear and apprehension. But I walked on down Gower Street to Hollywood Boulevard, where I found a small hotel. There I checked in, went up to my room, took a bath, and slept soundly the rest of the night.

The next morning I awoke with a feeling of relieved content. I lay in bed luxuriating in my aloneness. No one would order my day for me; no one would command and dictate and arrange. In fact, as I lay there I began to wonder just what I would do. Last night I had seen no further than the simple act of getting out from under the roof that sheltered my father. I had not considered exactly what I wanted beyond that.

I decided to ask advice of the Hotcheners, so I called them. They had been waiting for the call. Mother and Daddy had frantically knocked at their door within minutes of discovering my absence, and Helios and Henry had quieted their panic and discussed the problem with them. They had suggested that my parents do some serious thinking about their treatment of me, and had recommended that they leave me alone for a few days so both they and I could think things out. When I called, Helios invited me to go with them to their summer cottage at Long Beach, where I could have the rest and quiet they felt I needed. I accepted gratefully, and they drove by the hotel and picked me up.

A week later I returned home. Daddy was subdued; it was clear that I had given him a bad scare, and that he had been quite willing to think over the Hotcheners' advice that he begin treating me like an adult. He admitted, reluctantly, that it was perhaps not fully just that I should be the wage earner without having any of the satisfaction of spending some of the money. Yet it was with the my-hands-are-tied attitude of a man who feels himself deeply wronged that he deposited five hundred dollars in a personal checking account for me and agreed to give me the liberty I wanted.

Of course, I could not qualify as an adult, and I rapidly proceeded to fulfill Daddy's direst forebodings. I was totally unprepared and unequipped to direct my own life; I drank my freedom eagerly, unthinkingly, in great gulps, and it went to my head like a shot of brandy. I can hardly admire the picture of myself at that time. Those were years when Hollywood was notorious for its willful flaunting of convention, and I leaped eagerly into that heedless life. I became flippant and superficial, and I was satisfied that I was following the prescribed Hollywood pattern.

The temper of the record in my "line-a-day" diary changed. I was working on another picture for First National, an adaptation of the play *Forever After*; it was the best story I had yet had with that studio. I had to make a transition from the age of fifteen to about twenty-five, and that gave me a chance to show something of what I thought I could do. I was busy. I "hired a new maid"; "went to the library"; "went to Casa del Mar"; "stayed all night at the Inces." In the course of my work I met a personable young man named Bill Glass. He was fun; he was witty. He could make me laugh and forget, and if ever anyone needed laughter I was that one.

We were thrown together constantly in our work, and he did not conceal his admiration of me. I devoured it. The wound and the pain of losing Jack was far from healed, and though I had never heard of "rebounds," I was rebounding. Bill and I went to the movies, to dances, to the beach homes of people in the moving picture colony. I gloried in his attention, and in all the things that most girls of my age would simply have taken for granted—dating steady with a nice young man who had a Packard roadster, an engaging manner, and a host of friends with whom I could bubble and chatter.

After some of the all-night shooting sequences down at the

studio Bill drove me home. Weary after the hours of work, but exhilarated by the fun of being driven home by a young man at six-thirty in the morning, and secure in the knowledge that I had done nothing that even my father could have disapproved of, I boldly invited Bill in for breakfast. He made it quite clear to my parents that he thought I was a very special young lady, and he asked, in a straightforward and simple way, if he might be permitted "to take me out occasionally." Daddy shrugged his shoulders; he implied plainly that he was helpless to object, that he could not control this willful and selfish daughter. Bill was diplomatic; he clearly saw that the situation was a delicate one, and he invited the entire family out to dinner that evening.

Daddy accepted Bill with ill grace; both he and Mother, when the three of us were alone, pointedly discussed the fact that Bill was a "nobody," and, worst of all in their eyes, that he was Jewish. But their disapproval only hastened the inevitable. I was hungry for attention and affection; I was willing and even eager to defy the remnants of parental authority; and I vainly wanted to prove that my love for Jack had left no scars. On July 6 my diary reports, I "told Mother and Daddy that Bill and I are in love and that we are going to be married, and they said 'All right' and that's that!"

Both families were obviously unhappy about it. The slurs and innuendoes at home were redoubled. Bill's parents were more tactful and charitable, but they were good Orthodox Jews, and were clearly miserable that he was going to marry a Gentile. But Bill and I scorned their objections and merrily carried on in our young and tireless way. I flaunted my diamond solitaire; we posed for publicity pictures; we were happily swept along in the flood of telegrams and messages of congratulation (but I had a bad hour alone in my room when the telegram came from Jack "hoping the dear Goopher will be so happy"). We went to parties and made many new friends, and I convinced myself that I was happy. Our only argument was about drinking. I was vehemently opposed to it, for I now felt certain that alcohol had been the cause of the breakup with Jack. Bill was hardly a "drinker," but if he had more than one drink at a party we would have a row.

We had to crowd all our gaiety and activity into a few short weeks, for in the middle of August I was to leave for location in San Antonio, Texas. Since I would be away for only three weeks, we had no fears that our love would not survive our separation. We promised each other that we would each write a long letter every night, that we would send telegrams every few hours, and that we would make all the long-distance telephone calls we thought we could afford.

A few days before we were to leave, Mother suggested, with some hesitation, that she accompany me on the trip. "Please don't shut me out of my job entirely," she said, and I felt a twinge of conscience as I realized how much she must have missed the fun and excitement of going to the studios. It had, after all, been almost the only relief from the dull monotony of the routine imposed by Daddy. Partly from a sense of guilt, and partly because I was sure, in my new self-confidence, that I could manage her I agreed.

The special train bearing *The Rough Riders* location company, 150 strong, including actors, extras, stunt people, and a full crew of technicians, blared into San Antonio at two o'clock in the afternoon of August 19, 1926. The heat bore down as only Texas heat in August can, but we had no time to think about our discomfort in the noise and turmoil of our reception. The crowd at the station shouted; a military band blasted its welcome above the noise of the crowd; Mayor Tobin gained sufficient quiet to make a welcoming speech and present me with roses and gratifying compliments. Then a police escort cleared our way through the mass of people and guided us to the St. Anthony Hotel.

There Mother and I were installed in a magnificent suite on the top floor, a suite usually reserved for visiting VIP's or affluent bridal couples. In the living room stood a grand piano; almost my first act was to set my music on its rack, with a carefully worked out schedule for my daily practice—Chopin, Mozart, Bach, Czerny. And like a symbol of the life I had broken away from, there it stayed, untouched, as our planned three-week stay stretched into four, then five, and six—and finally into three months.

The weather was increasingly bad, rainy and hot, with a great deal of what we called "in and out" cloud conditions. We could not shoot except in full sun; close-ups were taken with "booster lights." So work was slow, and on many days we could not work at all. But we were never threatened with boredom. We were almost constantly entertained by the 1st Brigade Cavalry Regiment and the flyers stationed at Kelly Field. Another big company, the *Wings* company from Paramount, was also shooting in San Antonio, and when we weren't working the two companies merged into one. San Antonio was delighted with the glamour of movie making and movie celebrities; our company boasted such famous figures as Vic Fleming (the director), Charles Farrell, Charles Mack, and Noah Beery; and in the *Wings* company were William Wellman, Buddy Rogers, Dick Arlen, and Clara Bow.

We were lionized, partied, dated almost to death. On the days when we could work we hurried back in the late afternoon, hot and sweaty, for a swim at the country club or at Brackenridge Park, followed by a dinner and dance at the Gunter Roof or Kelly Field. The Texans were justly noted for their hospitality, and never a night passed without something to do.

Our suite at the hotel became the place to drop in, the place to bring up Spanish food and tequila. Mother could play the hostess to her heart's delight—and she did. I saw with more amusement than surprise that she was determined to take every advantage of her short respite from the prison of Temple Hill Drive. I did not see until later that she was also subtly urging me on into the round of dances and parties in hope of curbing my attachment to Bill. I didn't need any encouragement. I was twenty years old, a movie star, twelve hundred miles away from the oppressive shadow of my father, and I was having a wonderful time. I tentatively smoked a cigarette in front of Mother. No comment. I appeared one afternoon wearing lip rouge (yes, my children, at twenty!). Still no comment. Swept along in the crashing wave of excitement, I even tried an occasional drink; I discovered that I must laugh loudly after a dirty joke, so everyone would be sure that I "got it"; I found I couldn't tell them myself, because I fumbled and stumbled in an embarrassment; I learned that an occasional four-letter word was an infallible means of getting attention and laughs—given the proper audience. I happily became "one of the crowd." But I like to think that, with all my flippancy and flashy, superficial smartness, Lucile Langhanke was watching from a distance, behind a kind of veil, weighing this new girl, and ready to deny even a passing acquaintance with her if what she did became too painful.

Work on the picture had begun vigorously, and then trailed off. The first three days after our arrival we had worked hard. Vic Fleming was efficient; he had everything well organized and planned, and he was determined to finish the location work and get back to Hollywood. The rigors of those first three days almost finished some of us off. We were costumed in the Teddy Roosevelt period; I wore stiff corsets and petticoats and high shoes, and I was sure I would never survive the combination of heat and the physical activity that my part demanded. We survived, but only, I think, because the first three days were followed by ten straight days when the weather was so bad we couldn't work at all. After that the weather was spotty; we worked off and on. After a month there was talk of giving it up and going back to Hollywood. Then came a break in the weather, and we worked like slaves to make up the lost time. My diary records the fact that we did twenty scenes in one day, an almost impossible feat even for the silent pictures. Unfortunately most of the scenes were of me running down roads—comedy scenes where I was being pursued by an entire platoon. By the end of the day the corsets and heavy clothing and sweltering sun had taken their toll. I collapsed in a limp heap, and I was too sick to work for the next three days.

My sequences in the picture could easily have been shot in a week or ten days of concentrated work, but Vic Fleming had scheduled them so they were spread out over the entire stay in

San Antonio. This, I found later, he had done after a few talks with Mother; he agreed with her about Bill, and they both felt that the longer I was kept away from him the better it would be. They were right. Bill and I were already straining a bit, quarreling mildly in our letters and telegrams. And I found I was getting bored with writing him and receiving his letters. San Antonio was much more fun. *Don Juan* opened at a local theatre, and I made a personal appearance and was given a party. General Eltinge made me an honorary member of the 1st Brigade. I had no time to think about Bill, much less to spend writing letters to him.

And then Bill was completely crowded out of my mind. At one of the Kelly Field dances a very attractive young man, blond and stocky and strong, cut in on me. He was a beautiful dancer, and when I was not marveling at the smooth sureness with which we were gliding over the dance floor I was feeling dazzled by his quick and sharp wit. He put on a "local boy" act, telling me that he had seen almost all of my pictures, and that he thought I was wonderful, and how did I like acting, and did I think I would like living in Texas? I innocently accepted him as a local man, and had a fine time being coy and flirting with him. I was curious though, and I waited for a chance to ask about him. I had to wait a long time; he cut in on almost every dance. Finally I found myself dancing with someone from the company long enough to ask who he was—he hadn't even told me his name. The answer intrigued me. "That, dear child, is John Monk Saunders. He's the author of *Wings*, he's a Rhodes scholar, and he's an Olympic diving champion! And watch out!"

I didn't watch out. I fell—hard! I didn't completely fool myself; I somehow knew that I wasn't in love with Bill or Johnnie or anyone else, but that I was in love with love, and with the feeling of being important and necessary and wanted that went with it. Just the same, to be admired and pursued by John Saunders was, I felt, something special. He was the kind of man who seemed able to do everything, and do it well. Rhodes scholar and Olympic diving champion—these were only a part of his accomplishments. He was good-looking, but not too good-looking;

not very tall; blond, with strong blue eyes. His speech was soft, a little slow, with a slight impediment that was almost a lisp. Because he blushed easily, women thought he was "just darling," but he was a "wolf" of the subtlest kind. He always looked clean and cool; his clothes were always exactly right, and never wrinkled or unpressed even in the hot Texas summer. He was young for his many accomplishments, perhaps twenty-seven or -eight. He was highly gifted; everything in life seemed to come easily for him, including women. I think that life could have held no challenge for him, and that he must never have known the satisfaction of real accomplishment. That was the way life went for him, and the way it ended—he accomplished everything he wanted, without the sense of accomplishment. I remember how shocked I was, almost fourteen years after those days in Texas, to read that he had hanged himself in a clothes closet with a bathrobe cord.

Johnnie pursued me with a quiet but self-assured persistence. He had not asked for a "date" at the dance, but two nights later, when I was making a personal appearance at the local theatre, a large basket of flowers was sent up to the stage, with a card that bore only the initials "J.M.S." I returned backstage, and there he was, with all his bland self-assurance, carrying a corsage and my wrap. "We're going to have supper at the Roof," he confidently announced. So it began, and things were made easy for us. Vic smiled a knowing smile; Mother kept out of the way (she was, she assured me, happily entertained by a cavalry captain); rumors were carelessly but pointedly dropped that back in Hollywood, Bill was seeing a good deal of a former girl friend; and I didn't care whether we got home by Christmas.

We danced at the club, we swam in the pool in the moonlight, we took long drives into the country and dined at out-of-the-way places. We had all the trappings of romance that Hollywood itself could have demanded: a Texas summer, a harvest moon, dancing the "last dance" at the outdoor pavilion at the country club, a waltz with the lights out. And there were no questions asked, no promises made.

When I returned to Hollywood, Bill and I had a pleasant,

friendly talk, and we agreed to call off our engagement. I wanted it that way, not only because of Johnnie, but also because I was unhappy with what I found when I looked at myself. "What's wrong with me?" I began to ask myself as I wondered why I should have neither the desire nor the will to resist the attractions of personable young men and yet be unable to find any lasting content or satisfaction in them. Now as I look back, with all the happy benefits of hindsight, I think I can find part of the answer. It was more complex than the absence of any solid moral values in my training; and it was not simply that I instinctively sought any relationship, no matter how empty, that represented a loosening of the bonds that held me to my father. It was all this, but it was much more. It is hard to express, but I must try, for I am sure that it helps explain much of my conduct then and later.

My personality was what I could call "lopsided"; it had been formed first by my father's precepts and then by my reading. That part of it which could be forged only in the fire of experience was almost untouched. I was very emotional; I felt things strongly. But I couldn't express my emotion; I didn't know how. My reading had been extensive but unsupervised and undisciplined. At times I would devour ten library books a week, covering a wide range of subjects—psychology, biography, history, fiction, poetry, and the latest best sellers (the only reading matter that *was* supervised), which I had to read secretly because Daddy would not permit me to read such "trash." So much reading and so little doing had given me much to think about, but nothing to measure my thoughts and judgments by. My "thinking" had become purposeless and unconstructive; I could not err in it, but neither could I achieve anything by it. And this circuitous and aimless process could and did slip easily into emotional daydreaming. I think that for a number of years my thoughts and daydreams were more truly "me" than were all of my external words and acts.

My reading and daydreaming had led me to know the signs and conduct of "loving," but it had not brought me to know loving itself. I had experienced the shattering upheaval of physical attraction, but I did not know love, and I could not love.

The moment the fire ceased to burn brightly, the moment it flickered and began to die, I became restless, thinking that love itself was dying. The embers that glow warmly over the years cannot be described in books. I had never known them in my own family, and I had never been close enough to any other family to find that they existed.

So, feeling a strong but unlocalized discontent with myself, I broke away from Bill, and once more found myself fighting the familiar dreary battles at home. With a difference—for by now I had a much clearer picture of how things stood. I had read too much and talked with too many people not to be aware that Daddy was exploiting me, that my career was his livelihood. His bullying and criticizing grated now more than ever, but I bore it all sullenly, waiting for my chance to escape. I could not bear the prospect of settling completely into the old routine, the doing nothing, the reading, or taking a walk or having a manicure or playing the piano, the waiting for days when I could work so I would have an excuse to leave the house. I tried having friends in, with the usual discomfort and stiffness caused by Daddy's lack of cordiality. I went to an occasional movie with Charlie Farrell or Dean Markham. I decided to learn to play golf; that would at least get me out of the house on the days when we weren't working on the interiors of *Rough Riders*. Daddy made one feeble attempt to stop that. "What if you should get hit on the head by a golf ball?" he protested. And he meant it, quite seriously! But by now I had enough courage to laugh and say, "Why, I suppose I'd get concussion and have to be taken to a hospital, and my career would be ruined forever." Daddy turned away coldly. My career was too sacred a subject to be joked about.

August 6, 1926, is an important date in moving picture history. *Don Juan* opened with the first Vitaphone recording of background music. It was the beginning of sound. I gave no thought to its possible significance in the development of motion pictures or to the impact it would have on my own career. In my diary

I recorded only the fact that "the whole picture and its memories are very unhappy to me. I won't see it again."

The routine of existence went on, with little to disrupt its even sameness. Mother caused a mild flurry by becoming the proud owner of a Chrysler roadster and taking driving lessons from Parker. That inspired me to inveigle Parker into teaching me how to drive, secretly, of course, for if Daddy had known, he would never have permitted it. Parker still drove me to the studio, but as soon as we were out of sight of the house he let me take the wheel.

One day I had luncheon with my friend Menifee, who was now assistant casting director at Fox. At the table was a nice young man who was one of the assistant producers there; she introduced him to me as Kenneth Hawks, the brother of a promising young director named Howard Hawks. I thought no more about him; when he called a few weeks later to invite me to the opening of the Mayfair Club, I could only dimly remember even what he looked like. And even after the pleasant evening at the Mayfair Club he was almost immediately driven from my mind by an accidental but painful meeting with Jack at the Hotcheners'. For several days afterwards my diary records only brief complaints of "headaches" and "feeling low." Then my spirits and my social activities picked up. A happy series of dates followed, divided at first quite evenly between Kenneth Hawks and Peter Diege. Peter's name gradually drops out of my record; soon all my dates were with Ken.

We went together to see *Gentlemen Prefer Blondes*, and *Kid Boots*, and the USC-Notre Dame football game. I liked being with him; it was never hectically romantic, with the emphasis on sex. I liked his quiet good manners and his good taste. He was Ivy League—a Yale graduate—but he didn't overwhelm people with it. He wore good, tweedy clothes and smoked a pipe. He was tall, lean, and lanky; he was twenty-six years old, and had prematurely grey hair, very twinkling blue eyes behind horn-rimmed glasses, and a grin a mile wide. His family lived in Pasadena, but he and Howard shared a small home in Beverly Hills.

My dates with Kenneth were briefly interrupted when I began work on a new picture; we had finished *The Rough Riders* on November 26, and I immediately started working on *The Sea Tiger,* with Milton Sills. The studio had built a replica of a small Spanish fishing village on the beach at Laguna, and we were to do the exteriors there. Kenneth suggested that he and I go down in his car, but Daddy had already decided that he and Mother would take me. "Mr. Hawks wants to drive me down . . ." I told Daddy, and he thought he was being very clever when he said, "There are lots of hawks in this town who would like to drive you down." I didn't want to make an issue out of it. I was getting used to this new strategy; instead of storming and raging he now resorted to sarcasm and mockery. If he saw I was becoming angry or annoyed he would say something like "Oh, we must be careful not to distress the lady," or he would make an ironic comment about my knack for "upsetting the apple cart."

So Mother and Daddy drove me down to Laguna and saw me comfortably established in a little summer cottage above the beach. Then they left, and I was alone with my maid, a briskly efficient middle-aged woman who made the cottage cozy, kept a fire blazing in the fireplace, and cooked my meals. A maid in those days was almost a necessity, not only for these domestic duties, but also for the motion picture work. The studio supplied no hairdressers or make-up people, except for character or period work, and there was only a general wardrobe woman who supervised the packing and unpacking of costumes for location.

Work on the picture began pleasantly enough: I was playing a Spanish peasant girl, barefooted, wearing long braids and coarse, comfortable clothing. On the third day, the weather turned cloudy and threatening, so we shifted to the night sequences, with rain machines and wind propellers. The cold and occasional rain caused mechanical difficulties that slowed down the process of setting up the scenes; in the long waits between scenes I sat uncomfortably in the shelter of my portable dressing room, which was little more than an ordinary camping tent.

On Friday evening Kenneth appeared, loaded down like Santa

Claus, with flowers and candy and a portable phonograph and records. It required no very great perception to see that he had come a-wooing! And knowing what was on his mind, I was worried. That night, during the waits between scenes, we sat in my tent dressing room wrapped in blankets and played the little phonograph. He had chosen the records well, for the right mood and atmosphere—records like "In a Little Spanish Town" and "Shine on, Harvest Moon." But as we listened to the music and talked, I tried desperately to forestall the question that I knew was coming. I wanted to forestall it because my own short but lurid past weighed heavily on my conscience. I admired Kenneth; I knew that he was thoroughly decent and honest, and I could not have him loving me under an illusion that I was something that I was not.

I didn't know how to go about telling him. I made a few stumbling efforts to find an opening, but the opening just wouldn't come. But I knew I had to say it so he could change his mind before he committed himself. Finally I just told him. I told him of the long, desperate affair with Jack. I told him about Bill and Johnnie.

He was shocked, there was no doubt about it. He had been so completely unprepared for it. In his eyes I was sweet and virginal; no doubts or suspicions of me had ever entered his mind. But he told me he loved me for being honest with him, and we said no more about it during the rest of the night. We sat there listening to the records between scenes until he left at about two-thirty in the morning (we worked until three). Over the weekend I heard nothing from him. But on Tuesday he phoned me; he had checked with the studio and found we were finishing, and he said he would be down to drive me home.

On the way back we stopped in Santa Ana for dinner. We sat down at the table, and Kenneth didn't say much for a few minutes. I held my breath; I knew it was coming, and I thought I knew what it would be. Then he started talking. He said he had done a great deal of thinking, and he told me again, as he had on that Friday night at Laguna, that my being honest with him had just made him love me more. "Nothing that's happened can make any difference," he said. "Please, will you marry me?"

And then I found that I couldn't answer him. I had wanted more than anything else to be fair to him when I confessed my past to him in Laguna; I had to keep on being fair. If I married him I had to know that I would be an honest and faithful wife. In the light of my too casual romances of the past months how could I trust myself? I had found no trouble in being completely faithful to Jack, even during the year and a half of his absence, but that had been different. I asked him to give me time; I didn't want to decide right then.

In the following months one part of my life kept on in the familiar routine, but the part that was Ken brought a growing happiness and satisfaction. I finished work on *The Sea Tiger*, and again immediately began fittings and shopping for the next picture, *Sunset Derby*, another "pulp magazine story," as I called the drivel I had to do. We were scheduled for a good many location trips to San Diego, Tia Juana, and Riverside for exteriors, which were mostly race track scenes.

Ken was with me constantly. When I had days off, we went to dinner at Victor Hugo's or the Montmartre; we watched golf tournaments; we went to previews of the pictures Ken was helping produce. I learned a great deal about the technical side of movie-making from him: story conferences, cutting, audience reaction. When I was on location, he always managed to drive down to spend a day with me. He had a big Dusenberg, and he put a lot of mileage on it, as he said, "in pursuit" of me.

I met his family, and loved them at once. Mother and Daddy Hawks were wonderfully gracious people. His young sister, Grace, was very ill with tuberculosis; she was about my age, dark, with large blue eyes, and the hesitant, tentative manner of invalids. She was not in a sanitarium because Mother Hawks was a Christian Scientist and would have only practitioners, much to the unhappiness of the three brothers, Howard, Ken, and Bill.

Christmas came, and Kenneth gave me a beautiful diamond and sapphire wrist watch. Mother and Daddy raised their eyebrows at so expensive a gift, but Ken assured them that his intentions were honorable—"as soon as I can be sure of my contract with Fox—and *if* I can get the girl to say 'yes.' "

Mother liked Kenneth; she was impressed by his background and his manners, and she was sure that he would steady me and slow me down. Daddy liked him, too, but he especially liked the fact that I wasn't going to "rush into anything." He was not at all anxious that I should get married. Neither he nor Mother had ever talked much about my getting married. In the past, whenever I had brought up the subject to Daddy, his answer would be rather vague. "You don't have to think about that now. There'll be plenty of time when you're twenty-eight or thirty." And he *meant* it. He would have been completely happy if I had loved my work so much that I didn't want to marry at all. But I could hardly be so enthusiastic about acting while I was plodding along on the treadmill of trash I was called on to do. I was under contract, and I had no voice in the selection of scripts or stories.

At the close of 1926, I wrote in my diary, "What a different year than I expected it to be! It is indeed a new cycle, a complete change from the way I've lived before. But, oh, what a lot I have to learn! My only regret of the year was that it brought to a close the most beautiful thing that had ever happened to me, and ever will. And then several hectic, insincere romances. I've found I'm a very changeable young woman. I hope the next year will steady that a bit. As for pictures, nothing to speak of, and I'm discouraged. But most of the time—I'm glad to be alive."

Neither the Hawks nor the Langhankes were much surprised when, about the middle of February, I decided I wanted to marry Ken. We had built a wonderful companionship. He was a very real, substantial person, comfortable to be with. Wherever we went together we had good times. We worked hard, both of us, but we also found time for fun. My golf game had improved, and we walked the miles around Lakeside and Bel-Air and Flintridge and Riviera, arm in arm, laughing and gabbling like children. We began to accumulate a store of private jokes and silly pet names. We talked; we discussed pictures, and ourselves, and life.

I was on location in Riverside, and Ken drove over to spend the night. We sat in the dark in front of the fireplace in my room at the inn and talked everything out. Ken warned me again that we would have a wait of at least several months; we could not get married until he was certain that Fox would sign him to a long-term contract, at considerably more money than he was then making. I was not worried; I knew that he had been simply breaking in, in all sorts of jobs, first as assistant director to Vic Fleming and Art Rosson, and then as assistant producer. But I also knew very definitely that he was the fair-haired boy around the lot; he had a good sense of comedy, and a good story mind, and he was always well liked as a person. But not all our talk was serious and heavy. In his exuberance Ken could not very long repress his sense of humor. When he looked very solemn and said, "Darling, you've been honest with me. I can't let this go any further without confessing something to you," I braced myself. But even before I could feel the surge of panic that I am sure was coming, he launched into his confession: he walked in his sleep; and he had a tapeworm that he had grown very fond of, and had named Henry. I never did find out about the tapeworm, but I know at least that night he did not walk in his sleep.

Suddenly time was no longer a void to be merely endured. Dozens of interesting and exciting tasks had to be done, even though many months were to pass before our wedding. I finished work on *Sunset Derby*, and, for a welcome change, I was not scheduled to start another picture for nearly a month. Mother and Daddy went to New York to close up the Jackson Heights apartment and ship the furniture; I would need some of it when we had our own house. I spent many happy hours getting ready for our "nest"; I made chaise longue pillows, and bought and hemmed napkins, and bought linens and towels and sorted and arranged them with all of the glee of a miser counting his gold. I went to Sophie Wachner, who had made all my clothes, personal and professional, for many years; and we started planning my trousseau. It was to be a girl's dream come true—all satin and silk handmade lingerie, a traveling suit, and a good many hot-weather clothes, since we had decided on a trip to New York by train and then on to Havana and back to California by boat. We looked at houses—and it seems that we looked at hundreds, for *our* house had to be just right. We played golf. We saw Rein-hardt's *The Miracle*, and I wished I could be a part of something like that instead of perpetually playing the insipid ingénue in third-rate pictures. We heard Rachmaninoff, and then went out and bought all his recordings. We heard Fritz Kreisler, and then went out and bought all *his* recordings. We listened to our favorite popular quartette, "The Revelers," whose recording of "In a Little Spanish Town" brought happy memories for both of us. I bought a canary "for Ken and me when we get our house," and I called him "Marcabrun," after the twelfth-century troubadour. He *was* brown-marked—but that was also the name of one of the books that Jack had given me. Somehow I found that Jack was still lurking unhappily in the dark corners of my mind. We dined often with Ken's family, and bought out the stores in an effort to make Grace's weary existence a little pleasanter.

Buoyed up by the excitement, I found the courage to make my first important professional decision. My diary entry for March 16 tells the story—and reading it now, I remember clearly how proud of myself I felt when it happened: "What a day! Took things into my own hands and accepted the switch of Korda's picture to a picture for United Artists. Saw Considine this morning and sent a wire to Daddy in New York. Fittings and rush wig job at Westmore's and start work tomorrow." I hadn't asked Daddy; I had simply told him what I had done. I had actually made a decision about my work!

It was quite a good picture, too, and a very successful one; and it marked Howard Hughes' first venture into film making: *Two Arabian Knights*, with Louis Wolheim and William Boyd (now-adays better known as Hopalong Cassidy). The story was hilarious—about two World War buddies in Arabia; I was an Arabian princess who had been fished out of the sea from a ship-wreck onto a troopship. I spent several nights in the cold waters of San Pedro Harbor weighted down with a brocade dress and trying to breathe through a harem veil.

Ken and I were so happy in our own love that we projected a strategy of matchmaking to promote another romance. Bessie Love was a good friend of mine; we connived a dinner party to bring her and Bill Hawks together. To our delight, it "took," and for some weeks the four of us happily planned our activities and excursions together. Bessie played the ukulele well, and I remember one afternoon when we were lying around on the sand at the Beach Club, and Bessie started playing and singing a song they had written for her for a number in the show she was going to do with MGM. It was "Singin' in the Rain," and I never hear the song now but what I think of her explosive laughter and her infectious sense of humor.

In May, I celebrated my twenty-first birthday; I had come of age, at least in the eyes of the calendar and the law. Ken gave me a lovely negligee and a cashmere sweater—but he had one of his headaches, and since he was too sick to drive home he stayed overnight. He suffered from a chronic intestinal trouble; I believe he spoke of it as colitis, but he would rarely complain and he would not discuss it. His face would get white and strained, and a vein on his forehead swelled and throbbed. All he would do about it was to let me hold his head on my lap and put on cold compresses. How many times I did that, frightened by the color of his lips and face!

And so time was filled, until it seemed that time itself must stretch and burst from the strain of all we crammed into it. After the *Two Arabian Knights* picture was completed, I started on a comedy, with Mervyn LeRoy directing—his first picture. Until then he had been simply a "gag man" for the Colleen Moore pictures, with the job of thinking up visual comedy situations that could be added to the script plot. His first picture bore the title *No Place to Go*, and it was not until later that I realized how ironic the title was for me. For no doubt about it, I had places to go. There were fittings at Sophie's, for pictures and for the trousseau. Golf. Dinners. Movies. Company luncheons at the studio.

A preview in San Bernardino. Ken's family moved to Brentwood, so we saw them much oftener—Grace growing thinner and weaker; she had to be carried to sit out on the porch. We became closer to some of our Hollywood friends—Jack and Virginia Conway, Norma Shearer and Irving Thalberg (Howard Hawks was engaged to Norma's sister Athole), Victor Fleming and Clara Bow, and of course Bill Hawks and Bessie Love. I hired a new maid, the very efficient Marceil Sutherland, a girl who was to work for me for the next ten years, and who is still my friend. One Sunday I had my first flight in an airplane; we went down to San Pedro and flew over to the Isthmus in a plane with a "pusher-type" engine and an open cockpit, well forward, so we could look over the edge. And afterwards we joined the party on the Thalbergs' yacht.

As I look back over my diary for these months and read the record of our activities, our tireless ability amazes me. One weekend—not fully typical, thank heaven—will show what I mean. On Thursday, I worked, and then went to a dinner party at the Biltmore, where Irving and Norma Shearer announced their engagement. On Friday, I worked, and then went out for Ken's birthday dinner with his family. On Saturday, I worked, and then drove up to Santa Barbara to spend Saturday evening and Sunday with Vic Fleming and Art and Lou Rosson and Howard Hawks and Athole Shearer, and went out in Howard's Chris-Craft. I got home at ten forty-five that night, and I was up at six the next morning and worked all day in the August heat on the back lot. Today that routine would put me in the hospital for a week!

The relationship between Ken and me had become settled and comfortable and right. We had some time since decided that anything "shady" between us had to go, we would play it straight and wait until we were married. On a very few occasions we had spent the evening at his house in Beverly Hills, when Howard was shooting nights or was gone for some other reason, but we resolved to give all that up. And we felt much better about it. As time went on, the denial was hard for me; it made me nervous and edgy. I think I was hinting at this in my diary when I wrote, at the end of July, "Having a grand time, and working very hard. Only I don't like long engagements. I think they are a bit dangerous." Ken seemed not to mind; he was not a sensual person at all. He had none of the deep, fierce passion that I had known. He was very affectionate and demonstrative; often we sat in a big chair, with me curled in his lap, and read from the same book. He was tall, and I fitted just under his shoulder when we stood. And always we held hands; I loved his hands, large and big-boned and gentle. Once in a while Ken and I would have what we called our "small-town evening"; after dinner I would make fudge, and then we would sit in the swing on the upstairs balcony in the moonlight.

Another "unfortunate clash with Daddy" (as my diary records) was "too serious for me to remain home." I don't even remember now what it was about, but I do remember that I simply packed and left for Del Monte that night—we were to go there soon for location anyway. Mother must have been wearied by the atmosphere at home, too, for she stayed in bed, getting up only for dinner. Ken had been away, in New York and Canada, on business, and even though I had been working steadily on a picture I missed him badly, more than I had thought I would. When we finished the work at Del Monte, Ken wrote me to stay on, and he would meet me there. I must have been happily excited to see him again; in my diary I wrote, "Played eighteen holes of golf, had lunch, and started to dress for Ken at 3:30—he arrived at 7:00. It is so great to have him with me again." The next day we played golf together at Pebble Beach, and we had champagne because I made a hole in one on the sixth, I think it was—a notoriously tricky hole with the green almost completely surrounded by the surf. You either got into the surf or you made an easy par three.

And I find recorded in my diary then, and with increasing frequency and ardor as the months go by, "I love Ken so much. He is such a dear."

When I finished *No Place to Go*, I must have needed rest, for I went down to the Casa Del Mar Club at the beach for a week by myself. I slept until noon, and I read and walked along the beach, and Ken usually came down in the evening to take me to dinner and a movie, or to a preview of one of his pictures. I think I had arrived at a point where I just could not stand being at home if I was not working. After knowing families and visiting homes where love and trust and happiness were in the very air, the atmosphere at home seemed intolerably choked and deadly. Ken understood my feeling; he had recently had his first and last argument with Daddy. They were talking, quietly enough, about steering a car. Daddy did not drive, but he regarded himself as a master of the theory of the operation of an automobile; and when Ken said that "in backing a car you turn the steering wheel to the left to turn to the left," Daddy announced that such an idea showed the most abysmal ignorance. Daddy produced a pencil and paper to diagram it for Ken, and they both got a little red in the face. Ken just gave up—we were already late to see a play of Ruth Chatterton's—but he well understood what Mother and I meant when we said "Daddy is always right." He always was—even when he was wrong. Ken wisely never allowed himself to get into such a situation again. He was tactful, and he knew how to steer a conversation even though he didn't know how to steer a car!

Ken and I went to the season opening of the Mayfair Club, and for the first time in my life I had too much to drink. I didn't feel a thing; I was smugly congratulating myself on my ability to "hold my liquor," until we went out to the car and the night air hit me. Suddenly I felt as though I were going to pass out, and I made a desperate grab for Ken. He gave me a lesson in self-control. "Hang onto yourself," he said, "hang on, and just *decide* you're not going to!" I made it home all right, and the next morning I was rather proud of my first hang-over. I loved complaining about it in what I thought was quite a worldly manner. Except for that one experience though, our drinking was infrequent and light. If we went out with friends we would sometimes have a cocktail before dinner, and on a Sunday we might have a bourbon and ginger ale in the afternoon. Ken never had the second or third drink that would worry or anger me. Drinking at this level was something we could even joke about, although one of Ken's jokes backfired distressingly. We went to Irving Thalberg's and Norma Shearer's wedding, which was held in the garden of Norma's home. They were married in the Jewish ritual, and before the ceremony everyone was seated, chatting quietly. Herman Mankiewicz came out carrying what looked like a large champagne goblet. Kenneth gave an enthusiastic salute: "Yea-a-ay!" And somebody hissed at him, "Shut up! That's the Cup of Life." Poor Kenneth dissolved in embarrassment, and all through the ceremony I didn't dare look at him for fear I would explode into laughter.

I had been working with Joe Henabery in *Sailors' Wives*, another routine picture, memorable only because it was during my work on it that "Ken gave me the most beautiful emerald engagement ring—it's *lovely!*" And memorable too, perhaps, because it was during that time that Ken and I went to the opening of *Two Arabian Knights*, a splendid affair with all the Hollywood trimmings, and Jack Barrymore introduced me from the stage. I came off sweating.

The next picture was rather fun; it was a circus picture called *Three Ring Marriage*, and Lloyd Hughes and I were both "Wild West" riders. We traveled three stops with the Al G. Barnes circus—Phoenix, Yuma, and Los Angeles—getting our shots as they actually loaded and unloaded the cars, and set up and dismantled the tents. All the atmosphere was authentic. In Los Angeles we photographed the interior of the tent at a special show given free to the public. I had done very little riding, but the circus people were wonderfully helpful; they gave me an experienced little pony and showed me how to stand in the stirrups the way the professional girl riders did. The pony was absolutely quiet until his cue came, and then he was off like a shot. We did my scenes over and over again, as is the way with movies, and the next day I couldn't walk at all.

"Between pictures" meant little or no rest, for it was always time to start fittings with Sophie for clothes for the next one, and there were always publicity interviews and pictures. The fittings were fun now because each time Sophie and I worked a little more on my trousseau. Every stitch was handmade, and Sophie insisted on only the best imported materials. She even made my hats and bathing suits. For the wedding I wanted a simple afternoon dress with a sort of garden hat, but Sophie would not hear of it. "This is the only time you're entitled to wear a veil," she said, "so wear it and enjoy it." Besides, she wanted my wedding dress to be her present. So it was to be a classic heavy oyster-white crepe dress with Alençon lace (and—practical Sophie—it would be a perfect evening dress for later), and a veil that was a cloud.

I was getting more and more impatient. At the end of September I had written, "All I can think of now is 'when can we be married!' We plan now that Christmas will be about right." And it looked as though our plans were going to work out; throughout November, Ken became increasingly confident that the long-term contract with Fox would come through. We waited hopefully, and finally, on December 5, Ken telephoned the welcome news. He had it! And in my diary I exulted, "Ken got his contract and we're going to New York as we had hoped for our honeymoon! Wheeee!!!"

And as though life did not already hold enough happiness for me, Ken's boss, Sol Wurtzel of Fox, phoned about the middle of December and asked, "How would you like to play a tough 'gun moll' for a change?" *Would* I—after years of saccharine heroines, of just "looking beautiful," of hearing the tiresome repetition from the critics: "Mary Astor was lovely as the girl," or "Mary Astor was adequate." (One reviewer of *Beau Brummel* had been more forthright with his assertion that "Irene Rich as the Duchess of York would have undoubtedly made a better Lady Margery than Mary Astor. Miss Astor was seen to advantage from the standpoint of beauty, but she did not display any great histrionic ability.") So I had an interesting part in quite a good picture, *Dressed to Kill*, with Ed Lowe; I played a sultry but angel-faced girl who actually packed a gun.

In high spirits I began work on the picture during the week before Christmas. Then all our vigorous enthusiasm received a sharp setback. Two days after I started, Grace was rushed to a sanitarium, and the next day she died. Christmas, which was to be an event of such rejoicing and gaiety, was quiet and solemn. Ken sorrowed mostly for his mother; it was her second loss, for Ken's baby sister had died of food poisoning when she was four. On the twenty-seventh I "went to Grace's funeral this morning. She looked beautiful, but I think funerals are barbaric. It broke me up completely." I remember the way I felt, but I couldn't understand why I felt so miserable. Grace and I had never been close, for she was much too ill to be seen more than a few moments at a time, but I was crying uncontrollably when I got into the car.

The year closed with a quiet celebration. We canceled our plans for a party at the Mayfair Club and stayed home to see the New Year in with Mother's cider punch. And so "that's another year. I believe I can say without exaggeration that it was the happiest year of my life. Ken is the finest person imaginable, and he has certainly made me feel differently about a lot of things, chiefly myself. I toast *our* New Year. May it bring the happiness we desire; may it bring companionship, friends, success to us, success in our marriage. Dear 1928—be kind to us!"

The new year began as though it were setting about to fill my prescription to the letter. We set our wedding date for February 24; with so little time remaining, we quickened our pace of house hunting, and almost at once found the place that was just right. It was a sweet little house on Alcyona Drive, in the hills just above Vine Street, set against the hillside and well hidden from the street by shrubs and trees. We took a lease for a year, and I fell to work decorating and furnishing. It was the first job of that kind that was all mine to do, and I put all my heart into it. Ken and I had talked so much about what we liked and didn't like that I did not have to hesitate in my decisions. The drapes and carpeting could be the deep reds and greens that we both loved. For my bedroom I had the furnishings from the New York apartment, but there was more room, so I could add a chaise longue and end table and lamp; it was all orchid and pale green, with organdy curtains, feminine and lovely. Ken's room was furnished with some of his own things, a mahogany four-poster, a leather chair, a wardrobe, and bookshelves. I spent hours fixing the linen closet; I was like the mother bluebird I used to watch in the peach tree stump on the farm—busy, busy, busy. Arranging things, standing back to look, waiting impatiently for furniture to be delivered, putting in light bulbs, organizing kitchen shelves and cupboards—and being irritated on the afternoons when I had to go back to the studio for retakes.

Finally the time came when I could clean it up and set the stage for Kenneth's inspection and approval. A fire built in the fireplace, the lamps lighted and placed exactly where they belonged, a tray with cocktails—everything was just so. He loved it, and together we admired everything as we went from room to room, and then started again and went through the entire house once more. We felt that our little home was a perfect work of art.

I arranged with Marceil to stay there while we were on our trip; with her practical mind she would see that everything was in proper working order when we returned. I knew where I wanted the pieces of furniture and the lamps, and I knew exactly what color every rug and curtain and drape should be, but I had only the haziest notions of how much flour and sugar and supplies should be ordered. She could take care of that.

At the Temple Hill house, which I was to leave so happily in so short a time, the usual pre-nuptial confusion was taking over. Wedding presents were arriving, and careful lists of givers and gifts were compiled. The messages of congratulation were pouring in, and there was shopping, and there were showers. I went to a shower for Athole (she was to be married to Howard Hawks very soon) and the same evening fifty men from Fox gave Ken a perfectly planned surprise bachelor party—after which most of them joined the girls' party.

Despite the confusion and the turmoil the day finally came.

A string quartette played softly in the music room, and the far corner of the living room, with its arrangement of stained-glass windows, lent itself perfectly to tall baskets of flowers and tall candles. Marceil packed for me, and helped me into the beautiful crepe and lace wedding dress with its veil that was a cloud. And, with Menifee as my maid of honor, I felt like every bride in the world as I came down the steps on Daddy's arm to meet—my Ken.

And then there were photographs in the garden, and the wedding cake, and about forty guests milling around, and when I heard Daddy confide to a neighbor that it all "set us back a pretty penny" I wanted to say "*Whose* penny," but I didn't.

Even though it was *our* wedding, Daddy characteristically managed to have the last word. Howard was going to drive us to the station in his car, which Mrs. Hawks said was the customary thing to do. But Daddy insisted that Parker take us in the Pierce-Arrow. The Hawks side conceded gracefully, and Daddy felt very much pleased that he had "won." Poor Daddy—he was always "winning," and thereby losing.

We left on the Sante Fe at six o'clock. We sat in our drawing room and lived through the day all over again, and laughed at all the things that had happened. And everything was just the same, except that we were married. We couldn't quite believe it; we had been engaged for thirteen months.

But later I lay in my berth in my beautiful satin and lace bridal nightgown and stared out at the blackness, watching the points of lights of distant houses and hearing the descending scale of minor tones from the crossroad signals, and wondered. Because Ken had simply kissed me good night very tenderly and gone to bed in the upper berth. Well, I thought, we *were* tired. A bit tearfully I went to sleep.

Five

Our honeymoon was a whirlwind of laughter and activity. We had allowed ourselves a full month, but into that month we had to cram ten days of New York, with plays and operas and numerous side trips; a train-and-plane trip to Havana; and an ocean voyage through the Panama Canal back to California. Everything, even the haste and the inevitable mishaps, we enjoyed together and laughed at together. During our stopover in Chicago we decided to walk from the Blackstone to the Drake for lunch; the blustery Chicago wind caught Ken's hat and sent it spinning. He chased it for a full block, and we both laughed as though chasing hats were the most hilarious amusement life could offer.

Our ten days in New York were partly busman's holiday. Almost every day we saw a play, some of them memorable ones— Marilyn Miller in *Rosalie*, Edward G. Robinson in *The Racket*, Ann Harding in *The Trial of Mary Dugan*, Helen Hayes in *Coquette*. We went to the Met and heard Florence Easton and Scotti in *Butterfly*. And we saw my picture *Dressed to Kill*, which was playing at the Capitol. We shopped for presents for people at home. We saw newspaper reporters. We made a sentimental journey to New Haven to see the university, and Ken showed me his old room. When we met the boys living there, Ken had the usual reaction: "Aren't they awfully young?" And we met the fabulous William Lyon Phelps, who told me what I already knew —that Ken was a wonderful boy.

One afternoon at a matinee of a musical I was overcome by a violent attack of cramps, and Ken had to help me out of the theatre and carry me across the street to a taxi. At the hotel he administered a shot of gin, and I lay for a while in a hot bath as the pain gradually abated, leaving me limp but relaxed. It was my first attack in years, and I suspected that it had been brought on by sheer frustration; every night of our honeymoon Ken had simply kissed me affectionately and gone quietly to bed.

It was somehow not a subject Ken and I could discuss freely. He possessed a kind of natural delicacy that seemed inviolable. He strongly disliked dirty stories, although he was never prudish or sanctimonious in his disapproval. In our own relationship we were happily comfortable, but I clearly sensed the existence of an intangible line that I could not, and did not want to, cross over. I think now that it would have been much better if we had brought the entire matter out into the open and I could have explained to him the tension and repression I was suffering. It would have prevented a good deal of future unhappiness.

Our stay in New York had come to an end before we had a chance to draw a quiet breath, and we were off for Key West by train, and then on by plane to Havana. Our stay there was brief; we had only time to feel a suggestion of the enchantment, of the beauty of the vivid colors that were everywhere, and the funny little streets, and the speech. We went to the races, had dinner on the roof of the Sevilla-Biltmore, complete with Alexander cocktails, and learned the rumba—or the *son*, as they called the ballroom form.

At six the following night we sailed on the S.S. *California*. It was my first ocean voyage, and I found that I was an excellent sailor. I loved the ocean, with the rhythmic rise and fall of the water, and the endless stretch of the horizon. I relaxed as I had not been able to do for many months. We avoided the usual shipboard activities and crowds. We swam before breakfast, took snapshots, and sat and dreamed and watched the porpoises. By the strange working of chance Dolores and Helene Costello and their mother were aboard. We had dinners and long conversations with them; since none of them knew of my romance with Jack, I could talk without strain or embarrassment. I even felt a sympathy for Dolores, for I thought it quite possible that she would ultimately experience the hopelessness and unhappiness that my love for Jack had brought me. And one time when I was alone with her I asked, "What about you and Jack? Is that all over?" Perhaps it was an understandable bias, but to me her answer seemed rather sly and confident. "Not—quite!" she said. My sympathy was immediately transferred to Jack, and I thought, "You're hooked, my friend!" And another thought followed immediately: "It serves you right!"

In four days we were in Panama, where we were scheduled for an eight-hour stop. We spent a hazily dizzy sort of day, a medley of hurried sight-seeing, drinking countless varieties of strange and exotic drinks, buying quantities of expensive perfume cheap, and acquiring from a sailor a parrot that could say nothing but the Spanish equivalent of "Polly." Then came the beautiful trip up the coast of Mexico, with the coast line visible almost all the way. We docked in San Pedro on March 24, just a perfectly rounded month.

As if all this had not been enough, when we returned to our home on Alcyona Drive a glittering Packard roadster stood waiting for me in the garage. My own car! I could hardly believe in its existence. But whether I could believe in it or not I was all too ready to accept the undeniable fact that it was there. It seemed to confirm my new freedom, and it immediately became a means of exercising it. I had learned to drive fairly well, under the combined tutelage of Parker and Ken; but at home, even after I was finally permitted to go out alone, it was Mother's car that I drove, and inevitably my request to use it would evoke a lament about the great inconvenience it would cause her. Now I had my own car, and I drove it all over town, on any excuse or with none at all. I drove to visit people, and I drove to bring people to the house. The car, I felt, was the final step in my liberation.

I enjoyed being free to go where and when I pleased, but I also enjoyed being free to stay home, happily and comfortable, when I wanted to. Ken had hired a capable daytime maid for me, and we often had friends in for dinner, with no one to cast gloom over the party by an obvious desire to have everyone leave. It was grand, too, to have dinner at home alone, to sit in front of the fire with cigarettes and coffee, and then go to bed and read, usually in Ken's room in his big double bed.

Professionally I was still climbing. Now Fox was talking contract; I had only one more picture to do with First National, *Once There Was a Princess*, which was to start on May 2, and would finish by the end of June. Before the picture was half filmed, I had signed with Fox for forty weeks at $3750 a week. That, I think, was the top salary for anyone below a full star rating. However, Daddy was infinitely more pleased about it than I was. Ken and I had discussed the problems that might arise from my having an independent income, and Ken had made very rigid rules about it. The money I made I was not to use for any household or even personal expenses. Ken would pay for all that. I could buy presents with my own money, and that was about all. But I didn't need it even for that, as Ken also provided me with a private checking account. The result was that every cent I made after I married Ken was collected by my parents. Daddy assured me that it was all to be mine someday. He was using the money, he pointed out, to improve the value of the Temple Hill property (he improved it right out of sight, it turned out). He was also making small investments, but he lost money so consistently on them that he soon abandoned his career as financier. Actually I could not touch the Temple Hill property, and I had no voice in its management. A long while before, immediately after my first "blowup," Daddy had drawn up a "family document" that had caused much argument and discussion, but in the end Daddy had

had his way. The gist of the agreement was that each of us, Mother, Daddy, and I, owned one third of the property, and no one (meaning me, of course) could sell it or rent it without the consent of both of the others. This was designed to protect them against what they regarded as my willful and selfish whims.

About the first of July, I moved into my newly decorated bungalow dressing room on the Fox lot and started a sophisticated comedy called *Dry Martini*, directed by Harry d'Arrast.

It is not unusual for an actor to absorb and assume something of the atmosphere and emotional climate of the picture or play he is working in. I seemed especially sensitive to this contagion, although few of the pictures I had appeared in had a strong enough emotional atmosphere to affect me. This picture was different. *Dry Martini* was Paris, a gay and sophisticated Paris, the Paris of people with too much money and too much time. It was the story of a father who is shocked to discover that his daughter is carrying on an intrigue, and then finds that intrigue is not such a bad idea at all, after which he proceeds to get himself involved in illicit amorous situations. Today the Legion of Decency would label this one strictly Class C—"Condemned—Objectionable for All."

Mr. d'Arrast, a Basque, with great wit and charm, handled the situations and dialogue with a light touch. After the first week everyone in the company was infected by the spirit of the script. The conversation on the set, the stories and anecdotes, assumed the quality that we would have described as "sophisticated." I suppose that "sophistication" has a perfectly respectable meaning and use; but we defined it in our own way—as a superior attitude toward "ordinary" standards of morality. Its doctrine might be summed up in this way: appetites are meant to be satisfied; man's purpose in life is primarily the satisfaction of these appetites; the satisfaction is to be accomplished as efficiently and charmingly as possible. The properly sophisticated man could get blind-drunk if he did so in a good café and had friends to see him in a taxi. And he could sleep with anyone he liked as long as there were certain charming preludes and proper surroundings and a reasonable degree of "discretion."

To me it was a new and rather exciting point of view; with its specious doctrine of self-indulgence, it rushed into the vacuum of my moral sense and captivated me completely. Morality had at best meant to me a tenuous and indeterminate relationship between me and society—society as seen first by Otto Langhanke, but this view I had rejected when I found that no one else agreed with him; then society as seen by Ken with his school background of "what is done" and "what is just *not* done." The product of this background I liked, with its gracious living, even temper, and pleasant speech and manners. All its murky depths seemed to have been bred out; they had not, however, been bred out of me!

My marital relations with Ken were, in effect, non-existent; their infrequent occurrences were brief and unsatisfactory. Total abstinence was easier than this; but either solution caused me to be nervous and upset. We often slept together in Ken's big double bed; I loved him, and I loved the feeling of closeness, but it wasn't enough. I understood when his headaches made him feel too sick even to talk, but I could not understand when he was well and just fell asleep while I lay awake with my face buried unhappily in the pillow.

My frustrations found a partial outlet in the racy conversations and anecdotes on the set; this I accepted without concern, but when I found myself attracted to Russell Bradbury, one of the Fox executives, I felt the beginning of alarm. Mr. Bradbury was quite willing to recognize and respond to my obvious interest; he regarded Ken as a dull sort of man, too preoccupied with work and golf to have any talent or inclination for romance, even with his wife. He began a pursuit, which I resisted with all my very small might. The thought of infidelity to Ken appalled me; I could not believe that I was so abandoned that I could deceive a man I loved and respected. I wished I had someone I could unburden myself to, someone who could help me organize my uncertain notions of morality and strengthen my frailties of body and will. I knew that my girl friends on the lot would be no help; they would laugh at my scruples and say, "What are you waiting for?" Among themselves they discussed intrigues and infidelities as casually as they might discuss the weather.

But I had to talk with someone, and finally I unloaded my woes on Sally Eilers. Sally and I had become rather close friends during the work on *Dry Martini*, and I felt I had no other choice. She was a vivacious, dynamic girl, about my age, with a great deal of humor. And as I should have foretold, she was unable to give me any satisfactory advice. And so I started lying to my diary; I knew that Ken would never look at any private paper or document of mine, but I had memories of Mother leafing through the papers in the drawers of my desk, so I wrote: "Had a wonderful day at the beach all by myself. It was what I had needed for a long time. Feel infinitely better."

Even so, I was tormented by the guilt of treachery and deception. I told myself that I felt better physically for my deceit, that I was more relaxed, and freed from the intolerable frustrations of physical craving. I reminded myself that this affair was being conducted in the very upper brackets of "sophistication," in surroundings of luxury, with brilliant conversation and excellent food served by a discreet servant who quietly disappeared, and a late afternoon brandy flip which Brad constructed with great artistry and ceremony. Yes, it was all very "high-level" indeed; but ultimately I had to face the realization that I was pregnant and that an abortion is an abortion, whether it is accompanied by the music of Sibelius or by the caterwauling of tomcats in an alley.

I gave Ken the carefully prepared double talk that I hoped would answer his "But how could you be pregnant?" Since we had agreed that it was "too soon to have children" and (seizing on the words I had heard so often at home) "my career should come first," I determined to undergo a curettage. This too was accomplished according to all the canons of "good taste"; I went to a properly exclusive establishment that committed such crimes under the fiction of "therapeutic treatment." It was the first time I had ever been under complete anesthesia, and it was the experience of the anesthesia that interested me at the time more than anything else. I remember it very distinctly; a voice in surgery said "Have him call me on Monday," and the words were endlessly repeated as though in an echo chamber: "call me Monday . . . call me Monday . . . Monday . . . Monday . . . Monday . . ."

I now had a new burden of guilt to carry; a few days afterwards I was working in a scene with a darling baby about fourteen months old. I wrote in my diary that the scene was "difficult"; and I added that I "felt like a murderer." I think I must have also tried to relieve some of the pressure of guilt by an unconscious cruelty to Ken—of a more overt kind than the cruelty I had been perpetrating over the past months. I write of "tiffs"; and instead of the pride I had always felt when he won a trophy in tennis or golf, I express a vindictive pleasure in his defeats. "Watched Ken get well trimmed in the tennis finals at the club," my diary says.

Ken was being more difficult than he had ever been before. He was annoyingly ill; he had dysentery; he had too much to drink one night when he was out for dinner, and he passed out and had to have someone drive him home. That these might have been the symptoms of a man who was tortured by his wife's infidelity did not occur to me. I was sure he didn't know; I had covered my tracks too well. My worst time of remorse came some years later, when I learned that as a boy he had had a childhood illness which gave the doctors considerable concern. I also found from my mother's diary that she had taken it on herself to tell Ken about Bradbury. "Had a talk with poor Ken about Lucile this afternoon," she wrote. "I felt there were some things he should know. After all, people will talk."

A rough experience with surgery, a tonsillectomy that brought a good deal of suffering and bleeding and illness from swallowing blood, gave me a chance to straighten things out with Ken. I recuperated very slowly. Ken and I drove down to La Jolla and stayed at the Casa de Manana, drove along the Silver Strand to San Diego, and in general repaired our relationship.

My line-a-day diary at this point has fewer and fewer entries, and they finally stop altogether. The reason was that I had started writing more fully in a larger book, a black-covered ledger-type book, ruled in blue—almost identical to the books Mother had used for her journal. I had a fancy for an ink called "Aztec Brown"; the combination of colors seen at a distance by members of the press some years later gave them the impression that it was written in "purple ink." They were no doubt confirmed in this opinion by their supposition that the diary recorded events of that passionate hue. But that in its own time.

I tired of Russell Bradbury long before we finally stopped seeing each other. The re-established harmony with Ken made it still more difficult to rationalize my deception, and Brad became jealous and possessive; he would nag me about flirting with men at a party. My visits to his apartment became fewer and fewer because each visit involved detailed explanations of why I hadn't seen him sooner or why I hadn't called him.

And suddenly I found that I had professional problems that all but erased Brad from my mind. Something had been happening that most of us were paying little attention to—sound. Ken and I had seen some reels of Movietone, which was sound on film, but we had given it little thought. It was an interesting novelty, but obviously impractical. And then, to my surprise, I found that Movietone was on its way in—and I was on my way out. I had made several pictures for Fox; in April of 1929 the option on my contract came up. I was to advance to four thousand dollars a week for fifty-two weeks, and I had assumed that the renewal would be almost automatic. But most pictures were "part talkie" by then, and the studio requested a Movietone test before they considered the contract. My test was indescribably bad. I was nervous, and I hadn't the least idea of what I was doing. The sound equipment made my voice ridiculously low. Sol Wurtzel told my father that they could not renew my contract at the four-thousand-dollar figure; they were getting people with trained speaking voices, experienced people from the New York stage, who were delighted to work for five hundred a week. There was a spirited verbal battle. Wurtzel liked me, and he offered to keep me at about half of what I had been getting. Daddy was contemptuously indignant; it was an insult to offer me so "paltry" a sum. He turned it down. Sol capitalized on the chance to tell Daddy just what he thought of him—what he and the other producers thought of his judgment and his manner of doing business. And he told him very clearly and emphatically that in the future none of the producers would negotiate through him. They would deal with me directly, or with an agent, but not with him.

So I was out. And I stayed out for ten long months, while the industry moved into a new era. I missed the fun and excitement of working, but I enjoyed the leisure that brought no economic pressure and made no rigorous demands. Unrushed and unharried, I did the necessary work around the house. I took up drawing and painting with John Hubbard Rich, and I accomplished a few fair oils, and charcoal sketches by the ream. I brought home armloads of books, and read about method and technique and art appreciation.

Our lease was up on Alcyona, and we moved into a lovely newly built house on Appian Way, on the very top of Lookout Mountain. As the house was considerably larger, we kept a full-time maid and entertained often. I became an efficient hostess, although I was inclined to plan too lavishly. We had settled into a comfortable consistent group of friends, all married couples, who met almost every Sunday night for a buffet supper and games. There were Florence and Fredric March, Marian Spitzer, a writer, and her husband, Harlan Thompson, John and Kay Cromwell, and Gwen and Jack Blystone.

In this clique Ken and I were a "couple," a unit. But I felt that I also had a life of my own, a life I wanted to talk about apart from Ken. I could continue to write in my diary, but I could no longer talk with and confide in any of my close friends. Because they thought I was treating Brad badly they were not sympathetic confidantes. So I found a new girl friend to share my life with, Adeline Muir, whom I had met at the studio. But instead of pouring out my troubles into Adeline's ear I found myself listening to hers. She was deeply infatuated with a prominent Holly-

wood realtor; he was much older than she—thirty-eight or so—
and married. Because of his high position it was a very dangerous
situation. I became a third party, so they could have lunch together, and when Ken was busy I had dinner with them. Adeline
was a very innocent, gentle, and timid girl; now it was I who took
the role of the experienced woman of the world and dismissed
with scorn her misgivings and moral scruples. So the realtor decided I was on his side, and he repeatedly asked me to urge her
to give herself to him.

One Thursday in May he telephoned me and told me he
wanted to talk about Adeline. Since it was the maid's day off, he
suggested that we could find the necessary privacy in my own
home. He arrived, and after a few conventional pleasantries over
a highball I tried to steer the conversation around to Adeline; I
was becoming uncomfortably aware that I, and not Adeline, was
the object of his visit. Subtle evasive tactics availed for only a
time; then it became one of those ridiculous *La Tosca* pursuits
around a couch. When he grabbed me and kissed me, I slapped
him and almost literally kicked him out of the house.

I told Ken about it. I was so glad that I could tell him, that
I could be angry and guiltless about a man's attentions to me,
and that I could enlist my husband's help against the blackguard!
Ken was infuriated, and his anger was all the harder for him because he realized how useless it would be to go to the realtor's
office and give him a good beating.

I concealed this misadventure from Adeline as long as I could,
but when she kept coming to the house just to be able to talk
about him I was so irritated by her making a saint of the man that
I felt her illusions ought to be destroyed. So I destroyed them.
The following day he telephoned, icily angry. He told me to come
downtown with Adeline and meet him at his office at five-thirty.
His tone had frightened me enough that I did not think of refusing; when I met Adeline, her nose and eyes were red from
weeping and she was unwilling to talk. We met him, and he took
us at once into an inner office, where we would not be disturbed.

Then he tore into me. He told me that in his position as a real estate man he felt it necessary to thoroughly investigate the background of anyone with whom he was associated, even though he regarded that person as a friend. All their activities and associations were closely observed, so that if necessary he could "fight fire with fire." Then he called in a clerk, who handed him an envelope and left. He opened the envelope and shuffled through the contents, which appeared to be photos and negatives and reports. Then he turned to me and announced stonily, "I have here a full report on your affair with Russell Bradbury, with complete dates and times of your meetings. Here is a photograph of your car in front of his apartment, and here is one of you standing unclothed in his bedroom window." I had caused him the suffering of humiliation; now I should have my share of suffering, and probably mountains of disastrous publicity, with Ken divorcing me and naming Brad as corespondent. I was frightened, but I would have been less frightened if he had been less viciously belligerent. He pushed me just too far. When he informed me that as soon as he could he intended to turn all this information over to Ken, I suggested that perhaps he had things a little backward. Why, I asked, had he made the mistake of making a pass at Adeline's friend? "Because," he answered, "I knew that Adeline's friend would be easy to make a pass at." For the first time in my life I felt a total, all-consuming fury. I felt as though I were not a part of the scene at all—as though I were watching it, detached and disinterested, from a remote distance. Everything suddenly seemed to be a pale green color, and the furniture and objects on the walls moved slowly and rhythmically; for a moment I could hear only a sound as of a low vibration, and then I heard myself saying, "Why wait? Let's call Ken now. He's in his office." I wasn't bluffing; I meant it. The situation was intolerable. He suddenly looked a little less sure of himself, and hastily said that he didn't know the number. "I do," I said. "Get me an outside wire." In a few seconds I was talking with Ken. "Will you come downtown right away? Our friend here has something he wants to tell you." "Tell the s.o.b. to wait right there," Ken replied. "I'm on my way."

I announced that Ken was coming, and then I stood there stiffly, mechanically. I felt almost afraid to move, as though I were holding a bomb that would explode at the least jar. Then I felt that I could not tolerate his presence for another moment, and I went to an outer room to wait. Very shortly he came out and said, "Adeline is a very tenderhearted girl. She has convinced me that this would be a terrible thing to do. It could ruin both your careers, both yours and Ken's, and so when Ken arrives let's tell him that I simply want to apologize man to man to him. And I won't say anything further."

I had been willing to face disaster, but now I realized that all along he had been bluffing. Probably even his description of the photos and negatives had been a part of his bluff. I agreed with his suggestion; he had a smooth and diplomatic tongue, so when Ken arrived, controlled but pale in his anger, he had no choice but to accept the "apology" gracefully.

That night at dinner Ken looked up at me and said, "I wonder what he *really* wanted to tell me!"

Ken had been doing very well indeed, both in his job at Fox and in the stock market. He was cleaning up in the market. Every morning he was on the phone talking with his brokers. I can remember awaking to the sound of his excited talking; the conversations were quite unintelligible to me, and I never asked Ken to explain anything about them, since my father had convinced me that I was incapable of understanding anything about business operations.

And at Fox, Ken had finally achieved his ambition; he was given a job as director. He had a good story, called *Big Time*, about a vaudeville team, played by Mae Clark, a musical comedy star, and Lee Tracy, who had just come to Hollywood straight from his Broadway success in *The Front Page*. Ken asked me if I would help him with the picture; he explained that he had not had much experience in communicating with actors, but I think he did it mostly because he knew it would do me good to get back into the turmoil of a movie set again.

I was still making sporadic efforts to get a new contract, or even a picture, with any one of the various studios or producers. I went to see Irving Thalberg, to whom I was now vaguely related by marriage, but all I got was, in the common parlance, "the brush." Daddy exhorted me to "call" on various producers to tell them I was "available"—since he could no longer represent me. My failure to land a contract, however, did not prevent him from continuing to spend small fortunes on "improving" Temple Hill; it simply caused him to sulk and fret because I couldn't get a job and his income was consequently cut off. He seemed to feel that it was only spite that prevented my finding work.

During this period I experienced a perverse sort of pleasure in being cruel to Russell Bradbury. I had told him of the threatened exposure of our relationship, and I had used it as an excuse to break with him. But he persuaded me at least to have lunch with him at the Montmartre, and while we were waiting for coffee I went to the phone booth to make a perfectly innocent call. I even indicated to Brad by my manner that I was calling another man. He was outside the booth when I finished, and he was so angry he was practically in tears. He protested that he had loved me, and that he had been hoping that I would ask Ken for a divorce and marry him. Before he had finished, I walked away; I knew it was the last time I would see him, and I was relieved.

After that I settled down a little. I was worried about not working, and Daddy was groaning louder and louder about "no money coming in." But life was not boring. I worked at my painting. Bessie Love had broken with Bill Hawks some months before, but now they were reconciled again. I renewed my friendship with her; we went to the beach for swimming, and I gave a kitchen shower for her. And I found myself drawn strongly to one of the older women—Marian Spitzer. She provided the draught of intellectual purgatives and medicines that I sorely needed; she had been a newspaperwoman on the New York *Globe*, and was quite a good writer, with a healthful breadth and depth of interests. For the first time, my conversations with a woman were not confined to discussions of personalities and clothes. She had a special ability to think things through—and to see through things and people. Even in discussing people she was analytical rather than gossipy: she was interested in what they were like and what made them act as they did, rather than merely in what they did. She made many people feel uncomfortable; her speech was slow and hesitant, and with the talent of a reporter she could listen and draw people out, so that they revealed far more than they had intended. We shared the stories of our lives; when I had finished my sordid recital, she looked at me very keenly, shook her head, and said, "You're in for a lot of trouble, my girl."

She attracted interesting people of all kinds; her parties were always memorable affairs. I remember meeting Dick Rogers and Larry Hart at her house, and listening to some of their early successes, before they *were* successes. And one night I heard "Thanks for the Memory" for the first time, sung by a newcomer named Bob Hope. I remember many wonderful evenings when there were perhaps only half a dozen people left sitting around the fire and talking about everything in the world.

The stimulation of the mind seemed to lessen the nagging of the body; I became more settled, and my life with Ken improved immeasurably. Ken sensed my greater contentment, and he was warmed and encouraged by it. And I realized once more what an utter fool I had been to jeopardize our marriage. I didn't fully realize how very much Ken needed me at the moment. The panic was on, and he was losing money by the fistfuls. He talked longer on the phone in the morning, and he went into the bathroom to shave with none of the chatter and banter that we usually carried on. Fortunately he was in good shape professionally; his picture *Big Time* was very well received, and he was about to start another, with Warner Baxter.

And suddenly I found I was busy again. In November, Florence Eldridge, Freddie March's wife, had arranged for me to meet Edward Everett Horton. He was about to begin rehearsals on a play called *Among the Married*, by Vincent Lawrence. It was a comedy drama, with an excellent part for me, in which I would have a number of comedy scenes with Horton. Florence pointed out that working in the play might break my run of bad luck, and that I would just have to forget the fact that they paid only $150 a week. The salary was hardly what I had been used to, but at least here was a chance to do something, to be active. I took it.

I found that the thought of appearing on the stage was frightening; the days of training in Chicago and the war drama groups seemed remote and useless, or like something that had happened to someone else. But Florence encouraged me; everyone, she said, would help. The director came to the house, and we had a number of sessions of the most elementary work, learning to breathe, learning to project, learning to *speak*. I plunged into it with an "I'll show them" determination. I knew I had two strikes against me: I was a silent actress, and I had had almost a year of not being the busiest, highest-priced leading woman in the movies. My pride had taken a beating.

Opening night arrived, and I was armed with more self-confidence than I have ever known since. This is a typical reaction of the novice stage actor; he simply does not realize all the pitfalls. But the play progressed without my falling into any of the traps that I afterwards learned awaited the overconfident or inexperienced player; and the next morning I had breakfast in bed, drinking in all the glory of success, devouring the reviews and the telegrams, and surrounded by banks of flowers.

Within a week I had five offers from studios that had previously turned me down. I signed for a picture at Paramount with Freddie March, scheduled to begin late in January; the contracted six-week run of the play at the Majestic would keep me busy until then. And I signed at a good salary; it was about half of what I had received at Fox, but times had changed.

I enjoyed the life of the theatre. We were a good company. On matinee days Eddie and Florence and I and our husbands would meet at the Town House for dinner before the show. Then we would go on to the Majestic; the play became easy, and I found that it was fun to learn how to "get the laughs," especially with the good houses and responsive audiences that we had through the entire run. I would get home late, after Ken was in bed, and I would sleep late into the morning. Ken bought me a fluffy little kitten, whom I called Michael, and when Ken got up in the morning he would put the kitten into the bed with me.

Our Christmas was a happy one—for me. Bessie and Bill Hawks were married Christmas night, and I joined them after the show for their party at the Biltmore. The day might not have been so joyous if Ken had told me how badly he had lost in the market, but he had not breathed a word of it. Actually he had lost every cent of his capital; he had had to discontinue payments on a huge insurance policy of which I was the beneficiary; and the payments on the house were past due. But I knew none of this. And Ken had no reason for real alarm. He had a good contract with Fox and he was earning a thousand a week. It would not be difficult for him to recoup without either of us feeling any real pressure.

On New Year's Day we made our annual pilgrimage to the Rose Bowl Game—we never missed it, and as usual, Ken bought me a corsage of violets for my fur jacket. And then we went to Mother and Daddy Hawks' for an early supper so Ken could drive me to the theatre in time for the performance.

The next day, Ken had planned to photograph the parachute drop in the picture he had been working on. He had drawn the camera plan for me some days before: two Ford tri-motors were each to carry a camera and camera crew; one was intended for close-ups, and the other for long shots. They were to fly fairly close together, one a little above the other. They planned to take off from Clover Field and make a circuit around Point Vicente. A small two-seater would carry the stunt man, who would make the parachute jump between the camera planes and the land, which was supposed to represent the coast of England. They intended to make one trial run and then return to Clover Field to make any necessary corrections. It was quite simple, Ken assured me. In those days flying was not the casual matter that it is today, and I was a little distressed. But Ken calmed my fears. "If it looks as though there's going to be anything dangerous about it," he assured me, "I won't go."

As he left that morning, I waved to him from the bedroom window, with the kitten in my arms, and I pantomimed that we were going back to sleep. It was a matinee day, purely routine. There was only one set in the play, and after the matinee Florence and I usually stretched out and relaxed on the couches on the darkened stage until it was time to go to dinner before preparing for the evening performance. That afternoon as I was dozing off I suddenly realized that Florence had sat down beside me. She looked unusually serious as she said, "Mary, there's something I want to talk to you about."

"Sure," I said, "of course; get it off your chest. What's troubling you?"

She wasn't quite coherent. "There's been an accident, Mary. The planes—we've only just heard—they're not sure about anything yet—we've just got to wait."

With her first words I broke, then I recovered some self-control with her words of hope. And suddenly it seemed as though the whole company were there, all of them talking disjointedly. Eddie was saying that I should get my make-up off, and he kept repeating that he was going to find out something just as soon as he could. His insistence that I remove my make-up led to a short discussion about the show that evening. I told him that I felt all right and I was sure I could do it. But Eddie insisted that there were bound to be a good many morbid curiosity seekers and it would be better for me if I didn't. He told me he had got a call through to Doris Lloyd, and she had agreed to read through the part for that performance. That seemed to make sense, so I went into my dressing room and started creaming off my make-up, saying over and over to my reflection in the mirror, "It isn't so . . . it isn't so . . . it isn't so."

Then there was a knock at the door and one of the producers from Fox walked in. He was fighting back tears, and when he started to talk he couldn't; he just choked up. But he didn't have to say anything. I looked at him, and I knew. "He's dead, isn't he," I said, and he could only nod. I think I might really have broken then, but at that point Mother and Daddy burst into the room—true to form. They interrupted each other, explaining how *they* felt about it. Mother was almost hysterical, and Daddy explained over and over how badly she had been shaken by the news; he told everybody how she had wanted to drive through all the red traffic lights in her haste to get to the theatre. And my memory flashed back to other events when Daddy had worried over Mother's actions and had shown no concern for my unhappiness. The memory annoyed me, but it helped to steady me, and I said, "Please, Mother, don't make so much noise."

Daddy announced that they were taking me back home with them, and he told me, with something of his old brusqueness, to get my things ready. But Florence stepped in with firm authority and said in a tone that even my father did not want to argue with, "I think it will be best for Mary if she comes home with us for tonight. She can stay until she can decide for herself what she wants to do. And I don't think hysterics are very good for her at this time."

Florence had to do the show, so Marian Spitzer and Harlan drove me to the Marches'. Both Marian and Harlan were very quiet people, and they said almost nothing during the drive. But though he did his best, Harlan could not avoid stopping at signals at intersections where newsboys were yelling, "Ten die in film accident. Mary Astor's husband killed."

When we arrived at the Marches', I was shaking with chills; Marian and Freddie wrapped me in blankets, and fed me with hot milk, and sat with me in front of a big fire while Harlan told me what he had been able to find out. On the test run the two big planes had collided and exploded in mid-air. It was impossible that anyone could have survived. Even the chances of recovering bodies were slight.

I don't remember thinking or feeling anything. I just sat there. When Florence got home, I wanted to know how the show had gone. They put me to bed in the guest room, and they must have given me a sedative, for I slept for sixteen hours.

Six

I kept my grief under tight control; I was afraid to break down, afraid to let go. I felt as though I were someone else, outside myself, curiously and objectively observing my own dull motions. I was able to act and talk so normally that someone said, "She doesn't seem to know what happened." When I was alone I cried, but not violently or uncontrollably. It was rather as if I cried because I felt that I ought to. I remember everything very well—the day of Ken's funeral, conducted by Dr. Smith, the Episcopalian minister who had married us two years before. And afterwards we drove out to Point Vicente, where Ken's ashes were to be dropped from a plane. His body and four others from the plane he was in were the only ones that had been recovered. The other plane had gone off the undersea cliff beyond the Point, and not even any of the wreckage was ever found.

I stayed with Freddie and Florence for about ten days, while I tried to collect the splinters of my life and plan for the dismal future. About two things I was completely stubborn. First, I would never go back to our house, not even to get clothes or collect any of our possessions. It could have burned, with all the clothes and furniture, and I would not have cared. I was not even moved by the information that it would have to be sold for back taxes; that necessity simply solved for me the problem of what to do about it.

Also, I firmly refused to return to make my home with my family. That was another part of my life that I could not bear returning to, although for quite different reasons. This resolution resulted in a tearful interview with Mother and Daddy, filled with their saccharine clichés: "It will always be your home." "You can come back and be our little girl." I had had enough of being their little girl. In her diary Mother described this interview in somewhat different terms; she was bitter and jealous that I preferred my friends to my parents, and that I listened to them rather than to her. But the friends I had were good friends, and they had the sense to begin any discussion with the point of view of "What do *you* want to do?"

I had to face and consider some basic financial facts. The sale of the Appian Way house would bring little more than the taxes that were owed on it. The insurance policy—a two-hundred-thousand-dollar one—had lapsed. Nothing could be recovered from the studio for Ken's death; a suit was attempted by the widows of the men who had been killed, but negligence could not be proved. All Ken's capital had gone in the market crash; there were even small debts—from gambling on golf games.

No money had been saved from my own earnings. In the ten years I had been in pictures I had grossed very close to half a million dollars. I had three thousand dollars in my own bank account. There was Temple Hill, of course; someone talked with Daddy about the money that could be realized from it, but he simply laughed at the idea of selling it and getting something more modest.

I was unfit to keep house for myself; I couldn't even cook, and the mysteries of dusting and vacuuming I had never meddled in. So I had to have a housekeeper. I rented a small furnished apartment at La Leyenda Apartments in Hollywood and prepared for my first picture at Paramount. So far as I was able, I avoided everyone who had been intimate with Ken and me; it hurt to see them without Ken, and I couldn't help feeling that my very presence would be a constant reminder and constraint.

When all the details had been arranged, I left the Marches', moved into my apartment, and went to work at Paramount. It was my first "talking picture," and I can't even remember the name. I can remember very little of those weeks at all; I was dull and very thin—my weight had gone down to 110. One day I didn't show up on the set, and the assistant director found me unconscious in my dressing room. They gave me brandy and raw egg, and I was able to get through the day.

Within a month people had gone back to living their own lives and I was left alone. I went from the Paramount picture into another that Donald Crisp was directing; my work exhausted all my energy, and I was too tired even to accept an invitation to go out to dinner. Greta, my Swedish maid, cooked for me, then left for the night. I ate, then read and drank highballs until I fell asleep, usually to the horror of a nightmare about Ken. In one that recurred often, I saw him in the ocean swimming toward me; he was injured from the accident, but he was not dead, and he had been swimming for days. I would surge up to happy consciousness; and then, remembering, I would pour myself a stiff drink and try to go back to sleep.

I don't remember just when it was that Lee Tracy returned to town; he had been in Florida, and he had brought the camera bug back with him. Deliberately, of course, he set about arousing my enthusiasm. I bought a Filmo 16 mm. camera and experimented with various kinds of lenses, taking shots all around the studio. Lee got an editing outfit, and he brought it up to the apartment, where we would work for hours cutting and assembling film and lettering handmade titles. Lee roused me from my listlessness.

One day I noticed an odd rash appearing on my skin; there was no itching or burning, just scattered dull red splotches about the size of a plum. Lee took me to a friend of his, a Dr. Franklyn Thorpe, who had just come from Florida and was going into practice in a clinic in Los Angeles. Dr. Thorpe, Lee told me privately, was a grand person and I was sure to like him.

Dr. Thorpe examined me and inquired closely into my history —he had heard of Ken's death, of course. He told me he thought I was generally run-down because I had gone to work too soon after such a shock, but he was going to withhold final judgment until he had been advised concerning the X rays and the results of all the tests. A day or so later he came to see me bearing staggering news: I was not only suffering from malnutrition, but the specialist had advised him that I also had "incipient tuberculosis"! I would have to go to a sanitarium. I objected that I could not go, I couldn't afford it; but I promised to follow his instructions to the letter in my own apartment.

The treatment was to be rest and sun; a glass of milk every half hour (eight quarts a day), mineral oil, complete bed rest, and sun on the roof. There were to be no visitors, only my maid Greta and himself; no phone calls, no cigarettes, and no liquor. After about five days of this I slipped into a lethargic weakness that brought relaxation and a lightheaded feeling of contentment. I let go, unwound; I finally rested.

Dr. Thorpe called on me every evening on his way home from the clinic. As I came to know him better I found I did like him; I could lean on him. Our conversations became less professional and more personal.

He told me of his struggles to complete his medical education and become a good doctor, of bitter lean years, of interning at Marylebone Lying-In Hospital in London, and of a summer in Vienna. He was specializing in gynecology and obstetrics, and his great love was surgery. He was about thirty-six years old, a serious, gentle man, soft-spoken, but with a strange intensity in his eyes. Like our conversations, his visits soon ceased being professional and became personal. In a couple of months he relaxed the diet. By May, I had gained almost fifteen pounds; I felt wonderful and was able to go back to work again, on a lovely picture with Ann Harding called *Holiday*. And it was spring, and I told myself that I was falling in love again, and that he was, too.

I continued to call and see Marian Spitzer occasionally; the rest of the old clique had dropped away. Florence was annoyed with me for not keeping up with them, and for not bringing my "new friend" around. But I couldn't; I had to let them go. I couldn't because these were friends of Ken's and they were still a painful reminder. Gradually I heard no more from them, but I was content. I had lost my taste for "going someplace," for dancing and parties and crowds. I thought bitterly how futile it was that ten men should die for the sake of one miserable little scene in a picture that no one would remember a week after he had seen it. It was all monstrously out of proportion. And so, I thought, was the whole business, the long exhausting hours, the tension and the pressure and the worried rush, the scramble to climb the precarious ladder of Fame, as though it all meant something, as though it were important. My bitterness was a kind of sickness, I know now; I had lost any sane perspective toward Hollywood or people or even myself.

Life was empty, and into that emptiness came Franklyn Thorpe. I began to thrill that marriage to him might be a real solution for many of my problems. Now that I had lost Ken, I felt I had cheated myself of children; how I wished we had had a child! My "career" and a silly "affair" had taken care of that. If I had learned my lesson, if I had only grown up a little during those two years, this thing between Franklyn and me just might come out right. I resolved that I would fight for it.

I got a contract with RKO and sailed from one meaningless picture to another. Between pictures Franklyn kept cautioning me that, while my t.b. was "arrested," I must be very careful and get all the rest and sun possible. By now I had cut myself off from almost all my friends, partly because Franklyn occupied most of my time and partly because I was afraid they would gossip about my illness, and that would mean no work.

I moved from La Leyenda to a much pleasanter apartment on La Cienega; it had a big, high-ceilinged living room, with a bedroom and bath at the head of the stairs, off an open balcony; and it had a service entrance to the kitchen and an entrance from the garage.

For about a month I started picking up old threads of friendship. I went to a party at Bessie and Bill Hawks', and met a very prominent actor. Bessie and Bill were jubilant; they foresaw a match here, and they assured me that their friend had fallen very hard. If he had, I could find no response within myself. To be sure, it was a refreshing time; he had a beautiful home, full of books and good music. We had candlelit dinners and listened to Gilbert and Sullivan. Finally he told me that he had been separated from his wife for many years and he would arrange to get a divorce immediately if I would consider marrying him.

I told him no. I didn't try to explain it; I couldn't have explained it even to myself. There wasn't any rational explanation. All I knew was that I wanted Franklyn; therefore, I decided, I must be genuinely in love with him. So we were reconciled again.

As usual, I went on with my work; I had to show the demanding public that I was the successful, happy movie star. I believe it was then that I did two free-lance pictures for Warners—*Convention City*, with Adolph Menjou, Pat O'Brien, and Frank McHugh; and *Page Miss Glory*, with Marian Davies. The sequence of pictures during this time is vague; except during the hours on the set, I was more concerned with Franklyn than with the pictures I was making.

Most of his talk was about medicine; actually that was about all he knew. Since I wanted to please him, to share his life with him, I gladly talked medicine with him. That led to the most exciting and rewarding experiences of my life with him, for he allowed me to watch several of his operations.

My first experience was at Hollywood Hospital. I was capped and masked and gowned, and admitted as a technician. One of the nurses who had often worked with Franklyn on his obstetric cases knew me; she whispered to me, and asked if I had ever seen an operation before. When I shook my head, she slipped a bottle of spirits of ammonia into my hand. "Just in case . . ." she said. I was a little nervous, but I was too busy to think about it. The operation was a hysterectomy; it went with swift, machine-like precision. I had absorbed my anatomy lessons from Franklyn fairly well, and it was fascinating to watch the textbook illustrations come alive. I knew the names and uses of all the instruments, and I knew the routine, from scalpel to suture. And I loved watching the man I loved doing the thing he did best. Something fine happens to anyone when he does the thing he likes to do, and does it expertly—although perhaps that generalization should not be extended to include safe-crackers.

I decided I would work long enough to help him get an office by himself, and with my friends build up his practice. Then I could quit work and be a doctor's wife, make him a good home, and have children. It was as simple and childlike as that. If from the very first step on it could have remained only a pleasant dream it would have been all right. The trouble was that I had the determination and the energy to work at making a part of it come true.

And I had the money. I was back in the top salary brackets. I worked hard. I adhered to the rule among entertainers: "Never bring your troubles to the theatre or the studio." I gave reasonably consistent performances. I was liked by the producers, and I was always the director's pet. The people I worked with liked me, for I was never temperamental or affected. I was a worker among workers. RKO wanted to give me a starring contract, but I made the right decision and turned it down. Once your name goes *above* the title of a picture it must never come down, or your prestige is gone. I told them they could pay me the same money that the starring contract called for, but that I'd stick with feature billing. And I worked on the basis of two-picture or three-picture deals at different studios, and thereby kept the bidding high. I have always had much more sense about my career than I have ever had about my personal life.

So—we were married. We drove down to Yuma on Franklyn's birthday, June 29, 1931, and we were married by a justice at the courthouse. I remember writing rather sadly in my diary that it was a "beautiful June night, with the moon riding high—and the bridegroom never said a word." He was a trapped man.

We lived at the Cienega apartment for a while, and then found a pleasant house at Toluca Lake, with fine grounds. It was a relief to live in a house again. We had also found offices for Franklyn in the Security First National Bank Building at Highland and Hollywood. I was exultant; my plans were actually working! He seemed much happier, too. He brought some patients with him from the clinic, and I found several among my friends, though this source proved to be more difficult than I had expected. I took him to several parties to meet people, and we invited people to the house, but he just did not mix easily. This didn't bother me too much because I had just discovered that I was pregnant and was going to have the child I had always wanted.

One day Franklyn began talking about plans for a sailing cruise to the Hawaiian Islands. He reported that he had found the ideal ship—the *Henrietta*, a 67-foot, two-masted, gaff-rigged schooner. He could buy her at a bargain, and after our return put her back on the market, which was fairly good because of a lively interest in the sailing races to Honolulu.

We bought the *Henrietta* in January, and allowed ourselves three months to make all the necessary preparations for the cruise. All through January and February, Franklyn took navigation lessons. We went to Catalina and back many times. All the details of preparation, and there were many, made Franklyn a happy man. And I lay in the sun on the deck and thought about my baby; pregnancy had made me utterly content. Nothing worried me. I could eat anything, and I took a great many exercises, strengthening my abdominal muscles. (I made one more picture, with George Arliss, with the oddly appropriate title of *Successful Calamity*.) My job in preparing for the cruise was to stock the ship. I talked to restaurant people, to ship stewards, to chefs, to anyone who knew anything about quantity ordering. I made arm-long lists, and when the orders were delivered and piled on the deck the stack looked bigger than the ship itself.

According to our calendar, the baby would be born about the

middle of August; we were therefore to return in June, in ample
time for it to be born here.

We sailed under power from San Pedro on April 7, 1932. There
were six of us: Franklyn, myself, Franklyn's sister Clara, our
colored man who doubled as cook and deck hand, and two sailors
—Stewart, the mate, and a Norwegian boy whose name I've forgotten, although I remember that he proved to be the backbone
of the entire cruise. At the harbor light we sealed our engines
in case we happened to make a record run and upped sail. The
Henrietta was not fast—not with a 14-foot beam. We had counted
on picking up the Trades at once; they were supposed to be at
our back, but instead we hit them head on. For four days we had
rough, squally weather; everybody was seasick, and I was sickest
of all. I lay in the stern with blankets and oilskins over me, and
I didn't care whether I lived or died.

The weather cleared, and the days were beautiful. I liked the
closeness of the water, and the changing lights and the moods of
the sea. We passed through schools of porpoises, and two gulls
paced us for days. We were able to put up full sail, and there is
no sound like it. The boat was large enough so that even though
we had to grasp something to move about we could move upright.
That can make a great deal of difference in comfort; in a smaller
ship the crouching and maneuvering become dreadfully fatiguing.

All of us took our trick at the wheel; Clara's time and mine were
cut in half, but it was enough! We ate heartily and grew as brown
as nuts. I felt a contentment of well-being. My baby was moving
quite a bit now; at night, lying in my bunk as the ship rolled
gently, it would seem that she was groping with her hands to
find something solid. To feel that movement within me made the
baby seem even more real; already in my mind I was holding her,
cuddling her, singing to her. I felt I could not contain the happiness that welled up within me.

All of us got along pretty well. Franklyn's temper would boil
up occasionally, usually over trifles; and Clara would stay in the
bathroom so long that our exasperation blazed up at her once in

a while—but, as she explained, she *did* have to put on her mascara and the rolling of the ship made it difficult.

We knew we were approaching land. Even if our calculations had not told us, a great many other things would have. For two days gulls had flown about the ship; a pleasant, unfamiliar fragrance filled the air; more surface fish and bits of seaweed appeared about us. We stayed up late to catch the first glimpse of the Molokai light and drank coffee to keep awake. Just as the light showed its eye over the horizon, a squall came up. It hit us with no warning, with both fists, before we had so much as a chance to reef the sails. And then no reefing was humanly possible; the ropes were like steel, and twenty men could not have hauled them in. The ship hit the waves like a steam roller, now dipping her bow under the water, and then lifting sharply with a shudder to prepare for another plunge. We were in real trouble, for the connection—I've forgotten what it's called—between the wheel and the rudder broke. With no control over the ship, we were blown helplessly by the wind; we could only wait and hope desperately that the wind would change. By dawn we were close enough to shore to see the surf breaking like waterfalls pouring upside down against the cliffs. We all stood on the deck, hanging onto the rails, watching, and waiting for the inevitable moment when the furious wind would blow us into the cliffs. We couldn't talk; the wind and the rain snatched the words from our mouths.

As suddenly as it had hit us the wind let up and shifted. The men manned the sails furiously, and we veered ninety degrees to starboard in nothing flat! Stewart and the cook went below after helping to haul in the sails; we started the engine, and the two men lay on their backs with their feet on the rudder rail while Franklyn called directions down to them from the deck. It took us two hours to get through the channel and limp into Honolulu Harbor, just sixteen days from the time we left San Pedro Harbor.

We docked at Pier 6 at six o'clock—I can't help remembering that—and we scattered into Honolulu like chickens that had been cooped up in a pen. Franklyn and I made straight for a restaurant, where we gorged ourselves on lettuce and milk and steak. Food processing in those days was not what it is now, and we had no refrigeration on the boat; we had long since wearied of our sixteen-day diet of canned vegetables and chicken and ham.

The days on the islands blend indistinctly in my memory; I don't recall many of the things we did. There was the inevitable group that was too ready to lionize a movie star, but I pleaded my obvious pregnancy, and so escaped wasting time in the sorts of places that could be found any night on the Sunset Strip. We went to the Outrigger Club, and made one very good friend, Bill Hollinger, a half Hawaiian, who took us over and showed us a great deal of the real Hawaiian life that we would not otherwise have seen.

I loved Honolulu, the flowers and the fragrances, the sudden showers, and the moon rainbows over Diamond Head. The Hawaiian beach boys took care of me like brothers. I lay on my back on a surfboard while one of them swam beside me. I spent much of the time in the water; my own buoyancy and displacement made swimming almost effortless. Nonetheless, I listened and heeded when the boys warned me, "Enough now. You and baby take rest under umbrella." We made one trip to Kona on the western coast of the big island of Hawaii. But it was rough and uncomfortable; I was growing too big and clumsy to make my way around a schooner, so I resolved, "No more of that for me."

Franklyn seemed to be enjoying himself. He was busy, and he was worrying about money; the storm had wrecked the sails, and we had to buy a whole new suit of them. He decided we should leave for the mainland about the middle of June, and we booked passage on the *City of Los Angeles* for the fifteenth. In the meantime Franklyn had to round up a new crew to take the *Henrietta* back. One by one our company had left us: Clara frankly wanted no part of the return trip; she and Stewart left about the end of May. The colored boy said that Thelma, his wife, whom he had left in charge of the house, had sent him a wire saying his uncle was dying, and he had to get home *fast*. Only the Norwegian sailor was willing to return with the *Henrietta*. Franklyn finally managed to corral enough hands to man the schooner; and on June 14 we watched from high up on the Punch Bowl as the *Henrietta*, looking tiny and delicate, sailed toward Diamond Head.

That evening, Franklyn and I had dinner at Lau Yee Chai's; while we were still at the table, I felt a distinct contraction. We returned to the hotel to finish packing for our own trip home, and then we sat in bed and read. About every half hour I had another contraction; they were growing stronger, and I was becoming frightened, for the baby was not yet due for another two months. Franklyn had packed and shipped all his carefully selected instruments, and without them he could not examine me. But he had kept his drug kit with him, so he gave me a shot of morphine and I went to sleep for a while. Towards morning I began to lose water; my alarm turned almost to hysteria when Franklyn told me he would have to get me to a hospital at once. While I lay in bed crying uncontrollably, he notified an obstetrician and then called Bill Hollinger to come pick us up. Bill carried me into the car and drove as gently as he could to the Kapiolani Maternity Home. I was still crying while the doctor examined me; but when he had finished he patted me reassuringly on the shoulder and told me, "This baby is farther along than you think. We may be able to save it." I cheered up a bit, stopped crying, and settled down to the serious business of labor. In what seemed like a strangely short while it was time for delivery. This was a small, informal hospital, more like a nursing home, and the nurse said to me, "Do you think you can walk to the delivery room? It's just around the corner." I thought I could, and as we walked down the hall, Franklyn looked at me and said, "Good Lord, girl! You walk like a queen!" That was almost the last thing I remembered before I drifted into the blessed relief of semi-consciousness in the delivery room.

At about six-thirty that evening, June 15, my little girl arrived, battered and bruised, and weighing only three pounds six ounces.

I had not had an easy delivery. Even with so tiny a baby the narrow anterior-posterior measurement of my pelvis had made it rough on both of us. She was frighteningly frail, tiny as a doll, red and pathetic, with a bad bruise over her right eye from the forceps. But torn and shaken as I was, a half hour after delivery I was sitting up in bed drinking a cup of chocolate and chattering happily to Bill and Franklyn. I wanted to set off flares and wave flags. My baby was alive! Then the beach boys came with their guitars and serenaded me softly below my window, and I went off into a happy sleep.

I awoke the next morning in a room filled with fragrant leis—ginger, pikake, carnation. The nurse brought in messages and notes, and the Honolulu paper sent a photographer for a picture. And Franklyn sent off a wire, which I didn't know about until later, to our secretary, Martha Wright: "Baby girl delivered June 15. Please inform Mary's agent she will be ready for work in three weeks."

We had decided that the baby was to be named "Marylyn," but while we were still pondering the possible choices for a middle name, our indecision was resolved by the beach boys. From the first I had been deeply impressed by their evident concern and affection, and they now moved me almost to tears when they came into my room to tell me that they had been conferring about her name, for, since she was born in the Islands, she must have a native name. They were not satisfied with any of the usual names; it had to be something special, so they had delved into old tales and traditions, and there they had found what they were seeking. They handed me a slip of paper, and on it I read the word "Hauoli." They told me it could not be translated simply: it was an idea rather than a specific word. Then they told me a story about old King Kamehameha and his warriors, and how after winning a battle they sat under the shade of a hau tree and sang with the joy of their triumph. The emotion that they felt was "hauoli." I wondered how they knew—that she was indeed "triumphant joy"! And "triumphant joy" she would be always —Marylyn Hauoli.

But the first few days were filled with the agony of fear that my joy might not long remain triumphant. She was too weak to nurse, but I had plenty of milk, so my breasts were pumped regularly, and for two days I was permitted to attempt to feed her from a bottle. Even that was too much exertion for her; she was losing weight, and the nurse regretfully informed me that she would have to remain under constant watch in the incubator room, where I could be wheeled in my chair so that I might learn how to take care of her. Alone in my room I cried from the effort of willing her to live. She seemed so pitifully fragile; her head fitted easily in the palm of my hand. Without the normal baby fat her hands had a strangely mature and sculptured quality.

After five days she was showing marked signs of improvement, but she would have to stay in the hospital until she had attained a weight of five pounds. I was well enough to leave; so, happy in the certainty that my baby would now live but sad at the thought of being separated from her, I left the hospital, and we moved into a tiny house just under Diamond Head light, to wait, and to rest and lie on the sand, and to call the hospital twice a day to learn the news of "half an ounce today," or "a whole ounce and three quarters!" It could have been a happy time, but Franklyn was edgy, bored, and impatient to get back. He was still worrying about money; the trip had cost more than he had estimated, and he had received news of a bank failure (there were a great many of them at that time). He had spread money around in several banks, but we had suffered a loss of five thousand dollars at this particular one. With his preoccupation and irritability, I was doubly lonely, both for companionship and for my new baby.

When she was two weeks old she had held her weight for two days, and we could sail for home. The voyage was not a restful one; I was busy fretting over and caring for Marylyn. I padded a small basket for her crib, and by using the handles I could make a kind of tent over her to protect her from drafts and keep her warm. I was overwhelmed by the quantities of diapers that she used; the stewardess took pity on me and found me a hot-water pipe near the galley that I could hang them on. Daily I had to mix her formula with chemical precision, hand pumping my own breasts and measuring out dextrose and syrup and mixing them, and taking the bottles to the galley icebox, which I had gained permission to use. Franklyn maintained a professional interest in her, but he would confuse me by saying that I was making too much of a fuss over her or examining the bottles and pronouncing a professional verdict that they had not been properly sterilized.

I was kept so busy that I hardly noticed the passing of time, and it came almost as a surprise to find that the trip was ending and we were arriving home. We were met at the dock by Mother, who wept over the baby, and by a couple who were becoming rather close friends, Carol and Lasher Gallagher. He was the lawyer who had represented me in court when I had tried to salvage something from Ken's lapsed insurance policy. It was good to see familiar faces again, and to return to the comfortable familiarity of the house. And it was a relief to have some help. Thelma, our colored housekeeper, suddenly looked so strong and reliable! I did not entrust much of Marylyn's routine to her, but she could take over most of the heavy work, and coax food into me, and see that I got lots of rest. I was very thin and very tired.

Nevertheless, within a few days I went to work on a picture, *Those We Love*, with Kenneth MacKenna. The work was badly interrupted, for every three hours I had to retire to my dressing room for the breast-pumping routine. Miss Wright came over twice a day to pick up the bottles and get them back to the house for the baby's formula. Marylyn was progressing slowly but well, acquiring a healthy layer of baby fat as she gradually gained in weight and alertness.

Franklyn's practice, small as it had been, fell off considerably. This, I supposed, was the result of his absence. Fortunately Warner's offered me a long-term contract. The contract would put an end to my strong bargaining position, but it would mean a good and steady income.

Franklyn's temper was almost a worse kind than my father's. Daddy would explode, and then we would tiptoe around until he had finally calmed down, but Franklyn sulked and was querulous. I'm afraid I became more irritable, too, and we had a number of violent quarrels. The marriage just wasn't working. I even thought of instituting divorce proceedings, but we patched things up and I went back to stick it out for another two years.

I think it was about this time that the break with Mother and Daddy came. I should be, if anything, simply supporting them; but the fact was that they were living in a mansion with two cars and three servants while we lived very modestly, with only the servants we had to have to care for the house because I was working. And whenever we spent anything we had an argument with Mother and Daddy.

I finally screwed up my courage and went to Daddy to have a talk with him. I told him that I would give up my one-third right to the property, and they could have free and clear title to it— it was worth about seventy-five thousand dollars then. They could sell it, find a little business of some sort, live modestly, or do whatever they wished. But from now on they would receive no more money from me.

Daddy was tragedy itself. It was out of the question for him to think of selling "his" home. Surely I would pay for the projects that he had started; the grading had been begun for another driveway at the side, and what about the swimming pool that he had planned? I simply repeated my declaration: "No more money."

In the months that followed, I wavered occasionally and sent them a check, for I heard that Mother was doing all the work around the house and they had let Parker go. But then I found that Daddy was using the money to pay for his "improvements," so I opened an account for them at Wolff's Market. When the statements came in they included notations of "cash paid out," so I resorted to buying them food checks that they couldn't possibly transfer or convert into cash. Daddy finally put a mortgage of $22,500 on the house and went ahead with his swimming pool. It was typically elaborate, built into the side of the hill and shaped like a lagoon, about a hundred feet long and of varying widths and depths, with a little sandy beach at one end and overhanging foliage, and even a small bridge over it. It cost eighteen thousand dollars. Daddy was offered eighty thousand dollars for the house; he laughed at the offer and asserted that he would not take a penny less than two hundred thousand.

I was working at Warner's with Edward G. Robinson and Louis Calhern on a film version of the George S. Kaufman play *The Dark Tower*. One morning I was called to the portable phone on the set; it was a reporter, who wanted to know how I intended to answer the suit that had just been filed by my parents. I knew nothing of any suit; when I asked him what it was all about, he told me my parents were suing me for maintenance. I asked Lasher Gallagher to represent me, and he brought it to a quick conclusion. He told the court that I was willing to pay one hundred dollars a month toward my parents' support, and the case was dismissed. The reporters had rather a cruel laugh at Daddy's expense; they got him to pose on the little bridge over the pool, gazing sadly into the water, and they ran the picture with the caption: "Down to their last swimming pool"! Daddy mournfully put the house up for public auction, possibly under the delusion that he could get more for it that way, and it went down at twenty-five thousand dollars.

We had been receiving my full check for some time now, and we planned to build a larger and more comfortable house right on Toluca Lake. It was a lovely site, and the house we built was equally lovely. I rejoiced above all in the *real* nursery, with its own bath, for Marylyn; the room was off a long balcony with a high railing where she had a sandbox and could play in complete safety. Now we could afford a nice little nurse, and we also found our incomparable "Nellie," an Englishwoman, for our housekeeper. As I write it, this all sounds happy and idyllic—but the arguments we had over that house would fill a book. It also cost about twice as much as had been estimated.

I was awfully tired. My contract had kept my nose constantly to the grindstone; the battle with my parents had worn me down further; and at home I could find peace and relaxation only in the few minutes each day I spent with Marylyn. When the Gallaghers suggested that I go to New York with them while I had three weeks free between pictures, I felt that the change would be healthful and refreshing.

The Gallaghers were going on to Bermuda, so they would just drop me off in New York, and I would be alone. My friend Marian Spitzer insisted that I take advantage of the trip to have a real whirl; she told me she had written two of her oldest friends, Bennett Cerf and George S. Kaufman, and instructed them to see that I had a good time. She predicted that I would like George and fall for Bennett, but she was wrong. I liked Bennett and fell for George Kaufman. And these were the pages of my diary that were published—the account of my romance with George. I was swept into a wonderful world of top people in the theatre and writing and music. I wrote that I felt as though I had been in a foreign country, and had suddenly found people who spoke my language. I met Edna Ferber and Moss Hart and Alec Woollcott and Oscar Levant. I went to a small gathering where people hung around the piano and listened to a new score that George Gershwin was playing for them; it was a new concept of opera, and was to be known as *Porgy and Bess*. I felt that I was accepted easily and without question; I liked their ideas and opinions and points of view.

But it was George Kaufman who took me in tow and accompanied me everywhere. Late summer in New York was enchanting, when most people had left for the country. We went for drives in the park in hansoms; we heard Eddie Duchin play at the old Park Casino; we went to see George's musical, *Of Thee I Sing*. George was an extremely attractive man, for all his ungainly frame and saturnine mien. His wit was not confined to the printed page; it touched all he did, no matter how trivial or ordinary.

Whenever I came home my only pleasure was Marylyn—she was growing noticeably week by week. And of course there was work to be done—a picture to be made. My professional status at least was substantial; it was one thing I could count on, and it was still growing. I made a picture with Clark Gable and Jean Harlow called *Red Dust*; it has recently been remade as *Mogambo*, with Grace Kelly playing the part I originated. I made a fine film with Paul Muni, *The World Changes,* in which I had a very interesting part that called for me to make an aging process from twenty to sixty-five.

I continued to see George Kaufman at every opportunity. He came West with Moss Hart and stayed in Palm Springs while they were writing part of their play *Merrily We Roll Along;* I went to Palm Springs with Dorothy and Dick Rodgers and stayed for a week. I made another trip to New York and sat in on some of the rehearsals of the same play. George had wanted me for the lead, but when I frantically tried to get permission and leave of absence from the studio they rejected my request.

By this time I was bored with Franklyn. Our life was a series of explosions, usually over minor things.

I began to talk divorce, and the talk was considerable. I knew that it certainly was not going to be what is called "amicable." Secretly I went to a real estate agent and rented a small house on Tower Road in Beverly Hills; and then I told Franklyn that if he wouldn't leave, the baby and I would move out. What followed brought my whole life collapsing around me in a pile of dust and rubble.

I had kept a diary for years and I had realized for some time that it might be used in a divorce action. The diary revealed not only all the details of my own life from the period of Russell Bradbury to the present, but it also revealed much that I knew about other people. The lives of many people would be affected. I finally decided that the best thing to do was to submit to divorce on Franklyn's terms. Marylyn and I moved to Tower Road— Franklyn wanted only her legal custody—and he got an uncontested divorce in 1935.

Seven

When people asked me, "Why on earth did you keep a diary? How could you be so foolish?" it was much too complicated and too simple to explain. I'm not sure I could have explained it even to myself then. But now I think I can better understand my motives. I kept a diary because my mother had kept one in identical ledger volumes. I wanted to talk about my own activities and my opinions of other people and the things they did. I wanted the assurance of individuality and reality and substance that the diary gave me. The diary was a consolation and a reassurance. But when it was no longer in my possession it was suddenly transformed into a monster that threatened to devour me and my friends, and, worst of all, Marylyn.

Even under its ominous shadow I tried to maintain a normal life and a semblance of calm with Marylyn. For a while I was rather happy with her in the little house on Tower Road, as happy as I could be under the circumstances. Then my lease ran out at the same time I was called away on a location trip for a picture at Lake Tahoe, and I was faced with a dilemma. It would not be wise to try to find a new place and leave Marylyn with a nurse in unfamiliar surroundings, yet there was little else I could do. My problem was solved for me when I found that "Nellie," the Englishwoman who had kept house for us before, was now taking care of the Toluca Lake house for Franklyn and I could leave Marylyn there.

I was gone a long time. One trouble followed another in filming the picture: we were snowed in; everyone got the flu; one of the men died, and I came back to Los Angeles in an ambulance with pneumonia. I stayed at the Château Marmont for a time, convalescing; but finally Franklyn said it would be more convenient for him to take a small place in town and I could move back into the Toluca Lake house. And Nellie and Marylyn and I had a peaceful home.

I had begun a new two-year contract with Columbia. It paid well, but it meant constant work on a great many insignificant pictures. I worked on three and even four at a time, meaning retakes on one, costumes for two coming up, "art" and publicity for current production. On very rare occasions I had a week or two weeks off. It was dull, but at least I had little time to brood over my troubles.

At the beginning of the actors' fight for a union I had renewed my acquaintance with a well-known actress; this was before we built the house at Toluca Lake, and I had had time to serve on committees and attend meetings that finally gave birth to the Screen Actors Guild. My friend had a little girl about Marylyn's age, and now I often took Marylyn up to the actress's lovely home on a mountaintop, where we swam and rested and talked theatre while the children played together. Several interesting people were usually there—Norma Boleslavsky, a pianist who was the wife of one of our fine directors; Marcus Goodrich, the author of *Delilah*; Werner Janssen, and a few others. As time went on, I gradually told my friend something of the situation surrounding my divorce and the diary. She is a very vital woman, and a fighter, and she was indignant that I should be forced to submit to such conditions. She had a lawyer whom she praised highly to me,

Roland Rich Woolley. She urged me to at least tell Woolley the story and see what he thought of it.

I was not happy at the prospect of publicity and scandal that would almost certainly grow out of any further legal action, but I yielded to her constant pressure and took my story to Woolley. He was a genial, sympathetic man, and he had a mind like a steel trap. He flinched when I told him the details of the diary, but after he had thought over all that I had said to him he told me there was an excellent chance that he could keep the diary out of the case. In general, he pointed out, the situation was very favorable for me. Marylyn had been with me for a year, and under my care she was well and thriving and happy. He suggested that I sue for custody of Marylyn. But he warned me that he would need a good while to prepare the case.

While I was waiting for the case to come up I had a great stroke of luck. Columbia was loaning me to Sam Goldwyn to play the role of Edith Cortright in *Dodsworth*, with Walter Huston and Ruth Chatterton, and William Wyler directing. There was only one possible hitch: the companies were protecting themselves at that time by requiring all their players to take a physical examination for insurance. I was anxious for the part; it seemed a shame to lose it, and I thought that since I had been in good health for so long perhaps the tuberculosis might no longer be a threat. Marian Spitzer suggested that I see her doctor. I went to him, and told him frankly that I had an arrested case of t.b., but that I was sure I was well enough to do the part if he would approve me for the insurance. He examined me, fluoroscoped me, and X-rayed me. He called in lung specialists, and there were more examinations and X rays. Then the doctor called me into his office for the final report. In my mind I was already on my way to a sanitarium. But he told me that if I had ever had an arrested case of t.b. it was completely dormant. "Your lungs are as clear as a bell," he told me.

With this fear once and for all killed, I went into *Dodsworth* with gusto. Wyler was an inspirational director, tough and exacting, but sensitive. I loved Ruth, and we became close friends. And I admired Walter Huston.

After work I had to spend many long hours talking to Woolley; it took a long time to tell him all that he wanted to know. Finally our case was on the calendar—for night sessions since I was working during the day. The papers handled it very mildly at first, until the reporters smelled out the fact that a diary was involved. Then they began to display more interest. My mother was going to be there, and the papers played that up, too.

I remember the opening session of the trial. As I was leaving the studio, Ruth stopped me.

"Do you have anyone with you?" she asked me.

"Mother will be there," I said, "and Mark Goodrich is working with Woolley."

"No," she said, "that's not what I mean. I mean someone to sit in the front row, someone you know is on your team and can give you a wink of encouragement."

I laughed. "No, there's no one like that."

And she said, "May I drive you down and be with you?"

She did, and she was, to the bitter end. Woolley said she should have been a lawyer; he seemed to enjoy matching minds with her, and they had many a heated discussion in the office.

Judge Goodwin Knight was presiding, and from the first I felt at ease with him. But after the first five sessions the cameraman on the picture complained that I was showing the strain too much and I was becoming difficult to photograph. Since the case was settling down into a battle and it looked as though it would continue for a long time, Judge Knight discontinued the hearings until I finished the picture.

The reporters were becoming a dreaded daily ordeal; they were thick at Toluca Lake and outside the studio—which had put on extra police protection. So I went into a kind of protective hiding. During the rest of the work on the picture I stayed in my bungalow on the lot; it was a small home, with kitchen and bedroom, dressing room and living room, and I didn't have to set foot outside the studio.

The papers were clamoring for the diary, and Woolley was keeping it out as irrelevant. Then one day Franklyn's attorney showed me a single page cut from the diary and asked me to identify the handwriting. Woolley stopped that at once. After the session that day he told me he thought he had the answer to the diary problem, but he wasn't quite ready to tell me what it was. He had to be sure first. He began to intimate in court that he might be willing that the diary should be admitted as evidence. I was startled; he had said that he would keep it out, and it surely would injure my cause—but I had enough confidence in Woolley that I was not going to worry about it.

With the avowed possibility that the diary might enter directly into the case, publicity flared. I later found that it was my Hollywood realtor friend, whose own peccadillos with Adeline Muir were recorded in the diary who blew up the importance of that document to the point where it had the entire motion picture industry in an uproar. One night I was called to a meeting in Sam Goldwyn's office, where I found an assembly of the producers from all the studios, with their lawyers. There were A. H. Giannini, Thalberg, Warner, Cohn, and many others. Everyone was whispering and conferring, and I sat there wondering what all the furor was about. Thalberg was the spokesman. He told me they thought that Woolley and I were making a grave mistake. If the information they had received was true, the trial and the diary would create a vicious scandal. The scandal would give the industry a bad name, and I would probably lose the case and the child too. It would be wiser, they suggested, to drop the case, or at least attempt an out-of-court settlement. I looked at Woolley. He shook his head, and I said, "I'm sorry, gentlemen, but I shall proceed with the case, as my lawyer has advised me." I looked upon it as all too boring and a little pompous; besides, Walter Huston and some champagne were waiting for me in my bungalow.

The next day, Woolley told me what it was all about. A certain person who knew that he figured prominently in the diary was not at all happy at the thought of its being admitted as evidence and had substituted a forged version and his lawyer had shown it to the producers in an effort to pressure us into dropping the case or rejecting the diary as evidence. The forgery was lurid; it contained a "box score" of practically every male big name in the business, and it was loaded with pornographic details. Fragments of this forgery were "leaked" to the press, and the papers and national news magazines gleefully quoted them. The press had a Roman holiday with it. Out-of-context phrases appeared, jumbled and joined with dots, put together to make the omissions sound unprintable. I could not sue the entire fourth estate, because, of course, each paper was "simply quoting" material from another paper. I could only beat my fists on Woolley's desk and cry futilely, "There *wasn't* any 'box score' and I never called the damned thing 'Dear Diary.'" Rumors and quotations from the diary also went around town like wildfire, and it became a standard joke at parties for some man to come in looking furtive and frightened, with his coat collar up, and say, "I'm leaving town —I'm in the diary!"

A few pages of the authentic diary had come into the possession of the *Examiner*. This was mostly the account, romantic and sentimental, certainly not pornographic, of my friendship with George Kaufman. The entire association as revealed by those papers should have been interpreted as nothing more than a close friendship. But when people thought of "the diary" they thought not of these rather mild pages, but of the lurid lines quoted from the forgery.

It was becoming a circus. The courtroom was packed every day, and food vendors sold their wares in the halls. I had a few good moments—and some bad ones—on the stand.

They hammered at me about Kaufman. "Weren't you seen leaving the Trocadero with Mr. Kaufman at the wheel of a car?"

"No. Mr. Kaufman can't drive a car."

But finally they succeeded in making me angry, although Woolley had constantly cautioned me against losing my temper, and

I carelessly used a word which might be construed in a sinister sense. Woolley was a discouraged man that night.

I was always exhausted after the sessions were over; I was numbed by the whole mad merry-go-round. I hated the headlines, and the incessant flash bulbs, and the gaping, curiosity-seeking mob. Every afternoon I went home under police escort, and Nellie fixed me something to eat, and I had a good masseuse come in to undo the kinks and stroke my back monotonously until finally I fell asleep. The next morning it would start all over again.

I lost some valued friends. One of them was a girl I called on when I was first having my conferences with Woolley; she knew much about me, and I thought that she could help me pin down names, dates, and places. But when I called her she turned me down; she would rather not become involved. She was going to have a baby, she said, and this effort would make her too nervous.

Mother proved to be no help at all, and now she was sulking because after two days in court Woolley had told her it would be better if she stayed away. She had joked and chatted with the reporters, and had played up a sentimental act. Only Florence March, who had known me a good many years, and Ruth Chatterton appeared as character witnesses, and gave me some solidity and dignity by their presence. And dignified, prim English Nellie got up bravely on the stand and testified against Franklyn because she believed he was wrong. For her pains and her loyalty she was rewarded with the tag of "a tattling nurse" by a national news magazine.

Finally Woolley played his trump. He called for the diary, and expressed great amazement that it was not there in its entirety. He called every one of Franklyn's witnesses, and asked each of them the same question: "Have you ever seen this volume as a whole?" None of them ever had. A mutilated document cannot be used as evidence in court. It must be presented in full or it cannot be used at all. Therefore every reference to the diary was thrown out. Woolley knew when they had shown me the single page that someone most certainly had destroyed all the pages that concerned his own actions and shortcomings.

We were thirty days in court. Judge Knight finally ruled on a divided custody, nine months with me and three with Franklyn. The petition to set aside Franklyn's divorce decree was rejected —but the sword of Damocles was lifted. Nothing remained but to pay the bills—and they were plenty. And the abdication of the King of England, "for the woman I love," took our place on the front pages of the paper.

The diary was impounded by order of Judge Knight. The original and a photostatic copy were sealed in a bank vault, where they remained for sixteen years. In 1952 they were removed and burned, unread, by court order.

For a long time after the trial I was shy of people. I was afraid of what the notoriety might do to my work; others, I knew, had gone under as a result of scandal, and I prepared myself to take up some other line of work. I talked to the head buyer at Magnin's, and he assured me that with my knowledge of clothes they could use me as head buyer in Paris. But the effect was almost the opposite from what I had feared. When the studio was asked if they intended to exercise the morality clause in my contract, Sam Goldwyn put it best: "A woman fighting for her child? This is good!" *Dodsworth* helped, too. The character I played was a charming and gracious woman; the public could not match her with the luridly immoral woman the tabloids had painted. Wearing glasses and wrapped in scarves, I went one night with Mark Goodrich to see the picture. My first line was spoken off screen, but the moment they heard it the audience burst into spontaneous applause. Nothing has ever warmed me so much. I was told that it happened at every performance at that theatre, and that it happened in many cities.

The trial should have taught me a lesson, but it didn't. I felt that I was justified in my actions by the applause in the theatre, the encouragement and reassurances of my friends. The kindest feelings about me were that I had been very foolish and had made some bad mistakes, but for the sake of keeping my little girl I had been brave enough to admit them and had won a tough battle with the odds heavily against me. This was the picture that I fostered, and I tried to convince myself that it was true. The only truth that I cared to face was that I loved Marylyn and knew that I could be a good mother to her. The other truths about myself I chose to ignore. I do not think I could have borne it, to face myself as I really was—sick, spoiled, and selfish, prowling like some jungle animal seeking momentary satisfaction. Sexually I was out of control. I was drinking too much, and I was brought up short when I found myself late in the evening thinking someone was "terribly attractive"—and wondering the next morning, "Why, why!"

So the only result of the trial was that I sharpened my wits and became more cautious. Whenever possible, I avoided public places and stayed close to Ruth, to her home and friends. She maintained a constant "salon"; people came and went, and good food and drink were always plentiful.

The success of the trial was partly due to her efforts and help. The trial was often the subject of conversation at dinners—they were never "parties," but there were always six or eight at the table. When they discussed it, I often felt like a bug under a microscope, because the talk was quite frank. Usually, though, I felt overwhelmed by this rather brilliant group. The conversation frequently switched from English to French to Spanish and back again. But I listened well, and though I might be the subject of the conversation I was content to remain well away from the center of the stage. Of course drinking helped. In this house to be without a drink in your hand made you look a bit odd. But it was well-behaved drinking; I never saw anyone drunk at Ruth's, even though the nights, with their lively, intense talk, often stretched well into the early hours of the morning.

It was balm to my battered pride that at least these people understood what I had gone through with Franklyn. I was strengthened by their indignation that my side of it could never be properly told.

Shortly after the trial, at Ruth's home, I met a very remarkable woman, Auriol Lee. She was a rather famous English director; she had directed all of John van Druten's plays and several of Noel Coward's. She was an amusing little woman, cocky and witty; she wore a monocle that was always falling out, and her speech was rapid-fire. She was honestly very fond of me, as I was of her. She gave me credit for some intelligence, and often drew me out in conversation. She helped me relax and forget for the moment about the trial. And she was a matchmaker.

"You need a steady beau, ducks," she told me. "Somebody in your own class." Then with a few choice sentences she demolished people she didn't like. She was very English, very "class-minded"; when she talked of a "steady beau" she was talking about a "gentleman." "Don't want to blueprint it for you, ducks, but you're a lady. Don't care how you were born or how many men you've slept with. A lady's a lady. Can't mix *class*." Well, it sounded good, and I admired her. She was much older than I and, I was sure, much wiser.

She was not so crude as to "put it on the line," but she talked a great deal about one "Manuelito," a young man she had known since he was born. She had been a close friend of both his parents; his mother, now dead, had been a great beauty, and a prominent figure in European society; his father, who was half English, had been in the diplomatic service in Mexico City. Manuelito had gone to Cambridge until the family fortunes had run out, and he was more British than the British. He had been a bank clerk in Mexico City. He had a great ambition to do something in the theatre, writing or producing. At the moment, he was serving as a secretary to Auriol.

I remember the evening we met—it is about the only time I remember what I wore on a specific occasion. It was a Saturday night gathering at Ruth's; I was wearing a beautiful Vionnet plum-colored jersey evening gown of a long, classic cut, with long sleeves, and I was introduced to Auriol's Manuelito—Manuel del Campo. He was very handsome, rather shy, soft-spoken, with his blue wide-set eyes and brown hair. But he was so young! Twenty-four—and I was thirty.

There was no game to be played. It was all set; we simply went through the motions. A luncheon engagement. Dinner at my house. And we decided we were in love.

Eight

I was delighted with Mike. I felt comfortable about him because Auriol and other people I respected had given him their seal of approval; I was beginning to realize that my own judgment in these matters was hardly to be trusted. I loved his youth and enthusiasm, and I was determined that I would help him all I could. Just how I might help I wasn't sure; I couldn't, after all the publicity, suddenly say, "Look, everybody! I've got a new man!" I was reluctant even to appear in public with him. One night when we had gone to the Trocadero, I was embarrassed by the attention we received.

So we stayed out of public places and spent our time together at Ruth's house or at mine. We never ran out of conversation, and alone we had more chance to talk together. He told me about all of his life, of his devotion to his exquisite and important mother, and his desolation at her death. His sisters and his father, he told me, were extremely religious; they were all Catholics, of course, and he too had been brought up in the Church.

Thanks to Auriol, he felt he was on the way to doing what he wanted to do, to work in some area of the theatre or movies. He had a rich background in the theatre and its history; he had read plays in all languages, and he felt he was equipped to contribute something.

Christmas of 1936 was a good one. I had a lovely tree, and Marylyn received mountains of beautiful presents. She was at a particularly attractive age, blonde and chubby and loving. Mike was wonderful with her; they romped and rough-housed together, and she always squealed with delight when she saw him. Mother drove in from the small town of Lancaster, near Palmdale, California, for a short while on Christmas Day. She and Daddy were practically out of my life by now; with the money that was left after the sale of the house they had bought a small farm in Lancaster, where they were growing almonds and breeding goats. Daddy was off on one of his dreams again: they didn't just sell goat milk; they had nothing but pedigreed animals. Mother met Mike and observed and approved—Mike knew how to make someone like him. But my relations with her were still badly strained, and I was relieved when she was gone. Mike and I went over to Beverly Hills, to the big Christmas at Ruth's. She had the biggest tree she could get into the house, and a huge yule log burning in the fireplace, and presents and food and drink everywhere.

Auriol got a job for Mike as "reader" for Selznick. It is one of the humblest and poorest-paid jobs in the industry; it consists of reading innumerable scripts and writing very short synopses, to be scanned by the producers for material. But it takes some ability, and it is usually the gateway to a writing job. Then Mike was first exposed to acting, and that really spoiled him for anything else. He was having lunch at, appropriately enough, the Cock and Bull Restaurant. Bart Marshall was sitting at the next table and overheard Mike talking; he came over and introduced himself, saying that Mike's voice and accent were just what they had been looking for, for a part in a big radio show. They were doing a play by Noel Coward, and an unactory British accent was hard to find. Mike was thrilled, and from then on any job that was not an acting job was merely an unsatisfactory stopgap.

All our plans, professional and personal, were suddenly changed for us in the first few weeks of the new year, 1937. We had been so very discreet; we had plans to be married, but they were vague, with no definite time set. I didn't want to hurry things because I was tired of living on the front page of the newspapers. Everything seemed quiet; all the excitement had died down in the last few months, but I didn't realize that I was still news and the papers were watching my every move.

Then Mike's father had a heart attack, and was dead within twenty-four hours. It was a severe shock to Mike; of course he would have to go to the funeral, but he was afraid that he might have to remain in Mexico City.

He was packed and ready to leave on an evening plane for Mexico City. We sat miserably in the living room, feeling very despondent and hopeless about everything. It seemed nothing was ever going to go right for me. I loved Mike very much, and now I would probably lose him.

And then everything seemed so simple. Of course! Why hadn't we thought of it! We could fly over to Arizona and get married secretly. No one would know. Within half an hour I had chartered a private plane and phoned the airline that Mr. del Campo would join the flight at Mexicali.

We drove to Grand Central Airport and picked up the little plane. The flight was very romantic, with a full moon over the silver desert. A great deal of ready cash got us a taxi and a justice of the peace, and we were married in about five minutes. Then we drove to Mexicali and still had fifteen minutes to wait before the plane came in from Los Angeles.

While we were waiting, a phone call came for "the Senora." It was Edwin Schallert of the *Times*, a very old friend.

"Didn't you just get married, Mary?" he asked. "Or are my spies off the beam?"

I lied, laughing, "Way off, Ed. It's true we're going steady, but I just came down to see him off."

I was fooling nobody. Mike was panicky. "Stick to the story,"

I told him. "If anyone asks you about it when you arrive, deny it." Then the plane came in, and he was gone.

I drove back and found my pilot, and we took off for Los Angeles. I was feeling very seedy and hung over when I arrived in Grand Central, about seven in the morning. And I had forgotten my lipstick—nothing makes a woman feel more dowdy than not having her lipstick. I stepped out of the plane into a barrage of reporters and cameramen. Smiling my best smile, I borrowed a lipstick from a girl reporter, laughed at "all the fuss," and said "Of course not!" to all questions. When I got the evening papers I felt a little foolish. Mike had lost his head at the Mexico City Airport; first he had denied his elopement, and then he had admitted it. There were photographs of him and his sisters, veiled in mourning, trying to evade the cameras. I felt bad about it for his sake, because I knew how embarrassed he must have been. Then the telephone started ringing; I had calls from Auriol, who was cheering loudly, and from Roland Woolley, who didn't seem as pleased. He and Mark Goodrich had been trying to head us off, he told me. The report had come in as soon as I had chartered the plane. "It's just damn foolishness," he said—and after all they had done to get me out of the last mess! But I would not let their dourness spoil my happiness.

I spent the first few days getting used to the idea that I was married. I felt very happy, very young, and very much in love. *This* was going to work. The weather was rainy and cold, but I was warm and safe at last. I kept a big fire going in the living room and played jack-straws and drew pictures for Marylyn. I wondered how I was going to explain it to her. I tried to put out feelers.

"You like Manuel, don't you?" I asked.

And she answered, "I like potatoes too."

I decided to let it ride for the time being.

We wrote each other daily, passionate letters of the agony of separation. He described in detail how badly shocked the family had been by his behavior; that he should marry a divorced woman, outside the Church, was a great grief to them. But he hastened to add that he had absolutely no regrets. He would be considerably delayed by financial matters that needed his attention, the financial matters being that after death taxes the Del Campo estate simply did not exist. And, "Do you mind, darling, if I send up my books and personal things?" It is odd how an endearing habit of speech can turn later into an irritation. Mike was always saying "Do you mind" about something one couldn't possibly mind. I didn't mind; I was having a wonderful time, cleaning out closets, arranging drawer space, ordering new linen with "M. del C." initialed on it. Mike had drawn up a good plan for a bar in the library, and I went ahead with that. I had a carpenter line an offset in the room with curved eight-inch planks, and then had them painted a dull black, so they looked like the inside of a charred barrel. In back a mirror with shelves held bottles, and the front was enclosed halfway up the "barrel" to form a counter. And I removed some unattractive stained glass that Franklyn had liked and replaced it with clear glass. I always did like the making of a "nest," and although this one had had a previous occupant I did my best to eliminate all signs of it.

To evade the reporters when Mike returned, I told him I would meet him in Mexicali with my car; then we could drive somewhere and have a few days of privacy. The plane was late getting in from Mexico City; I walked up and down the platform, and to my satisfaction saw nothing that resembled the press. But as the plane circled for a landing there suddenly seemed to be a number of passengers arriving and checking in at the counters inside. Mike got off the plane, and I was in his arms, and behind us it was all being recorded for posterity. Since Mike had to clear customs, the reporters had time for some questions. I was as evasive as possible about where we were going, and finally we managed to shake them off. And we had a lovely three days in La Jolla. As soon as we arrived home, the papers started calling again. I told them to come out and bring their cameras and notebooks and I would talk to them and give them a drink and some food if they would then please let us alone. They promised, and they did.

I felt a great need to love, without restraint or reserve. And I could love Mike; he was easily pleased, responsive, and sensitive. It was easy to defer to his wishes, to give him anything he wanted. He was always grateful. He worked off and on at the job of reading scripts, of wading through "tripe," and we sat in the little library and discussed his future by the hour. He needed people, and he needed to impress people—just how much, I was to find out later. He often had time on his hands, which he would spend in Hollywood playing tennis. He was a camera addict, and he turned the dressing room into a laboratory, where he worked endlessly at developing and printing and enlarging. I was working on *The Prisoner of Zenda*; it took several months to make, so that I had a good deal of time off, and Mike and I could frequently spend an afternoon horseback riding. Riding was his greatest skill in sports; he had had horses since he was a child, and his mother had been quite a horsewoman. He showed me photographs of her jumping her lovely little mare that she won many prizes with; she always wore a habit for sidesaddle, complete with topper and veil.

Unfortunately by this time I was learning to drink more and more. The period in La Leyenda Apartments after Ken's death and the year following the divorce from Franklyn were the only times I had done any steady drinking, and then it had only made me sleepy. Now I was learning the habit—and I didn't know how well I was learning it. Most of our friends were the type who look for a bar immediately upon entering a house. A drink is the first amenity. Not "How are you?" or "What have you been doing?" but "What will you have to drink?" We had been going quite often to parties at Humphrey Bogart's; there were always a number of congenial people there and Mike always had a wonderful time.

I decided that it was time for me to become one of the crowd, and I announced one night that I was seriously going to set out to get drunk. The announcement was received with cheers. Mike had gone off to another room with some other men to play poker. One of the young actors and I remained at the bar and played a game called "drinking to the Emperor." Within half an hour I had drunk twenty brandies—the little glasses were lined up on the bar; my drinking pal was out cold, and I was complaining that "I didn't feel a thing." Mike and Bogey cautiously led me off the barstool as though I were a bit of fragile glass. Mike got me into the car, and as we drove home I was still discussing drinking quite clinically. I pointed out that there were three lights on the lampposts and I had heard that one only saw double. At home Mike went in to fix me some bicarb; he said I'd better upchuck or I'd feel awful. Disdainfully I went upstairs, under my own power, to my dressing room; I sat down to remove my make-up and missed the chair completely. Mike came bounding up the stairs and into the room. I looked up at him from the floor and said, "I didn't fall. . . ." And that was the last thing I remembered. Never had I had such a hang-over. For a long while afterwards I went back to spacing my drinks.

Mike was waging a campaign against the Toluca Lake house and he was waging it effectively. As he pointed out, I was getting a great deal of money from my contract with Columbia and I had additional income from a number of radio shows. We could afford something better. And Toluca Lake was out of the way; it was hard for people to get to. Besides, he said, he disliked the ghosts about the house; he could never get over the fact that it had been Franklyn's home. Some friends of Auriol's were selling their house and moving East, and we could have the house at a marvelous price. The price was marvelous all right, but the house at 1441 San Remo Drive was beautiful. It was a great Georgian house, with white pillars and a portico, set back from the street among lovely old shrubs and trees—a jacaranda and a cork tree and many deodars. The design was formal: a large living room and dining room, each with a fireplace, and divided by an entrance hall with a fine sweeping staircase leading to two master bedroom suites with a library between them. It wandered back to a kitchen and breakfast room, with a rear staircase to four smaller bedrooms and two baths. Of course it was too large for only one servant; Nellie sniffed and said it was "too big," so I got Marceil to come and take over the upstairs and serving. The house swallowed up the furnishings from Toluca Lake and greedily demanded more, and I obliged.

On moving day Mother came down to help; she had moved so often that she knew better than I what had to be done. She and I and Nellie and Marceil worked like beavers, and in my fatigue I was annoyed with Mike because he stood around smoking a pipe and looking helpless.

The process of decorating and getting settled was a long one. When the repainting was finished and the draperies were hung, there was nothing left to do but wait for the carpeting. Since we had a decorator who could oversee the work we decided we needed a holiday; so in May, Mike and I with Marylyn and Nellie sailed for the Islands to spend two weeks in Honolulu.

This time it was to be more fun. We sailed on the *Lurline*, and I had Nellie to take care of Marylyn, who was nearly six years old, and all over everywhere and into everything! We stayed at the Moana Hotel, and swam and rode in the outrigger canoes. The beach boys welcomed back their little Hauoli—I have some wonderful pictures of Marylyn with them. I took her to Kapiolani Maternity Home and showed her where she had been born, and the nurses made a fuss over her. I was content to spend most of my time swimming and sunning on the beach. We met a young divorcee who had a house at Diamond Head. And it didn't help any when I had to sit back and watch her and Mike carry on a flirtation. When I objected, very mildly, Mike just laughed and said, "Darling, don't be stuffy." I looked forward with more eagerness than I would have thought possible to the day we were to begin our trip home.

Running San Remo was a big job. Like a car on a cold morning, it sputtered and coughed, and seemed as though it would never start running smoothly. Marceil and Nellie had a fight, and Marceil left. Nellie was graduated to nurse, and we hired a manservant for a while. But it was too much for one person, and we began a frantic search for someone to take over and get the household operating efficiently. Auriol knew "just the person"—a woman who had worked for her in London. Without consulting us further Auriol brought her over at her own expense and proudly presented her to us. She would be "simply wonderful." Now Auriol had very defective vision, but she would not bring herself to admit it. She would rather peer at you than wear glasses. Mike and I put up with Briggs, Auriol's "jewel," because we didn't want to hurt Auriol's feelings. But Briggs was unbelievably dirty, and her food was typically middle-class English—tasteless "veg and a joint." She always poured the remains of all the soup bowls from dinner into the stock pot. She hung a turkey on the kitchen porch until it was so "high" we couldn't go near the kitchen. The end came for me the day she made a fancy English pastry, a "trifle." She showed me how smart our new English setter puppy, Sheila, was. Sheila was obligingly cracking nuts with her teeth, and Briggs was cooing "Now there's a love" and putting the meats into the mixing bowl. English customs or not, Briggs had to go. Our relations with Auriol were a bit stiff for a time, but we just couldn't tell her that her eyesight was so poor she had simply never seen how dirty Briggs was.

I was again in a picture with a long shooting schedule; it was *The Hurricane*, one of the happiest engagements I have ever had. It was a very difficult picture technically; the whole "island of Manakura" was built on the back lot of the Goldwyn Studios; while we were doing exteriors, one or two shots a day was the normal pace for the picture. Thomas Mitchell, Raymond Massey, Jerome Cowan, and I usually sat on the porch of the "government house" and played cards or talked, and at teatime John Ford, the director, would join us. It became a little ceremony every afternoon. Mike would often join us, too, after tennis or a swim at the Westside Tennis Club.

Mike was making contacts—he was very good at that. He had played tennis several times with Bramwell Fletcher and invited him to the house for a drink. Bramwell was planning a summer production of *Tonight at 8:30*, the series of nine one-act plays by Noel Coward, to run for six weekends at the Lobero Theater in Santa Barbara, and he suggested that I play the lead in as many of the plays as I would have time for. His wife, Helen Chandler, and Barbara O'Neill would alternate in the others. I agreed, to Mike's infinite satisfaction, for there is a small part for a "young man" in each of the nine plays, and he was to cut his theatrical teeth with them.

Rehearsals were no problem; I had plenty of time off from *Hurricane* for that. We did most of the work at San Remo, and then had a few days of the final work at the Lobero. The company, including Mike, stayed in Santa Barbara the whole time, but I had to commute. Looking back on it now, I don't know where I found the energy and stamina. We were doing the storm scenes in the picture, and I had to be soaking-wet the whole time. Marceil was working with me—at her old job—and she had to change me into duplicate clothing several times a day. I had been given permission to do the plays in Santa Barbara, with a guarantee that I could leave the set at five. As soon as I was finished I got into the car, and while Marceil drove I removed my make-up and put my hair up in pin curls. We would arrive at the theatre in Santa Barbara with just time enough for me to put on stage make-up; Marceil would bring me a sandwich and a split of champagne so I could eat while I was dressing. I would do the show, have supper with Bram and Helen and Mike, grab a few hours of sleep, drive back to Hollywood in the morning, and get made up and dressed, ready to work at nine. I did this Friday and Saturday nights for six weeks. On Sunday I could rest until the Sunday night show, since I didn't have to be back in Hollywood until Monday morning. As I remember, I did it with no strain at all; in fact, to me it seemed a most pleasant summer.

Mike had a wonderful time; it was just one long party to him. He was thrilled at being an actor. He had even taken a stage name—Michael Field, compounded from his nickname and the English translation of "del Campo." The only trouble was that he couldn't act. Both Bram and Helen tried to help him; they had had more stage experience than I. He had a beautiful voice and excellent diction, but he was wooden and artificial, and he could not learn how to move. He was the kind of actor who, as professionals say, "makes a date with a chair." It's like a fighter who telegraphs a punch.

During the five months it took to film *Hurricane,* we had one layoff period that enabled us to take the show to San Francisco. Some changes had to be made in the cast; Estelle Winwood took over the parts that O'Neill had played. Estelle and I did *Still Life* and *The Astonished Heart* together, and I learned a great deal from her. One morning when we were having coffee at a café near the theatre, she said to me, "You really want to act, don't you." Since I knew what she meant, I was not offended by her disregard of eighteen years of film work, and I assured her that I did indeed! So she coached me. She would put her hand firmly on the top of my head, holding it still, and command, "*Now* say your line." She taught me not to lean on chairs or a divan or a doorway: "Don't touch that door when you come in." I had to learn how to stand apart from other people on the stage. All this is contrary to movie technique; before the advent of the wide screen our "proscenium arch" was from four to ten feet, and we were accustomed to composition with other persons in the shot. And to lift an arm in an "open" gesture is an act that has to be learned for the stage. Estelle also solved the mystery of "projection" for me; it isn't simply "raising the voice" or speaking louder. The trick lies in listening to natural pitch and intonation and then boosting it with breath and diaphragm.

We were successful in San Francisco, so successful that another management took us, and put us into the Biltmore Theater in Los Angeles for two weeks. Mike continued to walk through his bits and to dream of days of stardom. But no producers came bidding.

Our life was completely keyed to Mike's temperament and needs. We gave a great many parties. He always handled the invitations; he loved calling people on the telephone and saying, "What are you doing Thursday? Come for supper half past seven-ish." And I would prepare for ten or twenty, with drop-ins after dinner. I was a wet blanket because I would make my excuses early and go to bed. Mike would be irritated, but then he didn't have to get up at six o'clock. I often fell asleep with the noises of the party coming up through the heating grill from the room below; and later I would awaken to the sound of cars departing and noisy farewells. Mike would come in and sit on the edge of my bed and tell me what a marvelous party it had been and what a shame it was that I couldn't enjoy myself.

I never had enough time with Marylyn. I left the house at seven in the morning and rarely got home before seven in the evening, sometimes for weeks at a time, before a break came and I had a few days off. Then I could take walks with her and get to know her again. She was healthy and robust; when I put her into a nursery school, she quickly adapted to the other children.

We had many friends I enjoyed being with, friends we had made while I was working in *Hurricane* and *Tonight at 8:30*, especially Bart and Lee Marshall, and Bill Gargan and his wife, Mary. Bill and Mary were good practicing Catholics, and they got into many discussions with Mike about religion, but most of it went over my head.

We had finally found a colored couple, Thad and Constance Brown, who could keep San Remo in smooth running order. We also had a full-time gardener. And two cars. And our clothes closets, including Marylyn's, were loaded. We had good horses; Mike had a jumper, "Little Nipper," and I had a polo pony, "Grey Fox." We belonged to the Riviera Country Club. We always rode on Sunday mornings, and served brunch to innumerable people. There was usually a caterer from the Derby, and we averaged about a case of liquor per Sunday.

I was a rich woman, but not *that* rich. Our expenses were absorbing all our income. We didn't even know how much was coming in and how much was going out.

Mike had met a man named G. Weston Rogers; after we had talked to him, and had been impressed by his evident honesty and ability, we engaged him as our personal business manager. He slowed us up considerably and began putting some of our money into annuities and insurance. The knowledge that our financial affairs now had control and direction was a comfort.

Now I could say to someone, "Can I afford this?" and be quite content if I was told I couldn't. The responsibility worried me because so much depended on my earning power.

The danger of this situation was fully brought home to me while I was working on a picture for Metro, with Judy Garland— a trivial thing called *Listen, Darling.* On one of my days off Mike and I went down to the stables and had our horses saddled for a ride. Mike was already mounted and had started for the ring for a warm-up. My grey pony was always a "spooky" pony; I was not firmly seated, and I had leaned over to point out to the groom that I thought Grey Fox's mane was getting a little shaggy and needed pulling. Fox saw a "ghost," and without warning he reared up. I grabbed for his poll and tried to hang on, but he shook me off and I fell on my back onto the concrete covering of the area near the stalls. I was unconscious for a few minutes; when I came to I was in excruciating pain, except for the dead numbness of my legs. People were running around in the irrationality of excitement, but at least they had the sense not to move me until the ambulance came. At the hospital I was X-rayed, and to my relief, they told me I had broken no bones. But I had to stay in the hospital for four days before I could use my legs, and even then I could walk only with great pain and for short periods. I was in a wheel chair for two weeks. The picture was held up, of course. When I went back, a double did all the walking long shots, and the shooting was arranged so that most of it could be done in close-ups. The entire incident gave Mike and me something to think about—I was vulnerable to accidents and illness, and if anything happened to me most of the money would be cut off. The thing to do was to get Mike started in the picture business.

I took matters into my own hands and went to Eddie Mannix at Metro. "Do this for *me*, Eddie," I told him. "Get Mike some kind of work at the studio—anything." He understood without my having to spell it out for him. After he placed a phone call or two to various departments he said, "Tell him to report to Blanche Sewell. He'll be her assistant."

For a time Mike found the job interesting enough, though

often at home he complained that "Mary Astor's husband" should not have to work "as a lowly cutter." Being a bright boy, however, he learned the job very quickly—and the training helped him earn a living in England after the war; he became a film editor at Denham Studios, and was head cutter on some of the early Burt Lancaster films.

Christmas of 1938 was a production! As always, I loved Christmas; the Christmas days on the farm were still sharp in my memory. I wrapped tons of packages, decorated the tree and the house, put a huge candle on the newel post of the stairway and a small tree in the upper hall. And I was especially happy because I was going to have another baby.

I worked one more picture—*Midnight*, with Claudette Colbert —before the baby was born. I tried to keep my pregnancy a secret so that I might work as long as possible, but the eagle eye of a wardrobe fitter discovered it. I was getting thick over the hips. I told the producers that I had been unaware of my pregnancy when I signed for the picture, and they condensed my scenes and got through with me before I began to show too much.

I was happy to be able to quit work and enjoy my pregnancy. Mike was gone during the day, working at Metro, and I spent happy hours with Marylyn, playing with her and talking about the baby. In the happy tranquility I was able to find myself again, to relax in my little sitting room upstairs and knit and read, to walk around my beautiful home and enjoy it, to plan the nursery, to sit in the garden and feel the sunshine and listen to the wind in the trees and be aware of living. I had an excuse now to avoid the strenuous cocktail party and night club activity, which had long since lost its savor—the same tired faces, the same smoky rooms and round of dirty jokes and loud laughter. Mike spent most of his Sundays, since I had curtailed the house parties, at the Westside Tennis Club—he *had* to be with people—playing tennis or swimming or playing backgammon.

Auriol had come to stay with us. She had returned from New York, where she had directed a play, and she was going to be in Hollywood for the summer, working in an advisory capacity at

Paramount. We installed her in Mike's room, and since I had a king-size bed in my room, Mike moved in with me.

My last effort at "going out" was a small party that Bart and Lee Marshall gave for my birthday in May. I had been doing very well, though I was getting heavy and unwieldy, and preferred sitting in my blue chair in my room and reading. I had a fine obstetrician and my pregnancy had proceeded uneventfully, except that he told me I must stay quiet, as my history of very premature delivery was not in my favor. A few weeks later Auriol decided I should get out a bit, and she took me for a drive down to the Miramar to visit her niece. Auriol was an appalling driver; because of her bad eyesight her stops and starts tended to be jarringly sudden. When I got home I felt none too well. I was sure the baby had changed position and had descended. I called the doctor, and he told me to get into bed and stay there. About two in the morning I was awakened by slight cramps and a seepage of water. I shook Mike, trying to awaken him, but he grunted and rolled his face into the pillow. I cautiously slid out of bed and crept on my hands and knees to where Auriol was sleeping. She was awake in an instant. I told her I couldn't waken Mike, and she cursed roundly and called the doctor to tell him she was driving me in. The jarring ride to the hospital did nothing to improve my condition; when I arrived, they had a beautiful room ready for me, but I only caught a glimpse of it from the hall. As soon as I was prepped I was sent into the labor room.

Auriol sat beside the window and read a newspaper. Mike came in during the afternoon, abject in his apologies, but I was beyond caring. The doctor was worried. The baby was five weeks ahead of time, and he warned me that he couldn't give me much medication. There'd be no relief; I'd just have to grin and bear it.

The rest of the day, and all the next night, I spent in the labor room. The following day, Auriol was back in her place by the window. Suddenly a strong contraction shook me; as soon as I could talk after it had passed I called over to her, "I think you'd better leave, darling. I'm going to be sick." She scurried out of the room and sent in a nurse, who briskly put up the bed railings. This scared me, but I soon knew why she had done it. The pains became dreadful, and with my teeth grinding I flailed and twisted. The doctor came in, and he stood over me with tears in his eyes, saying, "I'm damned sorry, lady, I'm damned sorry." By evening I was rolled into the delivery room, and the doctor took the mask from the anesthetist's hands, and as he put it over my face he said, "It gives me great pleasure—breathe deeply, dear lady."

Then I was in my room, limp, but wonderfully sleepy and relaxed, and a little nurse whispered, "You have a beautiful son, Mrs. del Campo."

I said, "Thank God," and I went back to sleep.

Nine

The recounting of my life has carried me through many love stories, cheap and tawdry and ephemeral. Now I am hesitant, filled with a humble apprehension, for I have come to the point where the great love story of my life began. It will take a long time in the telling, for I am "foolish and slow of heart," and it will have no ending. The outer fabric of my life, with its pattern of recurring mistakes; my talent for rushing blindly, headlong into disaster; the shambles that inevitably resulted from my habit of acting first and thinking afterward, if at all—this should have destroyed me, body and soul. And destroy me it almost did, and would have, were it not for the unseen and unfailing ministrations of this Tremendous Lover. No language, be it ever so extravagant, can express my wonder and awe at His persistence. I have turned my back on Him repeatedly; I have disobeyed Him flagrantly; I have glimpsed the very edge of hell. I have carried the burden of sickening guilt, and felt it lifted, felt His touch like the cooling breeze of the sea when I cried, "I have sinned exceedingly . . . Forgive me."

He reached me first when I was about to lose another, infinitely lesser love; yet He did not burst upon me with a blatant declaration that He could supplant and supersede that love. He entered subtly, through a shabby side door—the door of idle curiosity. Then one day, when I still hardly realized that He was there, He dazzled my mind with a flaming splinter of Truth, and from then on there was no peace for me. For though, in the grip of nature and habit, I was time and time again to turn away from Him, to renounce Him, to try to hide from Him, my ears could never again be entirely deaf to the beat of those "insistent feet, that followed, followed after."

But I must get back to the attic and continue my house cleaning. And a dirty job it still is. Much remains to be aired—unpleasant sordid ugliness. I must hold my lantern high and carefully search out the grimy debris that lies before me.

My son was born June 5, 1939, five weeks prematurely. He weighed just a little over five pounds. When I saw him for the first time, the next day, I was sure I had never seen anything so beautiful. This baby was fully developed; his skin had the coloring of a ripe peach; his head was covered with black hair, and he had black eyelashes. As we had planned, he was named after Mike's two uncles, Anthony and Paul, and he was to be called "Tono."

I had had another rough delivery. The doctor said he would have done a Caesarian if he had been in time, but he could not do the Caesarian after the amniotic sac had ruptured. He had done considerable surgery on the perineal wall and the cervix itself, so I could not look forward to a rapid recovery. For two weeks I felt as though I were sitting on a cactus! I was in the hospital for eighteen days; during two thirds of this time I ran a temperature every morning. I could have no visitors except Mike in the evening for a few minutes. Then one day they had to take me to surgery to do a clean-up curettage, which knocked me out completely for a couple of days, but after that my recovery was rapid.

I enjoyed the peaceful, long days in the hospital. I usually awoke very early, turned on the radio, and rested in a blissful peace and contentment. I had a wonderful nurse on the early shift; she was Jean Hoffman, the girl who had given me the little bottle of spirits of ammonia when I attended one of Franklyn's operations. I had kept in touch with her, and we had planned that she would take care of me when Marylyn was born. She had missed out on that because it had happened in Honolulu, but she had said she was going to take care of me this time, no matter what! She had even timed an appendectomy so that she would be recovered in time for my delivery, but I had rushed her badly. With Tono's premature birth, she didn't get the month's recuperation she should have had. She was cheerful and bright-eyed, always wearing a happy smile. She would come in every morning and brew me some special coffee—"hospital coffee is slush"—and get me bathed and cleaned in time for my breakfast, the doctor's call, and my morning visit with Tono.

Mike was a very proud parent. "Do you feel any different now that you're a father?" I asked him, and he answered, "Of course I don't," very positively. He was exceedingly pleased that the baby looked like him; I later came to feel that that was the greatest source of pleasure he ever found in Tono. He usually stayed only a few moments with me. I prepared for him hours before he was due, with clean bedding and a clean gown, my face and hair carefully done, and the room sprayed with cologne. But he was always hurried; he was on the town, dressed and already a little drunk, anxious to be on his way to some party.

When the time came for me to take Tono home, the doctor recommended that we have a trained baby nurse for a few weeks. This caused an immediate domestic crisis, for I could not keep poor Nellie and a couple and a nurse as well. I told Nellie that she could have her job back after the three months that Tono needed special care, but she couldn't understand, naturally, and she left for good. I engaged Martha Wright for the job for three months— and she stayed for three years! She was a quiet, capable girl, and both the children loved her.

I remember the day I came home. Mike was driving, and I

was very weak indeed—thirty-five miles an hour seemed nerve-shattering. Thad and Constance had great grins on their brown faces, and I regretfully handed my boy over to the starchy, official Miss Wright. How different it was from the day I brought Marylyn home! That beautiful house, Tono's own nursery, with all the best equipment, a nurse in her own room next to his. I had nothing to do. It was just as well; my own bedroom, cool and dark, was a welcome sight!

I hadn't seen Marylyn for almost three weeks; she came in as soon as she was permitted, to tell me all about the wonderful birthday party she had had. And she couldn't stay out of the nursery. She let it be known that a new baby brother was the best present I could possibly have given her. I tried carefully to avoid offending her through the usual stupidity of people who come to see a new baby—everyone clamors to see the baby, while an older child is painfully ignored. I told Marylyn that she was to help me; when people came in, she was to drop whatever she was doing and come and offer to show them her new brother. She was to take them upstairs herself, and she should see that they did not stay too long. With this responsibility, she was as happy as a seven-year-old little girl ought to be.

Not long after I had brought Tono home, Mike began to talk about having him baptized. I looked upon it as simply a sort of social honor he wanted to confer upon his son. It was all right with me if he had him baptized or if he didn't, but I did nothing about it. When Tono was three months old, Mike became insistent. I saw no reason why he should fret so about it, but I went out and bought Tono a lovely white silk outfit, a kind of suit. He was much too big for the usual white christening gown. And I suggested to Mike that it would be nice to have Auriol as his godmother; after all, I pointed out, she was our closest friend. He looked at me blankly—Auriol couldn't possibly be Tono's godmother, friend or not. Tono had to be baptized in the Catholic Church and Auriol wasn't a Catholic. We would ask Bill and Mary Gargan to be godparents. It was my turn to look blank. Bill and Mary were not really close friends. Did it matter what church

Tono was baptized in? Wasn't our friendship for Auriol more important? I said, "After all, what difference does it make?" Mike replied, "You couldn't possibly understand. It makes a great deal of difference."

So arrangements were made, and Tono was baptized at St. Monica's Church, and Bill and Mary Gargan had their hands full, trying to hold onto a candle and a big, squirming, protesting child. But it was accomplished, and Bill and Mary came back to the house with us, and we celebrated with some drinks. But I still couldn't understand it.

I asked Mary, "What is there about your religion that makes people act like that? I can't see how anyone as unconcerned about it as Mike can still be tied so securely. It's weird."

Mary smiled and said, "Well, if you ever really want to find out, let me know."

And we both laughed. I had enough to worry me without adding religion to the list.

I had Mike to worry about, for one thing. I was still irritable and edgy from my delivery, and I resented Mike's insistence that I start going out—because "it would do me good." After he had urged for a few days, I gave in, and regretted the decision before the night was half over. Ciro's had just opened, and we were there with a party that included about six others. Before we left the house I had asked Mike to forego his usual table-hopping and stay close by, and to call it an evening by eleven-thirty because I knew I would be tired. He had agreed completely. At Ciro's I was not especially happy. The noise and the chatter grated on me, my drinks had no effect at all, and Mike did not stay at the table more than a few minutes at a time—he had to go over to see first this person, and then that one. By twelve-thirty I was exhausted. I excused myself to the people at the table, got a cab, and came home. Mike phoned when the place closed. He apparently had not missed me until then as I coolly pointed out when he tried to tell me how embarrassed and angry he had been.

We rarely quarreled, and the few quarrels that we did have were usually when we were both tired. We still had our long talks in the sitting room upstairs, where we had installed a handy little portable bar—it was a nuisance to have to go all the way downstairs! Mike's bitterness would well upwards as we sat and talked. I realized that he hated his job, that he resented the fact that he could do nothing overnight to impress "the people in this town." He was bitter at what he regarded as my "superior" position—and at the fact that I didn't have to work to get attention. It annoyed him that I could sit in one place at a cocktail party and people would come to me, whereas he had to circulate constantly. I tried wearily to explain that twenty years of hard work lay behind my "position." It worried me that he attached so much importance to it. I tried to show him how much he had—my love, a son, a beautiful home, and a job that had fine potentialities if he stuck it out. But he received my arguments with ill grace; he wanted prestige and position, not in any remote and questionable future, but now.

My own position seemed a little uncertain when I had regained my strength and was ready to go back to work. Getting back to work is not easy after a prolonged absence from the studios. Producers seem to forget the existence of anyone who is not constantly under their noses. It was finally a stage offer from Elliott Nugent that brought me back into action. Earlier I had done a picture with him, and now he was arranging to try out a new play in California, one he had written with James Thurber, called *The Male Animal*. Elliott would direct and play the lead, and I was cast as his wife. The play needed some rewriting, but he thought it would turn into a very unusual comedy.

After three weeks' rehearsal we opened in Santa Barbara. Thurber and Nugent immediately started rewriting, and we took the play all over Southern California, one-night stands at Redlands, Long Beach, Huntington Park, Riverside, trying out different things—a new second-act curtain, changed dialogue, scenes deleted and replaced with new ones. It was very difficult, learning and forgetting, but it was fine experience. We played the Biltmore in Los Angeles, and then went to San Francisco for two weeks, and finally closed. After more rewriting they left for New York, and Elliott wired me to ask if I wanted to do it with them there. I didn't want to leave my baby; even a short run would mean at least three months, and that was too long to be away from the children, not to mention a husband. So I turned it down. *The Male Animal* turned out to be a great hit; it ran three years in New York and a year in Chicago, and is still a favorite repeater for stock companies. That is theatre!

Early in 1940 I had a good role in pictures again. *Brigham Young—Frontiersman* was a big picture, mainly about the Mormons' journey from Illinois to Utah and the founding of Salt Lake City. I played the role of Brigham Young's first wife, a long-suffering character, and not particularly interesting. It was another long picture; it seemed that it took forever to make. We went on many location trips, to Big Bear and the surrounding country, to Big Pine, and to Elko, Nevada, where we spent two days I shall never forget. I took Marylyn with me for a week at Big Bear. We had a log cabin, where I could cook breakfast for us very early in the morning, and Marylyn would chase squirrels and bring me pine cones. She had a wonderful week, marred only by the fact that she had to keep up her schoolwork with the teacher who was on the set for the children in the cast.

Later, when I had returned to Big Bear after bringing Marylyn back to Los Angeles, Wes Rogers called me to say that Mike had been in an accident. He had been driving my car, a Lincoln convertible, and he had crashed into a wall on Sunset Boulevard. The car was a total wreck, and Mike had a slight concussion, although the doctor who examined him reported that it was not too serious. Nevertheless, I told the director that I would have to go to him. The company car drove me down to Los Angeles, and I arrived home late in the evening. Mike was glad to see me—he had been very lonesome, he said. He was wearing a dressing gown, but he was up and around. He explained that the doctor told him the concussion was *very* mild. He would be away from work about a week, however, and had to stay in a dark room. I had assured myself that Mike's injuries were not serious, and I was back at work at Big Bear the following noon. Wes forestalled a suit by the people whose wall and newly planted trees Mike had hit; we replaced the trees and repaired the damage to the wall, and all was well. Insurance covered the car. Mike said he was so tired after work that he had fallen asleep for an instant.

The work in *Brigham Young* was difficult physically—the heavy costumes, the dawn location calls, the scenes in the uncomfortable covered wagons that shook us to pieces, the long hot waiting in the trailer dressing rooms, and a director with a bad temper who drove people unmercifully. But worst of all was the filming of a single episode in the picture—the miracle of the sea gulls, which saved the colony from a plague of crickets. The cricket scenes could not all be faked. Near Elko, Nevada, was a place that had had such a plague yearly for the past five years. The government had partially controlled it; they had limited it to an area about five miles long and a mile deep. There we went for our scenes. We were scheduled for four days, but it was so horrible that the shooting was finished in two. As we went into the area, the feeling was oppressive and eerie; the usual good spirits and kidding that you find in a location troupe were non-existent. The crickets cast a dull gloom over everything. These creatures were no little friends of the hearth; they were about the size of my thumb, and they had eyes that seemed to keep watch, like a fly's. Since they could jump only to a height of about three feet, tin fences were set up around the cameras and lighting equipment. Wardrobe had made the women players a kind of pantaloon, with rubber bands around the legs, and the whole garment sewed to the hems of our long costumes, so the crickets could not crawl up our legs. We had to go right into the spots where they were worst, with brooms and sacks, beating at them in the tall grain. Two days of this were all any of us could have taken. It was nauseating to walk through them, piled to a foot deep in some places, and the stench was awful.

At the local hotel I shared a suite with the script girl, Barbara Spencer; I think it was through mutual suffering that we became good friends—in addition to the horrible crickets we had to endure temperatures of up to 110 in the shade. After the ordeal of the first day's work we both felt the need of a drink. It was the odd beginning of a friendship that has lasted up to the present. Not for many years had I had a chum, a close friend with whom I could blow off steam. I loved Auriol, but the difference in our ages was too great for real intimacy. Now Bobsy and I found we had much in common, including attractive husbands. Back in Hollywood we became a rather happy foursome. Mike and Freddie Spencer got along well, and we spent many pleasant evenings together, having dinner at their place or ours, or playing cards, or going to parties.

The Brigham Young picture was a financial lifesaver. And the atmosphere at home always cleared with work and less drinking. Both of us were naturally even-tempered, and we never bickered. I was actually the more irritable, especially about getting my rest. I could not afford to look tired and drawn; there is no more penetrating eye than that of the camera, and a director can become very impatient if the make-up man has to repair dark circles too often. Mike could do his work in the cutting room after four hours' sleep, but I could not.

After the long grind of *Brigham* I was a little tired, and Mike suggested that we take a two-week vacation in New York. Production had slowed, he said, and he was sure he could get the time off. It was summer, and a change sounded good. It did not turn out to be really a change, though we did see some theatre. Mostly it was the usual round of luncheons, cocktail parties, dinners, after-dinner night clubs—people, eating, drinking, dancing. I think my party tolerance was reached during those years with Mike. I always tried to play up to the occasion, and was just as gay as anyone else, and then Mike would say, "Now you'll have to admit that you enjoyed yourself. You were having fun." And I would say, "I wish I could get the fun out of this sort of thing that you do."

When we returned to Hollywood we found that Mike had lost his job. The studio was strongly considering making him an associate producer but, alas, it didn't come off.

This was rough on his pride, and I didn't make it any easier for

him. I had coddled him like an erring but dear child, and now I
was pretty well fed up. I told him to stop bleating about it, and if
he really wanted to "show the people in this town" he could do
it by getting another job and working hard at it.

Since Tono's baptism the Gargans had become increasingly
close friends. They were at San Remo more often, and we spent
several weekends with them at their little house in Palm Springs.
I listened with growing interest when they discussed religion with
Mike, and now, instead of remaining discreetly quiet when they
talked about things I did not understand, I asked questions: After
all, I told them, my son was a Catholic, and I felt I ought to be
learning something about his religion. One evening when Mary
Gargan became entangled in explaining a point that was completely clear to her but that she could not make me understand at
all, she gave up in good-natured disgust. "You ask too many questions that I can't answer, Mary," she told me. "I'll have to bring
Father O'Dea over to see you. He's a good friend of ours, and I'm
pretty sure he'll be able to make some of these things a good deal
clearer to you."

A few afternoons later Mary brought him to the house. Father
Augustin O'Dea was a warm and hearty man, who soon dispelled
my shyness of the Roman collar. "Don't look at me as though I
were going to eat you up," he laughed. "Believe it or not, priests
aren't out to grab off everyone who comes by, like a spider in his
web." I relaxed, and we had a pleasant visit. Father was not at
all doctrinaire or dogmatic. We didn't talk very much about religion; he told me he had some books that might answer some of
my questions. "They'd better be good, Father," I told him. "My
main trouble right now is total ignorance."

I read the books, and then returned them to him at Nazareth
House, in the Valley, where he was director. I came back with
another armload. "Don't try to read through all of them," he said.
"Just skip around and find the things that interest you." A series
of trips between San Remo and Nazareth followed, and I found
myself "skipping around" in an impressive number of Father's
books. It was interesting, as travel in a foreign country would be

interesting, but that was all. "You can be interested in a trip through France without becoming a Frenchman," I told myself. And just as the condescending traveler might look with amused curiosity on some of the customs and manners of the French, I looked with amused curiosity on much of what I read of Catholic doctrine. Some of the points seemed obvious enough; I had no trouble believing in God, in the usual rather vague way. If I thought about Him at all, I thought of Him as a kind of Law that held the planets in place, or a sort of Perpetual Motion Principle that had set the universe spinning, and had then sat back to watch it spin. I had heard of moral law, but I looked upon it as a set of social conventions—an evolution of tribal ethics and customs that had changed as people became better educated and more civilized, and that had changed in different ways in different places. If you were English, there were certain things you did and certain things you did not do. If you were Spanish, there were quite different things you did or didn't do. And if you were a Tahitian, the whole thing was different. Well, I thought, here is just another set of conventions and customs, a good deal less realistic than most. But interesting.

In Palm Springs, I went to my first Mass with Mary and Bill. I didn't understand much of what was going on, but there was something "comfortable" about it, an easy, real quality that I had never felt when, in the dim past, I had gone to church with my parents. People didn't put on a special face, or turn and bow to other arrivals, or wear particularly fancy hats. They seemed absorbed, satisfied, as though this were a real part of their lives. I tried to talk with Mike about it, but he cut me short. "Darling— please! I've heard nothing else all my life."

Then my reading tapered off, and for a while my curiosity was dulled by a combination of professional and personal crises that left no time or thought for other interests. First, in December of 1940, Bette Davis called me on the phone to ask if I would play a part in the picture she was going to make, *The Great Lie*. She personally wanted me for the part, she said, and she apologized for asking me if I would mind taking a test. The actress who played the role had to look like a professional pianist at the piano, and she knew I played. "But," she said, "a few idiots have to be convinced." So far everyone who had sat down at the piano had played with "spaghetti arms." I took the test and got the part; and the next months, through February of 1941, were concentrated on nothing else, for it was the greatest challenge I had so far met in my career.

The theme of the picture was to be the great Tchaikovsky Concerto in E Flat Major. I was thoroughly familiar with it, but it was quite beyond my skill as a pianist. The concerto would have to be dubbed, of course, and it would be the first important effort at synchronization that had so far been made in pictures. I was excited at getting the part, and I entered enthusiastically into the whirl of tests for clothes and general appearance of the character. Sandra, the character I was to portray, was feline and powerful, a world-famous pianist, and completely ruthless. Edmund Goulding, the director, summed it up well: "She is brandy, men, and a piano." After talking it over with Bette, I decided on a hair style that was to become famous. The current style was the "page boy bob"; I had Perc Westmore cut my hair in a sleek shingle at the back, brushed slick behind the ears. The clothes were magnificent, designed by Orry-Kelly, with long, classic lines, and a little bizarre.

I shall have to explain in detail how the dubbing worked. In the scenes where I was playing with a full orchestra, the camera would see my hands, though not too closely—about the distance of a person sitting in the front row at a concert. The close-ups of a woman's hands actually playing were the hands of Norma Boleslavsky, a concert pianist. The sound track was made by Max Rabinowitz, and it was with him I worked. Hours. Days and nights. The final five pages of the concerto, and three other passages, I had to memorize. I played on a dummy piano that had been rigged so that the keys would depress, and they had to synchronize with Max playing a live piano off stage. The chromatic runs and certain other passages were beyond the skill of anyone but a fine pianist, but I had to be at least within a hair of the correct note. I gave up practicing at the house; there were just too many interruptions, even at night. So the final week before the concert scenes were to be filmed, I had a bed and a piano moved into my dressing room, and I just stayed there, working at noon and at night until about eleven o'clock.

I think I shall never forget the sensation of practically "playing" with the orchestra on those few days when we did the concert scenes. I was no longer conscious of Max; the music was in my ears and in my heart. I took my tempo from the conductor. The section runs about six minutes, and at the finish the men in the orchestra rose and gave me a "concert applause," the violinists tapping their violins with their bows. It was wonderful. Max hugged me, and gave them the official "Okay for sync." Many months later José Iturbi himself told me he knew that anyone who played the concerto so well could not have spent most of her life making movies. "But you had me fooled. I couldn't tell that you were *not* playing."

The story for the picture was not very strong. The first day I worked with Bette, I felt uncomfortable about it, and she sat on the set swinging her foot like a cat whipping its tail. Finally she dragged me to her dressing room and put the problem directly to me. "Mary," she said, "I know you must realize that we have a perfectly *lousy* story the way it stands now. We've got to do something about it, and between us I think we can." And she told me how she thought it should be changed. The only interesting action in the story was the conflict between the two women; the rest of the plot was nothing. The part of Sandra had to be built up, with more scenes between the two women, and Bette was powerful enough to stop all production while we did some rewriting. We developed the story as we went along. Goulding sat patiently by, occasionally kidding us by saying "Only a couple of cats could think that one up," or "Well, ladies, have you decided what I am to shoot in this scene?" Bette and I had become as simpatico as a pair of dancers as we worked out the story, constantly by building up the importance and impact of the character of Sandra.

A year later, when I received the Academy Award for Best Sup-

porting Actress for my performance in *The Great Lie,* Bette wired
me from her home in Vermont, "We *did* it. Congratulations,
baby." People have said that I "stole" the picture from Bette
Davis, but that is sheer nonsense. She handed it to me on a silver
platter. Bette has always had the wisdom, rare in this business, to
know that a star cannot stand alone; she appears to much better
advantage if the supporting actors are good.

I don't know how I was able to shut out all the personal problems that piled up while I was working on the picture. Mike was
still a British subject, and he felt it was his duty to enlist in the
Royal Canadian Air Force. One or two of his British friends had
already enlisted, and soon he was talking of nothing else. I told
him I felt his first duty, at least until such a time as this country
might get into the war, was to me and the children, especially to
Tono. Moreover, and I put this into words, I felt that if he got to
England he might never come back. I wanted him to come back,
to come back and settle down to work for me and our family. I
was even beginning to think that we might be married in the
Church, and that, I felt, would give our marriage a solidity and
dignity that it had not had.

But World War II had begun and I had to let Mike go with as
much grace as I could muster. Bobsy and Freddie Spencer and I
drove him to the airport and saw him off on the plane to Vancouver.

I came home, and the great house seemed quieter and emptier
than I would ever have thought it could be. I went into Marylyn's
room and looked down at her for a moment, and then I went in
and looked at the sleeping Tono. I put some records on the phonograph, fixed a drink at the now quiet bar, and went out into the
garden. In the mist the soft light from the windows of the house
was blurred and diffused. The voice of Flagstad singing "Isolde"
reached me as I walked under the dripping trees, back and forth
along the driveway. My mind hammered painfully on a single
theme—Mike was gone, and he was gone for good.

Auriol had been down in Indio at John van Druten's ranch, which adjoined mine. She came up to stay with me for a few days while she struggled with a number of financial snarls that had to be untangled before she went East to direct John's play, *The Damask Cheek*, which they had been working out together. She insisted that she was going to drive to New York, and this alarmed us. Both Johnnie and I were worried about her driving, because her eyesight was so very bad. But to tell her that she couldn't drive would have been like telling her she should be put in a wheel chair. Johnnie was at least able to convince her that she should not drive alone, and he sent his ranch hand with her, with instructions that he was to do the driving.

One evening about three days after she had left, I arrived home from the studio to find both Johnnie and Wes at the house. Wes was at the phone, calling the airport, and Johnnie was choked up so that he could not talk. Finally it was Constance who told me: they had just received word that Auriol had been killed that morning in an accident near Hutchinson, Kansas. The highway was wet from the rain of the night before; she was driving; one wheel had gone off the highway into a soft shoulder; the car had turned over five times. The ranch boy was in the hospital, but Auriol had been killed instantly. Wes and Johnnie and Auriol's niece flew to Hutchinson on the first plane they could get. Auriol had asked that she be buried wherever she was when she died, so her grave is there. I still had relatives living near Hutchinson, and they have kept flowers on the grave and have seen that it is properly tended.

Auriol's death depressed and saddened me; she had been a source of strength and comfort for years, and now I had neither her nor Mike. I found myself longing for the comfort the sight of Mike would bring me, and as soon as I could get the time off I flew up to Vancouver to see him. He was still waiting out red tape, but of course he had taken ample precautions against getting bored during the wait—he had made a number of friends, and he knew his way around Vancouver. Among his new friends was one very nice couple who had a home in the country called Hope Ranch; they invited us to come out with them, and then they tactfully decided that they had to go back to town—to leave us alone to say good-by to each other.

As I got used to Mike's absence I began to settle down into a moderately comfortable routine. I had enough to interest me to keep from moping. I was determined that I would not sit at the dining table and give in to the empty-chair blues. I converted Mike's room into a very comfortable upstairs living room. I brought up the radio phonograph and installed it in a recess, and put a bright covering and cushions on the studio-type bed and turned it sideways to make a couch. There was already a large desk in the room, and a telephone extension, and a big leather chair—plenty of books, records, and pictures. I had a cozy room for myself. Good tray meals could be brought up, and I would not have to rattle around in a big house. I could go out occasionally, when I wanted to—to the Gargans' or the Spencers'. And I didn't have to go to night clubs!

Things were really going very well for me. I had a contract to do two more pictures for Warner's during the year, and there was a good demand for me in radio shows. The business affairs I had to leave to Wes; I tried to take an interest because he was very enthusiastic.

I renewed my discussions with Father O'Dea. I think I did not know how deeply my idle curiosity had involved me, but I found that instead of reading Father's books with a detached interest I was beginning to study them avidly. There was much that made my unused intellectual muscles cry with pain. I had always been inclined to jump to rather intuitive conclusions instead of reasoning an idea out carefully. My conception of God took on some new dimensions; I groped toward the idea that eternity was something more than "foreverness," or any of the words that are used to express time and duration. The great truths I knew I could not presume to comprehend, or to imagine more than a faint glimmer of what they must be; but I accepted the fact that their truth did not depend on my comprehension of them. One phrase struck me sharply, and made me laugh a little, because I knew why it struck me—and that was the idea of God as a "loving Father."

I went to Mass occasionally at St. Monica's, but I felt strange and ill at ease. Everyone else was so clearly a part of all that went on, and I was so awkward and uncertain. I was not yet at all clear about sin, and I felt very self-consciously that people knew a great deal about my life. I was sure everyone was saying, "What right has she to be in a Catholic Church!"

I was ever more eager to learn, and I pestered Father constantly. He told me to go slowly. If the gift of Faith came, it would come in its own time; meanwhile I must pray for it. I had a rosary, and I used it, although the meditations eluded me. I was much interested in the Little Flower, the lovely St. Thérèse of Lisieux. On the rack in church I had found a pamphlet containing a novena to her, with a petition for Faith and enlightenment, and I said the prayers regularly.

I first kept my rosary in a little antique porcelain snuffbox that Mike had given me; one night before he went to Canada I opened the box, and out of it poured a heavy odor of roses. I was startled—almost frightened. I smelled my hands to see if there was any perfume on them. There wasn't. I went into my dressing room and smelled every bottle. No odor was even similar. No roses were blooming in the garden; there were no roses anywhere in the house. I took the porcelain box into Mike's room, where he was reading in bed.

"What does this smell like to you?" I asked, and I started to hand the box to him.

But he waved me away. "I can smell it from here," he said. "It's lovely. Roses. What have you been doing, praying to St. Thérèse?"

He wasn't even surprised.

In great excitement I carried my news to Father O'Dea. "Calm down," he said. "There's probably some natural explanation for it." And he gave me a lesson in the attitude of the Church toward miracles, explaining how even at Lourdes carefully documented and impartial medical testimony was necessary before any cure could be regarded as miraculous.

Father was a patient teacher and a good one. He was experienced in drumming religion into the heads of reluctant boys. Not only reluctant, but difficult. Nazareth House boys are often a tough bunch, boys from broken homes or bad environment. He was even-tempered and patient. Nothing was too much trouble for him. I would bring up a question, and he would mount a little ladder in his library and come down with three books to answer it.

The great Mysteries I accepted. The Virgin Birth and the Immaculate Conception I finally got untangled. Christ's miracles I could accept without any difficulty; I felt that if God had made the world and everything in it He could most certainly do anything He wanted with it. Nature's miracles were occurring all the time right under our noses—the fusing of two cells, and their growth into a human being—what greater miracle than this! But all these remained isolated facts for me; there was no integration; I could not see them as a part of the pattern that led to something infinitely greater.

I was reading a biography of St. Thérèse one morning. I didn't care for it very much; it was a bit sticky and sentimental, so I was not reading with much concentration. I don't remember what the context was, but I read the words, "Jesus Christ was God," and something seemed suddenly to flash in my mind. I had heard this and read it many times before, but now I felt the illumination of understanding. The light seemed an actual physical brilliance that I had to close my eyes against. Things that had had no real meaning before assumed meaning. The Incarnation, the Resurrection, the Sacrifice of the Mass. I slipped to my knees and prayed.

Since Father had been so matter-of-fact about my little miracle of the roses, I said nothing of the sudden illumination that I had felt sweep over me. I simply told him that I thought I understood things a little more clearly; but as we proceeded, and my comments and answers became easy and simple statements of facts, he began to say that I had been given the gift of Faith. And there were more books, eagerly read, and Father was bombarded with more questions, and finally he agreed that I was ready for baptism.

But the matter of baptism was not going to be so simple. I told Father of the conversation I had had with Mike about being married in the Church. Father had a talk with the Bishop, who, in brief, thought I should be helped. Father explained to me later; my marriage with Ken had been valid, but Ken was dead. My marriage to Franklyn was invalid according to the Church. Mike, a Catholic, had married me outside of the Church; if we were ever to resume our life together we would have to be married in the Church.

I wanted Father O'Dea to baptize me, of course, but a problem of etiquette and protocol came up, and I had to be baptized by the pastor of my parish. Mary and Bill were my sponsors; they had been sitting quietly but happily on the side lines, cheering me on, and now they would be in at the finish. I knelt at the rail and made my profession of faith, and then I went back to the baptismal font, to be baptized in the Roman Catholic Church. The pastor urged me to go to confession immediately—and he *did* understand why I wanted to go back to Father O'Dea for my confession. It took only a few minutes; we had previously gone over everything in detail, and that made it much easier for me. Then, with Mary and Bill, I was given my first Holy Communion. I stayed alone in the chapel at the altar rail for a few minutes while Bill and Mary waited in the car. Even after I got in the car I couldn't say anything; I couldn't say anything at all until we were well on the way back to Bill's and Mary's house. They joked with me gently, "Come on, darling, you're as white as a sheet. A good drink will fix you up." We broke open a bottle of champagne to celebrate, and had something to eat, but I wanted to get home, where I could be alone, where I could quietly pour out my thanksgiving to Him who had brought me "safely to the beginning of this day."

Ten

It was *my* year, in every way. The previous May, I had been engaged to emcee a new radio show, "Hollywood Showcase." It was a talent show for young professional actors. They were given a chance to be heard; we had an audience jury, and the winner was given an opportunity to come back the following week, and also received a week's engagement at the Pantages Theater. I introduced the people, conducted a short interview, and played a six-minute spot with an actor or actress, giving them the better part. We had five people each week—four plus the show for the return-engagement player—and the program played for fifty-two weeks. It did not interfere with my picture work, for it required almost no rehearsal for me; the show was ready to go when I came in for "run-through" and "dress" early Monday evening. I loved the show; it gave me a satisfying "possessive" feeling. It was "my" show; the musicians were "my" boys—"my" sound-effects man, "my" director. It also made my stock go up for other radio shows, and I played in hour dramas like "Lux" and "Screen Guild."

And it was during this year that I had one of my best parts

with Warner Brothers, in a picture adapted from Dashiell Hammett's story *The Maltese Falcon*. It was John Huston's first job of directing—he had also done the adaptation—and my friend "Bogey," Humphrey Bogart, was to star. The picture was a completely new conception of the "gangster movie"; it was the story not of hoodlums, but of a group of evil though intelligent people playing for very high stakes. I played the part of a crook, an unscrupulous girl who changed her name as she would change her hat, and who at the end admitted she "had always been a liar." John proved to be a wonderful director, with his dynamic personality and his keen insight into people. You either loved him or hated him, but you worked hard for him; his enthusiasm affected everyone on the set like wine. He had the picture well organized, so that things got done in a miraculously short time. And we had fun—zany, lighthearted fun. We were an unusually "close" company; players usually like to get away from each other at lunch time, but we would all go together across to the Lakeside Golf Club, where a big table was set on the patio for us. The normally frowned-on pre-luncheon drink was a must. We often took an hour and a half, and still we stayed ahead of schedule. I remember one scene near the end of the picture, very complicated technically; it ran about six minutes—and six minutes of script is an average good day's work. We rehearsed the scene before going home one evening, and all the camera moves were carefully plotted. The next morning we shot it in one take and went swimming at Lakeside the rest of the day.

Not only was I having a wonderful time with the picture and radio show, but I was also riding the pink cloud of my baptism. Every morning at six o'clock I went to Mass and Communion at Nazareth House, breakfasting occasionally with Father O'Dea, and then went on to the studio, only a short distance away. I would sit at my dressing table in early morning sunshine, putting on my make-up, full of thanksgiving for all my blessings—my radio show that was doing so well, the fine picture I was working in, my bounding good health. Mike was stationed in Alberta for pre-flight training, and I wrote to him regularly, though I received not so regular letters in return. I was not in the least lonely. My house was well run; my children would pounce on me when I came home in the evening, and I could play with them until their bedtime; then I could have a quiet dinner and study my lines for the next day. Finally there would be time for reading, and time for praying, until it was time for bed.

And I thought, in my happiness and content, that I was quite safe, that some intangible kind of magic had created an automatic immunity against the wiles and snares of the flesh. I failed to realize that I was still myself, that temptations would continue to exist, as they always had, and that now I had a greater responsibility than ever before to struggle against them. But I was not in the habit of struggling. And I had not counted on the fact that too much to drink, admiration, laughter, attention, an attractive man who said all the right things simply added up to dynamite for me. I found I had no strength at all—and my confession was full of shock and fright. Father was gentle and kind; he knew I needed strengthening as much as scolding. Life, he reminded me, must be for most of us a perpetual struggle against elements of our nature, and we had to be on guard constantly. But in tears of humiliation and shame, I resolved that it would never happen again.

I know that during all the years to follow my Faith never wavered. The Truths were as unquestionable, as undeniable, as the sunrise and sunset. But there were many difficulties that I did not recognize. The greatest of these was the responsibility as an individual that the Church imposed upon me. Some things it could do for me: it could define moral values; it could impress upon me the distinctions between right and wrong; it could provide the channels of Grace to help me live my Faith. But the rest— the doing and the struggling and the fighting—this was up to me. I was a human being with urgent appetites and strong desires, and I was wholly untrained in discipline. At the time, I would have indignantly denied that last fact. I considered myself well trained in discipline, but to me discipline meant only doing my work conscientiously, being punctual, being responsible to others with whom I worked, being obedient to the director. This involved only what people expect of me—what they had a right to expect. I still had to learn to do what God expected of me, and the lesson was to be a long and unhappy one.

One power I had developed to a high degree—unfortunately: the power of rationalizing my actions, of convincing myself that, despite the opinions and judgments of others, what I had done was, if not necessarily quite the right thing, the only possible thing to do. This had so often led me into blunders and calamities that I should have recognized the utter stupidity of persevering in such a course. I tried to convince myself that what I wanted to do was the only possible thing to do, even though it should violate all I had embraced in my baptism.

I worked into it through gradual stages, gently, imperceptibly. For one thing, I had not yet learned to separate the priest from his personality. I applied every reprimand and reproach from the pulpit to myself—often with good enough reason, I suppose. I was especially resentful when pictures and picture people were criticized. Our pastor often called on me at home, and he always asked for money. I always gave it to him—fifteen or twenty dollars. That was all right, but I didn't like it when the following Sunday, I had to listen to comments from the pulpit about how wasteful we picture people were, spending all our money on clothes and night clubs and never giving anything to the Church. I often came home from Mass irritable and "huffy." This was petty, I know—but it was important, for it made the next step much easier.

I also felt guilty about my parents. Mother's complaints about their hard life, her attitude of smiling martyrdom as she looked about my beautiful home and talked about "poor, hard-working Daddy," made me squirm, even though I felt I was not to blame for the conflict between us. If there had been a fair and friendly discussion and settlement when I first left home to get married, if my parents had been satisfied with a reasonable proportion of my earnings, they would ultimately have had much more, and I would not have had much less. But Daddy had held firmly to my entire income, and this had gone on too long. I felt that if I was to have anything I had to be defiant and ruthless—*"no more money."* Not fully certain that I was right, I had rebelled against my father's dictates, and I had got him "off my back." Then I could do as I pleased. Now I was about to rebel against the dictates of the Church, infinitely less sure that I was right. And God forgive me, I got the Church "off my back." So I could do as I pleased.

My "Hollywood Showcase" people had become a kind of family; after the show we would usually go next door to Brittingham's for supper, or up to the Brown Derby on Vine Street. William Winslow, one of the publicity men, I liked especially well. Bill was an enthusiastic flyer. I was interested because of Mike; his infrequent letters talked of nothing else (except perhaps how good it was to be with Englishmen!). I decided I wanted to learn, and Bill, having an instructor's license, was interested in seeing if he could teach a woman. He said he wouldn't guarantee it— but "Let's try." So we would drive to Burbank or Glendale, and later to what is now International Airport, and be back at the studios by ten o'clock. I enjoyed it thoroughly—it was difficult, but exciting—and Bill and I became good friends.

We often put in some flying time in the early evenings. One evening we had made several take-offs and landings, and just before coming in Bill took the controls because it was getting dark. The sun was setting; little lights began to blink on far below; it was so beautiful and I didn't want to land at all. The spell lasted through dinner at Brittingham's.

Bill had to go back to the studio to watch another show, and I went home. After the show he phoned me, saying he wanted to come out and see me. None of us knew much about Bill; everybody liked him, but his personal life was something of a mystery. He rarely talked about himself. But he had a great need to talk— and that night he did, for hours.

We met many times and the flying instructions continued. He was constantly working on ideas for promoting new shows, and when I had returned home after my flying lesson he would phone me every hour or so, with "How does this sound to you?"

My friend Bobsy Spencer had moved in with me. Her husband had gone to Washington with the Coast Guard, and I suggested she give up her own apartment and come in with me. I needed someone around, for I could not tolerate solitude now. If I was alone too much I heard a Voice, and I needed something to help me stop my ears. So we sat around in the evening, in the upstairs sitting room, highball glasses in hand, and discussed everything in the world, but especially Bill.

As flying student and instructor, he and I had ample opportunities for fun. We flew to San Francisco in his plane for a convention. My permit did not allow me to land or take off a plane of higher than 80 horsepower, but I could and did fly it after take-off. The long hours of quiet companionship, with only the drone of the motor, safe, alone in the sky with the rolling hills or the ocean beneath us, were wonderfully relaxing.

I began to feel the tension that grips a student when the time to solo approaches, when he and the instructor somehow feel that he is "ready." I passed my navigation. I passed my aerobatics; stalls and spins and recoveries. But ideally an instructor does not simply say, "Today you are going to solo." It should just "happen." We had been flying out of Los Angeles Airport, and for days there had been either a cross wind or a wind from the east. These presented problems that should not have to be faced on a first solo; everything must be "just right." I had been pretty unbearable around the house—Bobsy cautioned the children that I was "kind of nervous." For days now my pilot log had read, "Take off and land, 4." "Take off and land, 3." "Take off and land, 5." Nervous: I was ready to explode! Constance and Thad just kept out of my way.

Finally, *finally*, there was a west wind. For about a mile along Sepulveda Boulevard, just before we reached the airport, there were strings of little pennants, real estate ads. They were our first anxious knowledge of the wind, even before we could see the wind sock at the airport. Today they were blowing merrily, pointing *east!* But, superstitiously, not a word was said. Something else might not be "just right." Together we got into the Stinson, taxied out onto the field. I made three good take-offs and landings. Instead of going around the fourth time Bill had me stop and let him out; he said he wanted to look at the cotter pin on the tail wheel. He came back and slammed the door shut—from the outside. "Okay," he shouted over the engine noise. "Take it away. Keep your nose down."

I taxied back to the starting position, gunned my motor, and the little ship lifted, nice and easy. I was air-borne and alone, and I felt like yelling my head off in sheer exuberance. I headed out toward the ocean, made my first right turn just before I got to the beach, "stick and rudder right together," checked my tabs, right turn again, following the ten-minute pattern through to landing. Bill was sweating and grinning as he climbed into the ship. "Danged if you ain't a flyer!" I got the customary treatment back at the hangar—everybody pounds and pummels the neophyte—and there was a great to-do. I phoned home that I had made it. Then I dropped Bill off at the station and drove back to San Remo, where Thad was waiting with drinks all set up. "You'll have to excuse me," he said, "but I'm going to drink with you. I'm that relieved."

November 25, 1941. By this time I was hopelessly enmeshed in my undisciplined emotions. I think I have never told anyone the full extent of my blind, all-consuming infatuation for Bill. I concealed it as much as I could even from him, for most men are afraid of being loved too much, and I loved him too much. A simple account of the things we did and the places we went would not even suggest the state I was in. When I wasn't with him I was counting the minutes until I could see him again.

We both belonged to a club of Southern California flyers who once every year took over a resort or hotel somewhere in the state for a weekend. This year the resort was to be La Quinta, and Bill and I flew down. It was a fine weekend, with a congenial crowd and bright warm weather, lots of swimming and dancing and talk about the Japanese and the threat of war. The group broke up

Sunday morning; Bill had to be back for a Sunday evening show. As we came in for a landing at Grand Central Airport, an odd sight greeted us: not a single plane was on the field; none was even in sight. A colored boy came with a step to help us down from the plane; he was babbling something about the Japanese attacking Pearl Harbor, and telling us to get our plane off the field and into a hangar. We got the car and turned on the radio—and of course there was nothing else on the airwaves. My pilot log concludes: "12/7/41—Japanese attack on Pearl Harbor—all civilian aircraft grounded."

The war changed everyone's life, even my insulated and well-protected one. The pattern was different. There was more work to do; show people always find themselves recruited for selling jobs. I went on innumerable bond tours, through camps and factories. I made spot-announcement records for radio to sell bonds, to recruit for Civilian Defense, to do any number of tasks made necessary by the war. The studios began to retrench, and since I was free-lancing my jobs in pictures became fewer; the studios were using only contract players. At Christmas time I made a picture for Paramount, *The Palm Beach Story*, with Claudette Colbert. And Mike came home for a two-day final leave before going to Toronto to await overseas orders. He was very handsome in his R.C.A.F. uniform.

We were casually friendly and sophisticated about our relationship. We discussed divorce amicably and decided to go ahead with one. Tono would stay with me.

Bill had gone to Washington to organize communication centers. "Showcase" was limping along in its final weeks. No one was much interested in young people with ambitions for careers; the war effort was the important thing. I went to MGM for two pictures, and while I was making the first of them, a comedy with Herbert Marshall, my father suddenly had a severe stroke. Poor Mother was almost uncontrollably frantic. I had Daddy brought by ambulance to Cedars of Lebanon Hospital and called Sam Hirschfield to take care of him. He had a private room, private nursing—the best care we could get. Since Bobsy had gone to Washington to work in OWI, I had Mother come to stay with me. She spent most of her time at the hospital, and I went each evening after work to be with Daddy. He was in an almost continuous coma; only occasionally was he barely conscious. Once he opened his eyes and saw me in the room, and he whispered, "You're a good girl." They were the last words he ever spoke to me. He was unconscious for about four more days, and then he quietly slipped into death.

I had called Father O'Dea to ask if Daddy could be given the last rites, but Father told me that since he was unconscious, and had never given any indication he wanted to enter the Church, there was nothing that could be done. It was out of his hands entirely. In my ignorance I felt this was unreasonable and unfair.

According to his wishes, he was cremated and the ashes interred at Forest Lawn. I had Mother move in with me. I arranged the upstairs sitting room into a bedroom for her and tried to cheer her by telling her she could be a help to me. Thad and Constance had left, regretfully and tearfully. They had been wonderful servants, but now Thad was going into aircraft work and Constance into teaching. And then began the ordeal of trying to work and keep the house in something less than complete upheaval. Help was scarce and poor. And Mother turned out to be a real drag. She was idle; time hung heavily on her hands, and when I got a couple in she would nag at them until they left. I tried to explain to her, in the by now well-worn phrase, that there was a war on and we had to be satisfied with people who were independent and incompetent. The house seemed much bigger now, and Mother fretted that she had to spend too much time there. Because gasoline was rationed, she couldn't get a car that enabled her to drive around as much as she liked. She was with the children all day, and she spoiled them; she would argue with me, in their presence, if I disciplined them. I put Tono in a nursery school, which helped some. But it had become a complete nightmare. I can't even sort out the order of events between 1942 and 1944.

For a long while I listened when Mother wanted to talk about Daddy. I knew how dreadful his loss was for her; the ground had been cut out from under her, and she needed someone to talk to. It is interesting to me now, in the light of my better understanding of them and their relationship to me, how they had drawn closer together after I cut them out of my life. Mother told me how much kinder Daddy had been to her, how rarely they quarreled after they moved to the farm in Lancaster. They had been happy, she said, in the rural atmosphere, the quiet desert, the almonds in bloom, the nights of peaceful calm.

But after a time her constant living in the past began to weary me, with its "Daddy used to say" and "Daddy used to do." I felt it was time to return to the present, to go on living. Younger people have their own special kinds of cruelty toward older bereaved people. And of course my precious privacy was gone again. If I came home, tired and irritable from work, and wanting a few quiet moments to mix a drink and stretch out on the couch in the library, there would come a knock—always "timid"—at the door, and Mother would open it and look in, with "*Excuse* me for bothering you. I know you're tired, but I think you should know what's been going on around here today." I became so exasperated with her criticism of the current help—"And I said to him . . . and then he said" kind of monologue—that I finally threw up my hands and said, "All right. *You* run the house. I'll be the visitor." Except that I would not tolerate interference with the children. I had never had any "bedtime trouble"; it was taken for granted that when the time came, off they should go. When they got older and could read the clock, I usually gave them a warning—"five more minutes." But Mother started in with "Oh, let them stay up just a few minutes more," and soon I had whining and dissatisfied children on my hands, and bedtime became a mess.

Like most civilian pilots, Bill and I had joined the Civil Air Patrol. Since I was on layoff from the studio and had time on my hands, I went down to Wing Headquarters and said, "I have two hands, and I can type a little. I have at least normal intelligence. Put me to work." The office was a little hole in the wall, with two full-time stenographers, badly overworked. They looked at me doubtfully, sure that I was doing it just for the publicity, but after a few weeks of showing up on time, of learning the filing system, of taking fingerprints and applications, I had earned their full approval. I remember that it was July, because Rosie (the head secretary) and I worked all the night of July fourth. We had received orders to organize a task force, a new base that was to be opened in the Southwest. Since the work was all voluntary, we had the enormous job of contacting, by wire and telephone, ninety pilots with private planes from the entire state of California. The paper work was endless—description of planes, listing of radio equipment, tabulation of the flying hours of the pilots. Bill was in Washington, but he agreed to volunteer for a thirty-day stint to help set up the base. The most serious trouble was that the office would be handled by local women volunteers, and our Wing Commander was fretting because there would be no one from Wing HQ to organize them. They wouldn't know any of the routine detail; they wouldn't even know how to set up a military letter, or how our cross files worked.

I had a brilliant and not altogether patriotic inspiration. I would—and did—get a leave of absence from "Hollywood Show-case" for four weeks, and I volunteered to go south myself. Everyone thought it was wonderfully patriotic and mysterious; they knew only that I was on duty with the CAP, but the location was a secret. In my uniform, and identified only as "Mary del Campo, plotting-board operator," I traveled high priority to the Gulf.

Bill had already arrived. He was waiting as I got off the plane, and it was so good to see him that my knees were weak.

There was lots of work to be done. I helped set up the office in town; then I was transferred to "Operations" at the field. "Operations" was a little three-sided building that had housed the airport fire truck. We had only a short-wave radio, a direct teletype to the main base in Florida, a crude plotting board, and heat and mosquitoes. The little planes were tied down all over the field; CAP hangars were still under construction, but somehow we managed to get two ships out every two hours from dawn until sunset.

The evenings we could devote to pleasure. The weather cooled slightly, and we could go for Mexican food to a little outdoor restaurant. The time was up all too soon.

In Hollywood we developed a new show for Roma Wines. I was again the emcee, but the show was a review. We had two comedy sequences, one with Mischa Auer and one with Charlie Ruggles, and we usually had a guest star. I read the commercials, introduced the "spots," and occasionally was a part of the sequence with Charlie or Mischa. It was a great deal more work than "Showcase" had been—a day's rehearsal before the show, and rehearsal on the day of the show itself. And I also had a fifteen-minute show, one afternoon a week, for recruiting WAVES. The several jobs and the constant driving between San Remo and the studios drained away energy, time, and gasoline that I could have put to better use. I had a sort of triangle of driving, from San Remo to Metro to CBS and back home again. I had to find some way to conserve both energy and gasoline.

I solved the problem nicely. I found a little apartment near Fairfax and Fountain, right in the middle of my triangle, quite new and pleasantly furnished. It was on the corner of the building, on the second floor, with a stairway in the rear by the garages. After I explained my gasoline problem I was able to rent it with no difficulty.

It was a refuge for me. I could get away overnight the night before the show; I brought the evening dresses that I wore so that I could dash over from CBS and change. I could be myself, away from Mother, whose constant chatter got on my nerves. And I always felt calmer, and better able to cope with the problems at San Remo.

At home I was worried by another situation I saw developing. Tono was becoming a fussy, petulant boy, the victim of having too many women around him. We had a woman housekeeper now, and there was Mother, and me, and various friends of Mother's who often came to the house. He was a beautiful boy, with irresistible short curls, and everyone made him aware of it. After some inquiries I entered him down at the Elsinore Military Academy. Mother thought it was "cruel," but I had talked to the headmaster and the housemother, and I liked what I saw. There was a pool—he would be taught to swim; there was riding, and camping, and boys of his own age. I asked the headmaster how such young boys reacted to being taken away from their homes, and he said, "You wouldn't be flattered if I told you how quickly they adjust." I drove down on the monthly visiting days, and even though I hated not having him with me it was consoling to see him brown and healthy, rough-housing with the other boys—being a boy.

Mother began to complain louder about being so far out, with too little gasoline. She wanted to be where she could window-shop, where there were people and life. There was too little to do. The house was too quiet. So I found an apartment for her, on the first floor of the same building I was in, and she had a place with neighbors, people to talk with. But this presented another problem at San Remo. Marylyn had been going to the parish school for several years, and she had to be taken there in the car. After Thad had left, I took her to school and called for her whenever I could. When I was making a picture, this was impossible, and later, with the two radio shows, there were three days a week when I was not able to. Mother said she would do it—"anything to earn my keep"—but now Mother was no longer there to do it. I tried to enter Marylyn as a boarding student at Marymount School, but they told me they did not accept children of divorced parents. So I entered her as a boarder in the seventh grade of the Westlake School for Girls. I was not very happy about it, but it was the best I could do. (It turned out to be a good "best"; she was happy there, and still goes back to alumnae meetings and keeps in touch with her friends.) The trouble was that I felt guilty about everything, about every decision I made. I questioned whether I was doing the right thing or whether I was simply shoving everything else out of the way so nothing could hold me back whenever Bill should whistle.

At the same time, and all the time, I was aware that Bill did not love me. Not at all. But it was another reality that was not to be faced.

Being with Bill, alone or discussing a program with the writers, just *being* with him, was the difference between living and not living.

I decided to shut up San Remo and move to the apartment. The big house was just one empty room without the children. I missed them sorely; that they were obviously thriving was a consolation, but it didn't make up for not having them. So I closed up the big house; the shutters were pulled over the windows, the furniture was draped with sheets, the utilities were turned off. I kept the gardener and hired patrol service.

I thought the cozy warmth of the apartment would help my loneliness, but my hopes were empty ones. Bill had left his radio job to take a position with a network, and he was busier than he had ever been before. He came to the little apartment less and less. Many dinners were prepared, only to be thrown into the garbage can because at the last minute he would be "stuck for dinner with a client."

I don't know when I began walking in my sleep. In the corner of the hall I had a little knickknack shelf with a few figurines on it. One morning I went into the bathroom, and there on the flat tile edge of the tub were the figurines, all in a row. Mother was quite capable of a practical joke like that, and my first thought was that she had slipped in and put them there just to let me know she had been in. But the front door was locked and chain-bolted, and the back door was hooked. That night, I put face cream on the soles of my feet and dusted them with talcum. The next morning prints led from my bed into the living room, and around and around in circles in the room.

I went to see my doctor and told him about it. And he told me that sleepwalking was often the symptom of an insoluble problem. It scared me; I was afraid I might go outside the building and be picked up by the police.

My self-imposed quota of two highballs after dinner began to increase steadily. And there were crying sessions after I went to bed. One night quite late Bill phoned; he had been working at the office, and he had phoned to say good night before going home. I was very drunk, crying and incoherent. He drove over, and came up and quieted me down. My shame was almost unbearable—that I should cause him any problems with my drinking!

My lease on the apartment was almost up. The Roma show had come to the end of its run. I no longer had any reason to live in town. So I moved back to San Remo. Mother made me feel guilty about it; with some strange logic she accused me of having moved into the apartment just to get her out of the house. Now that she was settled, I was pulling out. There was no pleasing her. She was getting a hundred dollars a month, plus her rent; she had a car and she was living in a pleasant place, accessible to all the things she wanted. It would probably have made her happy if I had become a little girl again, someone she could scold and watch over and "work her fingers to the bone" for. But I wasn't having any.

I hired a good housekeeper, a Frenchwoman, somewhat deaf, and with very little English. It was a good arrangement; I didn't want a servant I would have to talk much with. She was clean, a good cook—a real "old country" woman. She understood food coupons better than I ever had, and she could always wangle a carton of cigarettes—"*pour Madame*"—from the grocery store in spite of her language handicap.

A time of strange emptiness began for me, for Bill's job had taken him East. A beautiful house of fifteen rooms, and in it only myself, a deaf Frenchwoman, and a little dog. In a way I was content, or at least I felt something that passed for contentment. The tension about Bill was released; I no longer wondered every moment whether I would see him or hear from him. I had no friends, and I wanted none. The only people I cared about were Mischa and Joyce, and on Sundays I usually went out to spend the afternoon and have dinner with them.

This was late in 1944. On the advice of my agent I had signed a long-term contract with Metro. It had been my experience that I made more money and got better parts when I free-lanced. But with the war, policies had changed. Free-lancing no longer paid so well—the gaps between pictures were too long. Someday I must get a list of the pictures I made for Metro; I was in a good many of them, but they were an undistinguished lot. My vanity suffered; at thirty-eight I was being put into "mother" roles. That was all they could see in me. The famous jinx of receiving an Academy Award seemed to be upon me. I remember that I was Kathryn Grayson's mother in *Thousands Cheer*, Elizabeth Taylor's mother in *Cynthia*, the mother of a good-sized family in *Meet Me in St. Louis*. I felt tied hand and foot. A light flared briefly when Noel Coward phoned me from London, saying he wanted me to play the second wife in the London production of *Blithe Spirit* with him. But Metro said no; I was going into another picture.

In this emotional and professional twilight I had time on my hands—time for my evening routine of writing long letters to Bill, listening to the evening schedule of radio shows, putting away about a fifth of scotch a night, and crawling off to bed about two or three in the morning, to sleep until noon the next day.

There came an offer to do a play in New York, a new play by Clare Kummer called *Many Happy Returns*, with Henry Hull starring. I came back to life. This was a chance to be near Bill, so I decided I wanted to do a play. I went in and did battle for permission to go—and I got it.

They gave me a leave of absence for six months, I think it was, and I went to New York. I had always stayed at the St. Regis Hotel; through the years the management always saw to it that I had the same suite on the seventeenth floor. But the war had changed things, and I didn't know what I was getting into. I was lucky to get a room, and I could have it for only five days; that was now the rule in all hotels. I had been foolish enough to bring my dog, Miss Jo, with me, and since many hotels would not accept pets the number of places I could stay was still further reduced. But I could take it all in stride; nothing was too inconvenient, for I was in New York and I would see Bill.

I thought longingly of the times when we were both wearing old, greasy clothes, working around the plane on a little flying field in the desert, and of the dinners where we had eaten chili and put a coin in the jukebox to hear our favorite tune. Now it was Richelieu's for cocktails or the Barberry Room for lunch. And the clamor and urgency of New York were everywhere about us. He took me to the formal opening of the CBS television broadcasting; we left before it was over and rushed to his office, where he had a set. He tuned in the program, and I gasped in amazement. It was the first television I had ever seen.

In New York I was an asset to Bill in his job. I was decorative and important, and he liked having me meet his business colleagues. I was aware of this, but it was all right.

Then the play went into rehearsal. Henry Hull was not only starring in the play *Many Happy Returns* but also directing it. Rex O'Malley, with whom I had done a picture a few years before, Neil Hamilton, and Jayne Meadows also had major parts. We rehearsed three weeks in town, with Henry and the producer and the writer all fighting continually about changes in the script. It was a very light comedy, and couldn't take heavy handling, but Henry was trying to shift more and more of the play onto himself. He was the star, and he was trying to make the play a starring vehicle, which it never could be. We opened in New Haven to dreadful notices, and the rewriting began all over again. My part was well written and luckily did not need much change, so it wasn't too hard for me. The trouble was that once a play has opened and there have to be more rehearsals there is never time for proper rest.

After New Haven we went to Philadelphia for two weeks. There Henry Hull left the show. We had a new director, and parts were reshuffled. Then we went back to New York for more rehearsals. I rented an apartment in the Sixties—an awful place, dismal and dark, and atrociously furnished. But it was a place to live.

Rex and Neil and I stayed pretty close together. They both were good Catholics, and Rex, in a very pleasant way, saw to it that I got to Mass. I told him of my conversion since I had last seen him, but I added that I wasn't working at it and just didn't feel like going to Mass. "But you can't do that," Rex protested, and cheerfully escorted me off to Mass. The first time was in Philadelphia, on the Feast of the Immaculate Conception. It was a rainy day, and I was amazed at the attendance; even the aisles were jammed. I don't remember how I felt; I can't separate that day from the times I went to the same church in later years when I was in another play. But Rex did convince me that even though I could not receive the Sacraments, I could at least go to Mass. As I knelt at the Consecration, I would watch and envy the people going to the altar rail. Many years later, when I had made my peace with God, I was discussing my religion with a non-Catholic, a writer, who said, "It's the pageantry that appeals to you, Mary, because you're an actress." And I replied, "Well, why not? The Lord certainly knows what I am most sensitive to. His appeal is different to everyone." But actually there is not much "pageantry" in a six o'clock Mass of a Monday morning.

Finally we went to Boston, where we were to open on Christmas Day. It was a miserable time for me; I had never before been away from the children at Christmas. And Bill had come up for our dress rehearsal on Christmas Eve, but he couldn't stay for the opening—and that did nothing to cheer me up. I was also worried that the play might hurt me professionally; I saw that it had been a bad move, and I was about to call it off. But an actress I met in Boston, Jean Dixon, gave me some good advice. She told me to take it to New York; I had nothing to be ashamed of personally. The play would not run, but "Let them see you. Don't let them be able to tag you with the label of being an 'out of town' failure." I shall always be grateful to her, because it worked out just as she had said. The play was panned in New York, but the critics were kind to me. They accepted me as an actress rather than as a film player. "She has a flair for comedy, hitherto kept a secret by the movies"; "a magnetic quality for an audience"; "come back and let us see you again—in something good." We played six performances and closed.

After the play's demise I hung around New York hoping something might be going into rehearsal right away, but it was late in the season for new plays—it was February now, 1945. I went down to Baltimore with my agent, Gloria Safier, to see a play starring Franchot Tone; the leading lady was to be replaced. But it was a bad play, and I couldn't afford to take another chance. I did a couple of radio shows, but that was all. I tried to close my eyes to the fact that Bill and I were growing further apart; there was no change in him, but I felt that he was too busy for me. His life was his job, and only occasionally did he even seem conscious of me. From what he said, it looked as though his job would keep him in New York permanently. I was not at all happy.

And little Jo was getting thin and weak; she had not taken well to the traveling and the cold weather. Bill took a look at her one afternoon in the apartment and said, "You're going to lose your little doggie if you don't get her back home." It was true, and although I felt Bill was being more emphatic about it than necessary I decided to go back to California. Bill and Gloria saw me off at Grand Central. The train started to move. I don't remember anything except that I had some scotch in my suitcase, and safe within the four walls of that drawing room I was going to get very drunk.

For a while it was good to be back. I re-established contact with my children. Marylyn was doing very well at Westlake; she was bubbly and happy as she showed me her room and introduced me to her "suite mates." We drove down to see Tono, who was brimming over with the news of how well he could swim and ride.

Bill's letters to me were cheerful, always including a bit of gossip about someone we knew or a clipping that was amusing. They were the brief letters of a busy man, typed by his secretary. But they were important to me, and I learned to recognize the sound of the mailman's car in the morning.

Time dragged along slowly. Metro had nothing for me; I was still on my leave of absence, and no picture was scheduled. When I heard that workers were needed for the Arts and Crafts section of the Red Cross for Occupational Therapy at the Army Hospital in Van Nuys, I volunteered my services. After several indoctrination meetings, and a few classes, I was assigned to plastics work. I was very much interested, as I always am in learning something new; I learned to work with a band saw, drill press, and other power tools, and I donned my uniform, a green smock with the Red Cross insignia and the Arts and Skills button, and went to work with "my patients."

We worked in shifts of three days a week from nine until three. The workshop was a bedlam of sounds, made mostly by the power tools in our department. Most of the boys were under orders from the doctors to put in time in work therapy, and it was our job to get them interested. Sometimes it was pretty tough; many of them were crippled, battle-weary children. But it was rewarding to get a boy started on something simple, such as a picture frame that had only to be cut to size with a saw, sanded, buffed, and joined. And it was encouraging if he came in a few days later with a picture of his girl and asked to make a frame that would fit it. Or to start a boy on a molded salad fork and spoon, which began as a job to be done, sullenly and unwillingly; then, as it began to look like something, to watch him brighten and ask, "Say, do you think I could get this mailed to my mother?"

I had homework to do, roughing in models, sawing templates. Gradually I developed a little workshop in what had been the chauffeur's room off the garage. I got some hand tools, a small hand drill, a jig saw, a sanding machine—all kinds of toys! Toys to distract me, to work for others and take my mind off myself, to take up the slack of time.

One afternoon Bill phoned me. He was in town for only two days, but he'd get out to see me in the morning. In the morning! No, he couldn't come out tonight; he was tied up by business.

He came, and he was full of news. Television was on its way in; sales promotion demanded new ideas, new methods. I listened, and showed him my workshop, which he duly admired. But he was in haste, and I was frantic to detain him. "Will you call me after the meeting?" "Can't you have dinner with me?" No, he'd have to hurry on. He looked at me for a long moment and said, "You are a very wonderful woman." Nothing else. No "I'll see you." He just got in his car and drove away.

I sat on the steps to the entrance of my workshop, dry-eyed. I sat so still for so long, thinking nothing, feeling nothing, that when I rose my body ached. It was all over. I felt old and tired and lifeless.

Eleven

If this were a script from my own fairy tale world, we would now dissolve to our wretched Hollywood Magdalene, veiled in penitent grey, walking up the steps of St. Patrick's, with a shaft of high-wattage sunlight on her shoulders, accompanied by full chorus and MGM orchestra swelling to a triumphant fade-out.

Unfortunately it is instead the document of a woman who has had her wits blown out of her; who prays, perhaps—I don't remember—but if she does it is for the wrong thing. And God is patient, and permits her to choose her own futile consolations.

It was only a twenty-minute drive, over the pass on Sepulveda Boulevard, from the house of my friends Mischa Auer and his wife, Joyce, to San Remo. The pass was not then the heavily traveled road it is now; there was practically no traffic. Late on Sunday night I was driving home after a party at Mischa's; the white line began to split and form an X. I shook my head to clear it, but it wouldn't clear; and then I discovered that indispensable aid to drunk drivers—close one eye. It frightened me into making a firm resolution. To stop drinking? Oh no, that would have been sensible. But never to drive if I had been drinking. It was a resolution that stuck, however, and it probably saved quite a few lives, including my own.

For I was making the trip between San Remo and the Valley very often now. My Valley friends were a lively and congenial group—Mischa and Joyce, John and Barbara Mahin, Ann and Mort Greene, the Colonel Barrys, and several others. Among them, I could drug my memory. Everybody held perpetual open house; people were always dropping in for drinks and food and swimming. Then somebody would barbecue steaks, and Mort would play the piano, and it was all jolly good fun.

I couldn't return their hospitality, because my housekeeper was grumpy when she was put to extra work; besides, the house had no swimming pool, and it was too far from the Valley. The group preferred to circulate within its own territory. Everyone urged me to "move to the Valley," to sell my white elephant of a house and get a small home in their neighborhood so I wouldn't have to be alone so much.

Being alone was not good for me. I had settled again into a meaningless and dangerous routine. Except on Sundays, I would not take a drink until after five o'clock in the evening, but at night, after my tray dinner, I would turn on my radio for my evening schedule of shows, with a scotch and soda on the coffee table beside the couch. After the shows went off the air and the radio was silent, I would have several "nightcaps" as I sat there staring blankly at the book titles on the shelves, or watching the goldfish in the large replica of a brandy snifter going round and round, round and round. I never remembered getting to bed. I still walked in my sleep; just how often, I don't know, but I sometimes woke early in the morning to find I was standing at the head of the stairs.

I looked around for a place in the Valley, and found a lovely little house on Hayvenhurst set back from the street on an acre all planted in lemon trees. I can hardly remember how it looked then, I built on and altered it so extensively later. Wes and a contractor looked it over and pronounced it to be well built; the price was right; the whole thing was a sensible move. My Valley friends were happy about it, and helped me select shrubs and vines and flowers for the landscaping. I kept the furniture from San Remo that I would need, tagged it for moving, and sold the rest. I stayed at San Remo for a while, until the new bedroom at Hayvenhurst was finished. It was good to be planning something—and the thought occurred to me that this was the first home that I had selected. And it was going to be permanent, I told myself. "I'm through moving. Here I shall live, and here I shall die." With my children, until they grew up and left home, and then myself. I didn't want anyone else.

But my friends had other ideas. "You ought to have *somebody*," they said. John Mahin was sure I'd like a friend of his, a Sergeant Tommy Wheelock, in the Weather Service for the Air Force, down at Long Beach. I thanked him and mentally rejected the whole idea.

The children both came home for the summer, and I had to dismiss Frieda; she was too old and grumpy to cope with them. She referred to Marylyn as "dot girl"; she would chase them out of the kitchen with a broom, and generally complain about their mischievousness. On Sundays I often took Tono out to John's pool for a swim; there was usually quite a crowd of servicemen around the pool, boys from nearby camps. One Sunday I was introduced to Sergeant Wheelock. He turned out to be a big man who looked like a stuffed caterpillar in his uniform, not at all handsome, with very heavy eyebrows and heavy lines like parentheses around a thin mouth, all of which gave him the rather sad look of a St. Bernard. He had a pleasant voice, and he was most amiable. He talked with me during much of the afternoon, telling me he had known John since they were boys in prep school together. He had gone to Groton, and then to Harvard. "Never graduated, though. Too stupid." He hoped he would see me again —next weekend, perhaps.

And the next weekend he was there again, almost irritatingly attentive, lighting cigarettes, getting drinks, hanging around—and showing his drinks rather too much. He had a talent that he inflicted on people whether they liked it or not: he played Dixieland jazz on the piano. Now I know there are some people who think Dixieland is an art form, the real folk music of our country, and they speak of it in hushed tones. But I don't understand it and I don't like it.

While Sergeant Wheelock was hammering out "Twelfth Street Rag," I had a chance to say to John, "Is *this* the man you thought I might go for?"

He smiled. "Yep."

"Why, John," I said, "this is the dullest man I've ever met."

"He's a sweet guy, Mary—a great guy."

Well, I knew how often I'd been wrong in my judgment of men; perhaps I was doing him an injustice. So when he phoned to ask to take me to dinner, I accepted.

In civvies he looked much nicer, well groomed and clean. We had a good evening, away from all the hubbub at John's. He told me about his background, which was an impressive one, although he was modest enough about it. He was real Boston blueblood; his grandfather had held a chair of literature at Harvard. He had lived in China until he was ten, when his father died and his mother brought him to Groton. (John later filled in more of the biography. He had already lost a fortune in the market crash, but he was soon to inherit a large sum left in trust for him in China.) He had been a stockbroker in Chicago, but when the war broke out he had joined the Air Corps. Being over age for active duty, he had "fought the battle of Long Beach" in the weather department. As soon as he was discharged he hoped to go into some business out here.

I took him back to the house for a nightcap, and he looked at the furniture stacked up for moving. "Why fool around with movers?" he said. "I can get leave and move you in the station wagon. It'll be simple." I was ready to move. My bedroom was completed, and construction on the children's wing had begun. Wes had put San Remo up for sale. So I told Tommy to go ahead.

The move was rather fun, except that Tommy would show up early in the morning, while I was still at breakfast.

He was like the strong man in the circus. For a gentle man, not especially muscular in appearance, he handled the heavy pieces of furniture as though they were toys. Loads of books and furniture began to pile up at Hayvenhurst.

He seemed to be so much in love that nothing was too much trouble. He ran errands. He wouldn't let me lift a finger. "Just tell me what you want." He began to make himself a part of my life.

He told me he wanted to marry me, and he knew how I felt. "Of course you're afraid. But I want to take care of you."

"Frankly, Tommy," I told him, "I'm still sick. I'm trying to get over something that was serious. I need time."

"Well," he replied, "don't you at least want someone to be around while you're getting well?"

I thought this was the nicest thing I had ever heard. And I began to think of him, not in the usual romantic light, but as someone dependable, who could help me bring up my children. And I began to see all sorts of nice things about him. He was thoughtful, not only about me, but about Marylyn and Tono, whom he treated intelligently. He was always good-natured, never surly or belligerent.

He was discharged from the Army late in the summer. He took a room in a house near John's, but he was at my house from dawn till dark. It was like the fable of the camel who put his head inside the tent and soon had moved in completely.

I was working in a picture, a long, elaborate production called *Fiesta* (playing a do-nothing mother role, of course), that called for a location trip to Mexico City. I went down about the first of December. The children were in school, so Tommy said he would stay in the house until I got back and "attend to things." I was glad to have him do it, for there was much to be attended to—details about a new wing, a cesspool to be dug, a watering system to be installed.

I didn't like Mexico. It reminded me of Mike, and all the things he had said about it. I disliked the altitude; it gave me nosebleeds. I got dysentery, despite heeding carefully all the warnings

of drink only bottled water. I went to the garden canal of Xochi-
milco and was badly disillusioned. I had made a picture with
Richard Barthelmess called *The Whip*, for which the studios had
built a back-lot reproduction of the canals that had it all over the
original! I had reclined in a cushioned gondola in a beautiful
white gown, with a mantilla on my head; there were real flowers
and lovely music from the other boats. No dank odor, no banana
peels and other ugly refuse floating in the water, no pursuit by
boats selling souvenirs, no mendicant boys. The company moved
to Puebla for some bull-ring scenes, and the town was noisy with
celebrations of the approaching Christmas season. I went slowly
crazy in my room, trying to sleep. And in my irritation I drank.

I went to Mass in the beautiful cathedral there. It was the
largest I had ever seen, rich with gold and gilt and lace. I found
another reason to be annoyed at the Church—I had to find all the
"reasons" I could. I thought how wrong it was that all the poor
peasants, the women with their black rebozos and sickly, ill-fed
babies in them, should be dropping their precious coins into a
gold plate, while the priests and servers were dressed in elaborate
lace. If I had known anything of Mexican history I would have
known that those poor peasants were probably giving thanks to
God that they could openly attend Mass.

I was impatient to get home, and oddly enough, I was impatient to get back to Tommy. I was surprised to find that I missed
him; at least I missed his attentions, his doing things for me. His
letters were newsy and brief, with no sentimental nonsense—but
he did rather flatly inform me that "you're going to be a married
woman as soon as you get back."

I became Mrs. Thomas Gordon Wheelock on December 24,
1945. We were married in John Mahin's living room, with John as
Tommy's best man—and Marylyn as my bridesmaid. She could
hardly keep from crying, because "it is just all so *beautiful*, Mom-
mie!" She was a walking exclamation point at that time anyway.

Mother was there, and wished me happiness with a resigned
air. She had come to the house before the ceremony; I was still
in my white terry-cloth robe, with my hair up in bobby pins, and

I was having a "shortie" of brandy to brace myself. As she came in, I said, "Behold the bride!" I meant my general state of dishabille, but for a split second I beheld myself—doing the expedient thing, the unwise thing, and, although I tried not to think of that, the *wrong* thing. I had not even the excuse of being "in love." I took refuge in the present moment: get dressed, have a drink, be happy.

Tommy and I spent the rest of the day delivering Christmas remembrances around the Valley. Everyone was a bit cold to us; we had not invited any of our friends to the wedding. Because John's house was small, we had decided to have no one but my family and John's—Tommy had no relatives on the Coast. But we both had long lists of friends all over town, and we felt we couldn't confine our invitations to just a few.

In the evening we sat on the steps of what was now "our" home. It was a soft night. The kids were tucked away in the library. I felt a quiet hope that I had at last found my harbor.

The idea of Tommy Wheelock being broke was treated as simply one of those absurdities that happen occasionally in life. And so I accepted it. But it was no joke that five years after our marriage I had exactly $192.86 in the bank and we were over thirty thousand dollars in debt.

I had blown up another pink balloon that burst in my face. I had told myself that I would slow down our drinking after we were married. The summer had been confused and trying, with the dilemma of whether to marry or not, the move to Hayvenhurst, the parties. But now it was no better.

I enjoyed fixing up my home; I would not give up my hope that this house would be permanent, and the things I bought and developed for it were done with a view toward permanence. Tono's and Marylyn's rooms were planned so they could grow up in them. I bought some nice bits of early Americana—an old "flower clock" ticked comfortably on the mantel; a cobbler's bench with a red leather seat stood in front of the long couch. The original bedroom was now a library lined ceiling to floor with shelves of books. And in the living room was a spinet piano on which Tommy could hammer out his Dixieland.

It was all comfortable and friendly, but there was also conflict and frustration. I often walked in my sleep. I would awaken in total darkness, without the least idea of what part of the house I was in, completely disoriented, wailing tearfully for Tommy to come and get me. To help me he bought several small lights that could be connected directly into the floor outlets, but when I awoke, though I could see where the light was and knew where it was supposed to be, I was still completely turned around. In cold weather the glowing embers of the fire dying in the fireplace gave me the impression of being at the wrong end of the room.

In order to have the car Tommy always drove me to and from the studio. He was an early riser anyway; he liked to get up and "get going." I began to suffer more from hang-overs, and learned the comfort of the quick shot in the morning. It was wonderful to feel better, not to want to scream with nerves while I was being made up and having my hair dressed at the studio in the noisy tension of getting people ready to be on the set on time.

A few months after we were married, a neighbor of Mother's called us in the middle of the night to tell us that Mother had had a heart attack. A doctor had been called, and he had declared that she was in a very serious condition. We dressed and hurtled over the pass to Fountain Avenue. We found her conscious, but badly frightened, and we stayed until a nurse arrived. She had been given sedatives, and was asleep by that time, but the doctor told us that the attack was serious, and he recommended that I have a specialist in for her. She had never been herself since Daddy died. Always an emotional woman, she had never recovered from the shock of his death. When she had come out to the house, I had noticed that she was developing a number of nervous habits—fidgeting, playing with her necklace, always moving her hands and her feet.

We hired nurses to put in twenty-hour duty, and every afternoon I went in and stayed with her for four hours. She was made of tough material, and soon was able to be up for short periods and feed herself. Never had I, so naturally impatient, had such a lesson in patience. She had become even more garrulous and bitter; when I gave her her dinner I noticed that she was becoming like a little animal, picking up food in her fingers, poking and stirring around in her dish, taking quick little bites greedily. I asked the doctor about this personality change, for I was alarmed by it; he told me that such an attack often affected the higher centers of the brain. He did not hold out much hope for recovery, although she might live a very long time. But she would always need care. The only solution seemed to be a nursing home. Of course she resisted this, poor thing; she became very ugly about it, but the doctor and I finally persuaded her to go into a pleasant home on Beechwood Drive. She had a bright, comfortable room, and I brought as many of her personal things as I could in order to surround her with familiar objects. For a while she seemed to enjoy the presence of other women her own age she could talk to.

She had been there only a short time when the head nurse called me one evening after dinner and told me indignantly that they were neither equipped nor licensed to take care of mental cases, and that Mother was wandering around disturbing all the other patients with her screaming and groaning. Suddenly she said, "I'll have to hang up now—here she comes again." And I shall never forget the sounds I heard over the phone. I could hear her maniacal shrieks and groans. I was distraught; Tommy was in Arizona, and I didn't know what I should do. Then the nurse phoned again, and told me she had called the doctor and he had sent Mother to General Hospital.

John and Barbara Mahin went with me to carry out the grim duty of having her committed. I sat with a number of other people in a dismal hall; patients were confined behind bars while a judge, a recorder, and a physician went from cell to cell. Mother had contracted pneumonia, and she was mercifully unconscious. The judge ascertained that I had the means to put her in a private institution if she lived long enough to get there. She was taken to Rosemead Sanitarium, a fine place where she had wonderful care. She recovered from the pneumonia, but her mind deteriorated rapidly. Tommy drove me out there once a week, and I usually cried most of the way back home. Sometimes she knew me for a short while, but then I would become her sister or some friend, and I had to listen to some hair-raising tales about myself. She confided that "Lucile's husband, Tommy, committed suicide. She drove him to it." She was fastened to her bed by a kind of belt so that she couldn't get up. She complained that all she had to eat was cheese, and the doctor threatened to punish her by sticking her with a needle if she didn't eat it. To see her so made me sick with grief, and finally Tommy insisted that I pay her no more visits. It did her no good, brought her no comfort. And it was certainly not good for me.

Mother did not live out the year. Tommy took the phone call one night, and told me quietly that it was all over. It was a blessing that she had not lingered on, but still the shock brought tears and grief. Part of it was grief for a mother I had never had.

Her ashes were placed in an urn beside Daddy's, as she had requested. I called Father O'Dea and had a Mass said for both of them.

Her effects were few, and her sister disposed of them, except for a small sapphire ring that Daddy had given her, and that she had promised to Marylyn, and for me—her diary.

Tommy felt I needed a rest and a change; I was exhausted, emotionally and physically. So we flew to Chestertown, Maryland, where Bobsy was living. She had divorced Freddie Spencer, and now was married to a very fine New York lawyer, and had a beautiful estate on the eastern shore of the Chesapeake. Bobsy was an excellent hostess; she gave parties for us, and took us fishing in their cabin cruiser. And I drank too much.

When we came back home, I had a serious warning about my drinking. One evening Tommy and I were entertaining a doctor who lived just up the road from us, and with whom we had become quite friendly. I hadn't had a great deal to drink, but I suddenly felt quite drunk—dizzy and completely disoriented. The doctor took a close look at me and said, "This girl isn't drunk.

She's ill." He took my temperature; it was 105. Immediately they drove me to Queen of Angels Hospital, where, after a great many tests, I was informed that I had cirrhosis of the liver. I was very sick—but I was even sicker when the story "leaked" and our columnist Jimmy Fidler was able to tell the world about it. Cirrhosis is not necessarily caused by alcohol, but the two are closely associated in the minds of most people.

After I got out of the hospital I had to make regular trips to see the doctor and have liver-function tests. He told me my liver had been badly damaged and I must never drink again. I was frightened enough to accept his ultimatum. "If you say I mustn't drink, then I won't."

About three months passed before I was scheduled to see him again. When I took the routine tests, the results were excellent. He asked me how much I had been drinking, and I replied, "I haven't been drinking anything. You told me not to." When he said, "You mean you haven't had a drop in three months?" the note of surprise in his voice meant to me that my condition was probably not so serious after all. So when I got home I thought, "A bit of sherry now and then can't hurt me. He was just trying to scare me. He probably thought I drank a lot more than I did."

The sherry program didn't last long, however. I began to "taper on." Too much is rather sickening. And I began to take straight shots of gin for relief from the cramps that seemed to be getting worse every month now. I also caught colds quite frequently, and of course that calls for a hot toddy of good, high-proof bourbon. I read a number of articles in magazines and newspapers about alcohol and occasionally I read about a group of people who together find their answer in a fellowship based on spiritual principles. I knew that their numbers were increasing rapidly all over the country. One afternoon a friend of Tommy's came out to see him; Tommy told me beforehand that he was an "ex-drunk," and was now one of the "pillars" of this fellowship. I was surprised, when I saw him, to find that he was a hearty man who looked as though he had never taken a drink in his life. And one Sunday afternoon a woman of about my age was at the house; she told me that one of these fellowship groups met regularly in Studio City, right near Republic Studios. Since I was becoming more and more interested I told her I'd like to attend one of their meetings.

The first time I went with her I was very much impressed—and also shocked by the stories some of the speakers told. These were the stories that you read about, in the newspapers or in case histories in medical books. I went several weeks in a row, listening with sympathy, but with no sense of identification, to speakers tell their own stories. "These people," I told myself, "are certainly to be commended for their ability to lick their problems. But they have *really* had problems: the sordidness of sanitaria, drunk driving (I mentally patted myself on the back for having learned not to get caught at *that*)—these people had—what did they call it?—'hit bottom.' I haven't hit any kind of 'bottom' at all." My case against the group, for myself at least, was clinched for me when Bobsy came to visit us for a few days and she went with me to one of the meetings. In the audience near us were several "first-timers"; they reeked of liquor, were depressed and shaking. Bobs put it in her own emphatic way: "Mary—this is for *drunks*." Not for me.

I just "drank heavily," but when I was working on a picture I stopped drinking. At least I gave the producers no cause for alarm; I did no "nipping" during the day. I did my job. I had stopped drinking while I was attending the group meetings. It wasn't difficult, only boring. So I went back to my "rules about drinking."

Most of the time, while I was not especially happy, neither was I especially unhappy. I had achieved some of the goals I had worked for; I had a home, and I had my children near me. I had taken Tono out of Elsinore when I first moved to the Valley—he was just too far away. I entered him in Ridgeway Military School, which was only a few minutes away from the house. Both he and Marylyn could come home on Sundays, and once a month they had the entire weekend. Tommy would drive over to pick them up while I prepared a big Sunday breakfast, sausages and eggs and hot biscuits or stacks of pancakes. And we had a happy family atmosphere that made my heart feel good. We had a few very happy Christmas times too, with a big "old-fashioned" Christmas tree, a big turkey, and much opening of presents.

But I was beginning to feel chronically tired. I had a very good housekeeper, and friend, in Ebbie Davis, who came in daily during the week. But the work at the studio dragged at me. When I was not on a picture, there was always something the studio would call me in for—publicity pictures, or to help make a test with someone who was up for a part. It had all become just a routine job for me. If I had some sort of a goal to work for, if I could have felt there was some visible end to the race, I think I could have kept on.

When Metro put through its program of annuities for its contract people and they informed me I could retire with a good annuity at the age of fifty-five, Tommy thought this was a wonderful idea.

I began to develop all kinds of psychosomatic symptoms. Aches and pains all over. Sometimes my shoulders hurt so much that I could barely comb my hair. I had one symptom that was frightening: I would be able to inhale, but not to exhale. My lungs would fill to bursting, and I would turn blue; the only relief was for someone to give me a kind of artificial respiration, physically pushing the air out of me. There was a flowering weed growing around the house, and someone suggested I might have an allergy to it. Tommy went around with a spade and a wheelbarrow, digging them up, but it brought me no relief. It was emotional, and out of any real control.

I had had lots of work to do—*Cynthia* and *Cass Timberlane* with Metro, *Desert Fury* on loan-out with Paramount, and *Claudia and David* for Twentieth Century. The picture *Little Women* was about the end of me. I was playing the sad, gallant Marmee; Mervyn LeRoy was directing. It was in color, and the costumes were elaborate—and hot. I often felt that I was burning up. One afternoon I was lying in my portable dressing room on the set. I was having a very tough period, and my misery was multiplied by the corset and hoop skirt I was trussed into. I got up and stood in the doorway to watch the scene they were shooting—the scene of Meg's wedding, with guests dancing in a circle around the bride and bridgegroom. In the next setup I was supposed to enter and join in the circle. I watched the vigor, the pace, the swinging arms and the laughter, and I felt a weakness that made me break out in heavy perspiration. I began to cry, and an assistant called Mervyn in. "Merv," I said, "I can't do it. I just can't do the dance." He was very sympathetic and kind. "I believe you, Mary," he said. "No pep talk would help—I know you too well. You're too good a trouper just to lay down on the job. I'll fix it so you can just be in a shot watching."

At home I thought about myself as objectively as I was able. I went over my various symptoms—the little pains, the fatigue, the quick flare-ups of temper, the waking in the night weeping, finding a room "too hot" when others didn't—and I laughed a little. I had been married to a doctor for five years and I hadn't recognized the signs of menopause. I also realized that I was not going to have an easy change, and the doctor confirmed this. "You girls in pictures, with your emotional tension, do not build toward a placid and uneventful change," he said. He advised me to "slow down," to stay out of emotional situations, to find an interest in something outside myself, so I might escape the usual tendency to become completely self-centered. In a way I was relieved; I could accept symptoms instead of being alarmed about them. The one thing that was really troublesome was that my periods were becoming very frequent, with a heavy loss of blood that left me weak and listless. But this too, I felt, would straighten itself out, in time.

Everything would straighten itself out—but I needed rest and peace of mind, and could have neither. During the remaining work on *Little Women* my bitterness grew, my resentment built higher and higher. The hot lights, the long waits, the heavy woolen costumes, trying to be patient with the silliness of Mlles. Allyson, Leigh, Taylor, and O'Brien—it wore me down. I would sit quietly and wonder, "What am I doing here?"

I told Wes I wanted to get out of my contract with Metro, but he didn't think it was wise just now. But I persisted. It was night after night, day after day—Tommy argued with me, Mahin talked to me, everybody said I was foolish. My agent, Sam Jaffee, said he would do whatever I wanted. "Then get Metro to release me from my contract," I said. Metro suggested that I take six months' sick leave—a year if necessary. But I didn't want that; I would never get well if I knew that inevitably I would have to hear the phone ring and the casting director ordering me to report for fittings for the next picture.

My pent-up bitterness had blown like the cork on a warm bottle of champagne. I was sick of supporting people—beginning with my parents. But now I was fed up. Between outbursts I would shut myself up in the library and sleep—and drink.

Tommy thought I'd better see a doctor, and he took me to a wonderful man and a fine psychologist. I loved him, and I tried to co-operate with him, but he could not help me. He could try to help me get a better look at myself. I talked about working at Birmingham Hospital in Occupational Therapy, and how good it had been for the men, how rapidly they recovered when they were doing something with their hands. He picked this up—gently. "Could I suggest that you try it? You like working in three dimensions—maybe you could find some satisfaction in sculpturing."

It was mid-semester at Hollywood Art Center, but Mr. Lovins, with whom I had studied drawing many years before, accepted me, and I enrolled in the life class under Henry Lion. It was just the right prescription for me. I enjoyed learning how to work with the material—we worked in terra cotta, which has the cool damp feeling of sand on the beach that has just been washed by the receding surf. I learned how to make waste molds and working molds, to make "slip," to cast in plaster. I had Tono sit for me three days during his Easter vacation, and I did a very presentable head, which was accepted and shown in the Fine Arts Building at the Pomona Fair. I did a group of seals, a small garden piece; I had made sketches of the seals at the tank at the beach. The piece I liked best, although Mr. Lion disapproved of it as being too "representative," was a large cross, and clinging to it, facing it, was the figure of a man, his arms outstretched on the crossbar, and his head dropping and hidden in the angle of his shoulder. Into it I put all my own longing to return to the Cross, and subconsciously my own death wish—I even called the piece "Thanatos"; but like my longing, the figure could not survive the blows and buffets of experience. I sent it to an exhibition in Chicago; it was broken into three pieces, and returned to me.

The only trouble with the class work was the crowded room; I was very nervous, and the chatter and the impossibility of turning without bumping my neighbor with my elbows made me feel panicky. I rented some space—sculpturing takes lots of space—a short distance up the road from the house, and I worked there for a while. But even that was too noisy. A lady had an ice-cream stand next door, and when she wasn't chattering with her customers her radio was blaring. I told Tommy that I wished I could have four walls thrown together at the bottom of our lot, where I could go any time I felt like it and work in peace. Tommy jumped at this—and I took his word that it wouldn't cost much. In a short time I had an enormous place, with concrete floor, a cooling fan, electric outlets, space for my work bench and all my tools and cans of plaster and terra cotta, and shelves for all my pieces.

It was June 1949; Marylyn graduated from high school at Westlake. She had grown into a very beautiful, attractive girl; she was fun, and I loved being with her. She had her dates, and her passion for clothes and records. Remembering my own longing to confide in my parents, I shared every new "crush" or interest with her, at her level. I listened to her raptures over her latest and shared her tears when it was "all over." Then she fell in love with a boy I didn't like. Our relationship went out the window because I raised the devil with her. One night she got home about two hours late, and I was boiling, and before I knew it I had slapped her—hard.

Tommy was not much help. He didn't take it very seriously,

and thought I was making too much fuss about it. I believe he did have a talk with her, but whatever he said didn't have any effect. She went into USC in the fall, as a boarder, and Tono was back in school, and I had other problems to distract my attention.

I had taken on a job that was too much for me, although when I undertook it I didn't think it was going to be as bad as it turned out to be. Through the years I had kept in touch with a nurse who was an old friend of mine. She had joined the Army Nurse Corps and had been stationed with the Army in Italy, where she had seen a great deal of action much too closely. Her foot had been cut by a piece of shrapnel, and her whole leg had become infected. At this time, she had been writing me from the Army Hospital in Baltimore, where she had been for a year. Her letters were unhappy; there was little that they could do about her leg, and she was tired of the hospital and wanted to get out of it. Feeling that a good dose of California sunshine would bring back some of her brightness that I remembered so well, I wrote and invited her to come stay with us.

My heart went out to her when I saw her. She was on crutches; her eyes were big with suffering; she was thin to the point of emaciation. Tommy and I listened to her story, and it was pretty dreadful. One part of it she told over and over: she had been an "old maid," a very pretty one, but there had never been a man in her life; she had fallen in love with an artillery sergeant in Salerno and he had been killed the day before they were to be married. This and the fact that the doctors had told her that her leg would have to be amputated before she could get well had thrown her into a serious mental and emotional state. She had to take drugs by the handful to tolerate the pain; most of the time she looked like a lovely lost zombie.

She stayed for several weeks. From the way she talked, her sister and other relatives in Alabama didn't want her, and I didn't quite know what to do. She said nothing about going to them or going back to the hospital. I stayed up with her until late at night, comforting her in her pain, listening to her talk. It was wearing me down, not knowing just how to cope with her. Tommy finally said, "This is too much for us to handle. She should be with her family." He telephoned her sister and said that we were sending her on with a nurse; we simply couldn't go on caring for her. She wept when Tommy told her she was going home, but he was firm about it. "It's making a wreck out of you," he said to me, "and I won't have it."

I was able to exist, after a fashion, with my "symptoms." I was more sensitive to noise, and I would jump violently at the slam of a door or the sudden ringing of the telephone. I spent some time in my workshop and turned out a few pieces, but most of them went back into the clay barrel. I was so tired I had to sit on a stool at my modeling stand; my hands shook so that I couldn't control a modeling tool without sweating from the effort. I could relax somewhat in the pool, but the gentle rocking motion and the warm lapping of the water against my body would bring on a sensual feeling that was a torment. Tommy and I no longer lived as man and wife; I slept on the studio bed in the library. When I slept. I tried taking quantities of sleeping pills; I didn't know just how bad the combination of sleeping pills and alcohol was. During the day I drank beer; at night after dinner I would have perhaps half a dozen highballs. I would take a couple of seconals and go to sleep for an hour or so; then I would be wide awake for the rest of the night. I would read a mystery book until I went back to sleep, at about seven in the morning. Then I would usually sleep until eleven or twelve. I was very cautious about drinking too much around Marylyn and Tono. Sometimes, after Tommy got home, I had a couple of cocktails before dinner, and if I noticed that I was feeling them too much I simply said I was not well and I went off to bed. I had explained the "biological situation" to both the children, so my occasionally "feeling ill" was not of much concern.

Dust gathered in the workshop. I stayed in bed and read and drank until finally I was staying at a constant drunk-sober level.

Out of the haze Tommy appeared one day with two men from

the fellowship which I had previously rejected. Somehow they got through to me; I dimly remember one of them saying to me, "Wouldn't you like to get out of this rat race?" I agreed that they should take me to a sanitarium run by the fellowship; I remember crying bitterly through the whole drive. The sanitarium was a reconverted house; I had a room next to the kitchen—the only private room in the building. They put me to bed and gave me something, but after a while I got up and walked out into the kitchen, crying for Tommy.

I remember the odor of paraldehyde, a succession of nurses and doctors, and not much else. In a few days the terrible shakes subsided, and the psychiatrist asked me if I'd like to "do a little work with him." I took all the tests. When it was over he said, "You've got all your marbles, and very good ones, but you don't seem to have any aggressiveness at all."

"Should I?" I asked.

I hated the place, but I was docile—I ate what they brought me and did as I was told. I caught a glimpse of some of the patients, haggard and repulsive.

And the realization came to me that this was the kind of people the Fellowship was for—and I was one of them. I had hit bottom.

Twelve

The psychiatrist gave me books to read, books on alcoholism and on psychology, along with some lighter reading. Then he asked me if I ever heard of Thomas Merton; when I told him I hadn't, he brought me a copy of *The Seven Storey Mountain*. And it was through this beautiful book that I found my way back to the Church. It wasn't just an emotional spasm. During the long days in the hospital I carefully and deliberately went over the sins of the past eight years; I looked at them in all their stark ugliness, with coldly appraising eyes. I felt the indescribable sense of Presence. I said the almost forgotten Act of Contrition, and my contrition cut through me like a surgeon's scalpel, with white-hot sharpness that was too great for tears. It brought a dry, desperate firmness of resolution. One resolution stood out above all others: come what may, I would never again take my hand from His. No more would I try to flee "wildly down the arches of the years"; I would walk carefully and humbly, with Him.

Very soon afterward I left the sanitarium. I had been infused with a sudden vitality that startled the psychiatrist. "You look like a different person," he said. I walked tall. I could smile with a genuine joy that was only a feeble reflection of the joy I felt in my heart.

No longer was I on the "pink cloud" of my conversion. No longer did I have a serene and unquestioning confidence in myself. I had confidence only in God. I knew my weaknesses: I was proud and passionate and sometimes cruelly selfish, and above all, I was not very wise. I knew that it would not be enough merely to make a hatful of good resolutions. Good resolutions too often affect one's feet, so that they don't quite touch the ground. You have to be alert every minute, lest you stumble.

I knew that much repair work had to be done, within myself and in my relations with my children. I determined to go along with the fellowship program, for that would help me repair some of the dilapidation of my own body and mind.

I began to turn back to books that I had not been able to open for years. Fulton Sheen's *Peace of Soul* had just come out, and Father O'Brien's *The Road to Damascus*. I reread à Kempis's *Imitation*, and St. Francis de Sales' *Devout Life*. I got out my dusty rosary and recited it with the radio broadcast of "The Rosary Hour." I started going to Mass. But I was low in spirit because I could not receive the Sacraments. Of course I could not keep all this to myself, and there were many religious discussions at home. Tommy was an Episcopalian. I was not firmly enough grounded in doctrine to reply to all of his derisive questions; I did my best, however, with what I did know, and sometimes I surprised myself—although I converted no one.

At this point there are a good many unhappy "ifs" and "might-have-beens" in my story. Perhaps the greatest of these was simply "*If* I had not been the weak and spineless creature that I was"— but there was, I am sure, much more to it than that. If my old doctor had still been alive he would never have allowed me *not* to feel well, and I think he would have discovered that there was something organically wrong with me. The members of the fellowship had strongly impressed on me the principle that it takes a good while before the "dry alcoholic" has reached the stage where he can tend bar for a party and not want a drink for himself.

I found I could get along better with Tommy after I had a few drinks. I was more relaxed and more tolerant. It helped relieve the nervous strain. I was worn down with my periods; for about a week I would be exsanguine and exhausted, and I would rarely be out of pajamas and a robe.

I was increasingly concerned about Marylyn. Finally I had a long, quiet talk with her, and I told her that I had made a decision. I could no longer get through to her, and something had to be done. At the beginning of the second semester she was going to Mount St. Mary's as a day student. She surprised me with her willingness; and she told me also that she was in love with a boy who was about ten years older, a veteran. She had met him in a drama class at SC. Since Marylyn was only seventeen, I didn't take it too seriously. She'd forget him, I was sure, when she was no longer seeing him every day.

I also had registered Tono in Our Lady of Grace School the following September. He had a bike, and could ride to and from school and live at home. Everything was getting "right."

Everything except me.

The year was practically spent in bed. Ebbie would bring me a tray breakfast as soon as I had my shower and changed to fresh pajamas. There would be the morning paper and the mail, and then I would start in on books—best sellers and mystery stories, for anything heavier would tire me. About two o'clock I would give up and go to the bar and have a straight whiskey. I talked to no one on the phone, and we had no one at the house. I stopped putting on nail polish; my hands shook too much. My hair was blessedly curly, so I could let it grow and not go to a beauty parlor. I sometimes got into a shirt and slacks and wandered about in the patio. My knees hurt. My elbow, shoulder, and jaw were painful with neuritis. Sleep was miserable. I would close my eyes at night and clouds of colored light would float before me, and sometimes faces with huge mouths and teeth. Finally I had to keep the light on. I would get up and wander around the living room.

Tommy would appear and ask, "What's the matter, honey? No sleep?"

"No."

"Do you want to talk?"

"No."

"Take another pill."

"I've had three."

"Damn! Well, I've got to get up early—I've got to meet Smith (or Jones, or Brown). I think I can get it through his head that . . ."

And he would go back to the bedroom, and in a moment his snores would shake the house. Then I might go to the bar and pour about three fingers of bourbon, and down it, curl up in a chair, and go to sleep for a while.

I couldn't verbalize my prayers, but I prayed. Sometimes I could only hold my rosary clenched in my hand, but it was a prayer. I was sick, and I knew it. I was sick when I was sober, and sick when I was drunk, but somehow I did not despair. I felt that I was simply at a standstill, but that the time must come when I could move forward again.

The prospect of seeing the children would always force me to make a heroic effort to curtail my drinking—I would drink only enough to keep myself from flying apart. Tono was fine and healthy, growing, full of school and airplane models—at the stage where he never walked, but always ran. He never resented discipline, never pouted. If he did something that caused his movies or allowance to be cut he simply regarded it as "bad luck" and took it in stride.

Marylyn had undergone an astounding and gratifying change since she had been at the Mount. She obviously loved it and thrived on it. She talked with enthusiastic admiration of her friends and the Sisters. She took eagerly to the religious instruction; until now I had deferred to Franklyn's wishes about her being baptized. But she had always wanted to be, and she had the right to make her own decision about it now. And she could hardly wait to finish her instructions and be received into the Church. She was still in love with Frank, the boy she had met at SC, and she brought him over to the house when I was well enough to have guests. I felt that Marylyn was too young. I had hoped that she would go on with her college education, but I took one look at her determined chin and said I would give my consent if they waited until she was eighteen and were married in the Church. Since this is not their story, I won't go into details, but Marylyn was baptized a few days before her eighteenth birthday, and Father O'Dea married them at the Nazareth House Chapel. I gave them a Ford coupe and a thousand dollars for a wedding present, and they drove across the country and spent some time at Bobsy's farm in Maryland.

I had never lost touch with Father O'Dea. He never "bothered me"; he would simply make an occasional social phone call, asking no questions. I occasionally took discarded clothing over to him, which the Sisters were always eager to have to distribute; I would talk with him about my difficulties with Tommy, and he would say, "Poor fellow." That about summed up my feelings about Tommy also. There were times when I would argue with him and snap at him, but in the main I felt sorry for him.

My thinking was not very good—how could it be! I was sure of only one thing: if I could receive the Sacraments, if I could get rid of the burden of guilt that weighed me down, I could fight through the web of doubts and confusion that entangled me and find myself. I felt it had to be the Sacraments; no ordinary physician or psychologist could release me from my burdens.

In my talks with him Father discovered that Tommy and I had not lived as man and wife for well over a year. He asked me if it would be too delicate a matter if I asked Tommy to sign a paper agreeing to continue this relationship. He would submit this, with a statement that complex conditions, including finances and children, made a divorce impractical at this time, to the Chancery Office.

Tommy was very good about it; he said he was happy to sign

the paper if it would help me feel better. Father came to the house one afternoon; I was too ill to walk, or get out of bed. He heard my confession, simply and factually. He gave me absolution and said, with tears in his voice, "Welcome home, Mary."

And soon I was able to stop slopping around. I went to Mass and Communion. I decided to go to a doctor and see if I couldn't get in better physical shape. Tommy was on a new deal, one that looked good even to my doubting eyes—it was the conversion of a Navy vessel into a freighter. One of the men in the group with Tommy was a doctor; Tommy told me about him, and I went to him three times a week for shots and treatment. It did me a world of good. Sometimes I felt so well that I was sure the dark curtain was lifting and I could see blue sky.

Tommy had bought a third-hand Ford—little more than a motor and four wheels, but it meant that I could have the family car. So I got up the courage to drive again. I didn't venture far, however, a truck rushing by would make me shake with nerves. But I did get to Mass sometimes during the week, and I could get over to Santa Monica, where Marylyn lived after the honeymoon.

In March I became a grandmother; Marylyn had a little girl, Frances Jean. She had a very difficult and frightening time, and I was in a spin of worry until it was all over.

It was not a life that was conducive to peace and contentment. My nervousness was getting worse instead of better. I couldn't sleep. The doctor kept me well supplied with sleeping pills, but sleeping-pill rest is not good rest. Worry began to rule my life. One night when Tommy was out I caught sight of a bottle of vodka on the bar, and I decided that I would *not* be careful about how much I drank. I hoped I might pass out and at least find relief in oblivion. I began drinking, and the rest of that horrible night I recall only in disjointed fragments. I remember crying bitterly, and I remember thinking that I would take a couple of sleeping pills and go to sleep. Forget all about it. Forget all about everything.

The pills were in the bedroom, on the mantel above the fireplace. As I opened the box I jerked the lid, and I remember the white capsules falling all over the bricks and popping up like pop-corn. Finally I gave up trying to retrieve them all, and I walked back into the living room and poured another drink of vodka to wash them down.

The rest is secondhand. Father O'Dea says I phoned him and said, "I've taken poison—get help." He was too far to be of immediate help, so he phoned young Father Smith at St. Cyril's. Father Smith says he got there in about five minutes, and I was lying on the floor. He thought I was dead, or very near death. The quickest thing he could think of was the police. He called them, and they came with an ambulance—and they took a look at the pictures in the hall and recognized the fact that this was not only a Mrs. Wheelock, but Mary Astor.

I was taken to the Van Nuys Receiving Hospital, where the press got a good picture of me having my stomach pumped. It was printed the next day in the *Mirror*. And all the papers carried the story of "Attempted Suicide."

Consciousness came back painfully to me two days later in Culver City Hospital.

If there had been a pocket in my nightgown on that deadly night, I would not have been in the hospital. But how absurd to try to explain that it had been like the instinctive action of a woman putting pins into her mouth. It was my only shred of comfort—that there had been no conscious intention of suicide. I know this because I know that I had never looked on suicide as a "way out"; if I had I would have taken it long ago. My offense was simply that I had been blind-drunk. If I had been walking on the street and a truck had run over me, I would not have had the stigma of "attempted suicide." But there it was. And there it still is.

I was in the hospital a long time. Marylyn and her husband had taken Tono to stay with them until the uproar quieted down. Marylyn came to see me in the hospital—she was the only one who did—and her eyes expressed her deep shock. After I came home from the hospital, it became too expensive to keep Ebbie; we let her go in August, and I took over the care of the house. In many ways it was a good thing for me; it revived my interest, and gave me a sense of responsibility. Now I *had* to make decisions, even though they were only so slight as the decision of what to have for dinner. It was an effort, but I had to face it. I could no longer say to Ebbie, "I don't care—just anything."

I went to Sunday Mass, to confession and Communion. I saw to it that Tono went also. I knew that somehow, somewhere, the answer must be in the Church. The peace and content I felt after Communion was no mere emotional product of my imagination; it was a kind of clarity, an illumination, a great relief from the tight locked-up pressure that I felt most of the time. In the afternoons I said my Rosary, slowly and intently, and sometimes I remained for long moments afterward on my knees, my head and arms on the bed, loath to break the precious sense of stillness. In July I had made a five-day retreat at Holy Spirit Retreat House. Tommy had been so astonished at my appearance when he picked me up that he said, "Whatever it is, you ought to do it more often." Afterwards it took me a while to get used to the atmosphere of "friends" and drinking.

It was about this time that Mike showed up again. I had not heard from him directly since the war; Tono had had a few letters, and once in a while Mike had remembered birthdays and Christmas. We knew he had been working in London as a cutter, and that he had remarried, and that was about all. Now he was in Hollywood on business. He came out to the house to pick Tono up for lunch; he and Tommy had a drink, and everything was on a very pleasant, sophisticated level. Tommy rather liked him— said he was intelligent and amusing. As far as I was concerned, he was someone I had once known and hadn't seen for a long time. He was balding, still vain, and still full of news of people. He had a good time with Tono, and talked a great deal about taking him over to England some day. For a moment I felt bleak about the future. After all my efforts would Mike win Tono away from me and have the enjoyment of his maturity?

I continued trying to learn my job of keeping house; I bought an entire collection of cookbooks and read the women's magazines for household hints. I would have enjoyed it, except for my very poor health. Every two or three weeks I was knocked out with cramps and hemorrhaging. I tried not to complain too much; I presumed it was all part of the change. I had a great deal of insomnia, but naturally I was now frightened of sleeping pills. I prepared elaborate Thanksgiving and Christmas dinners, and 1951 came to a confused ending.

The following year was a morass of bickering and wrangling; I struggled painfully through it toward the complete disintegration that I knew lay somewhere ahead. When I felt well, I could bury myself happily in housework, taking the day and scrubbing and sweeping and polishing the house until it yelled. I took a home study course in doctrine from Woodstock College in Maryland, and the 96's and 99's I found on my papers when they were returned to me filled me with a cautious pride. I could keep myself humble by recalling the obvious fact that, despite the high grades in doctrine, I didn't rate nearly as well in behavior. I knew what to do, but I couldn't do it. But at least I had now formally prepared myself to be confirmed, and it was a happy day when Marylyn and I knelt to receive together the Sacrament of Confirmation. I made my nine First Fridays. I found a much needed friend in Jane James, one of our neighbors. She and her husband, Ed, were occasional visitors at the house, and they drew me closer into the activities of the parish church. Jane wanted me to join the Altar Society at St. Cyril's, and although I was reluctant to "join" anything I went to a meeting with her, liked it, and resolved to do my best as a member.

But these were only occasional firm spots in the bog. Worry about Tom and money, the constant pain of neuritis, always brought me back again into a slough of gin and bitterness. The house was my only symbol of security; when I came in the front door, it seemed to open its arms to me. There was something safe about it, and I went into a spin when Tommy talked about its value on the market. But debts were pressing heavily, and no money was coming in. By this time the house was fully mortgaged.

Something had to be done, and it was obvious that I was going to have to do it. In June, I called the Motion Picture Relief Fund to help us clear our financial muddle. The M.P.R.F. worker interviewed us and got a complete financial statement from Tommy, and I began to feel a new birth of hope that they would get us straightened out. It would not be just another loan; loans were no answer to our problems, and we had already had too many of them. But the report from M.P.R.F. once more dashed all my hopes to the ground. It seemed there was only one way out, an unhappy, hateful way. I would have to go to work again.

I had renewed my friendship—or at least acquaintance—with Menifee Johnstone, who had been my maid of honor when I was married to Ken, and who was now a movie agent in Hollywood. She agreed to try to find something for me, but we both knew that it would not be easy after I had been away so long. In September we got close enough to a TV series to discuss it for two or three weeks, and even to plan some of the details with the writers, before it fell through. Then nothing. Finally she got me a part with Warner's in *The Grace Moore Story*. It would not begin until December, and I tried not to think about it while I was waiting—waiting to return to the dull treadmill.

There was a hopeless void in my life where I wanted love and affection. Except for Tono. I could love him and feel secure in the love he manifestly felt for me. I could watch him grow and I could find satisfaction and pride in him. He was a normal, healthy boy, and of course there were the inevitable anxious moments that any son will cause. When, during his last year at Our Lady of Grace's, he brought home an "F" in deportment and courtesy, I had to remind myself that twelve is a difficult age. But he got through it, and I had the joy of watching him graduate from Our Lady's in June and registering him in Notre Dame High School for the fall semester.

My affection for Tono was coupled with the worry that his home atmosphere was dangerously bad for him. In November the kettle boiled over. Tommy had been getting home late for nights on end, and I spent the long evenings sitting alone in front of the fire, trying to think, trying to see a way out. Finally one night he came home and I exploded and told him I wanted a divorce.

The days dragged on. Now that Tommy was gone, I called the M.P.R.F. again, and they sent over a worker to help me straighten things out. I drearily began fittings for the picture at Warner's, and took a camera test—I had forgotten the Chinese torture that preceded five minutes of actual shooting. I tried to put off the bill collectors who were constantly at the door. I did the work that had to be done around the house. Tono kept me going—he was always cheerful and anxious to help. At least, I thought, I had the consolation that things couldn't be worse.

But they could be. Three days before Christmas, I was doing the wash. There was water on the steps that led from the service porch. I was hurrying, carrying a laundry hamper back to Tono's room. I was wearing rubber-soled shoes, and I slipped on the wet steps and fell, with my left leg under me.

I couldn't get up. White-hot flashes of fire seared through my leg. Tono finally helped me into the living room, and then called the doctor. He took me to his office and had the leg X-rayed. The fibula was broken, and I would have to spend six weeks in a cast. There went the Warner job.

The New Year looked bleak. I couldn't work. I couldn't drive. The market refused to deliver or even sell me any food until I paid something on the bill of about seven hundred dollars. I developed a bronchial cold that I couldn't shake.

Then I found that the world was not at all so lacking in love and affection as I had sometimes thought. Louise Fazenda sent me a loan of a hundred dollars. Two of the Altar Society women came in and cleaned my house for me. Menifee did my marketing; once a week she would bring in enough to last until the next shopping day. Jane and Ed James had me over for dinner.

Late in January the bronchial cold flared, and I was really sick, with a high temperature. I called Miss Quinn at the M.P.R.F. and told her I needed a doctor but I couldn't afford one. I was thankful that she knew my exact financial situation; without wasting any time in an investigation she took over. She sent a housekeeper to stay with Tono, provided a small weekly check to cover the expenses for food, and took me to the Motion Picture Relief Hospital.

It was a blessing to be able to let go. To stop fighting the dizziness and the nausea, trying to make a bed and to get supper for Tono; avoiding taking my temperature. I had bronchial pneumonia, but they got it under control very quickly. The six weeks on the cast was over; they took an X ray and removed the cast. I was shocked—my leg was like a broomstick, and I couldn't walk on it as well as I had with the cast. But I was getting well, and that was the main thing. The hospital was a beautiful place; every room is private, furnished in good taste with drapes and pictures. There is none of the "hospital" feeling. And there is no feeling of "charity." As the head nurse told me, "You just can't feel that way about it. You've been giving a percentage of your salary for years to this place. Look upon it as an insurance policy that is paying off."

I was about to be discharged when the doctor suggested that they get a biopsy of the uterus. My history of excessive menses was not good; the minor operation would keep me there only two more days, and it would be wise to eliminate any possibility of cancer. As soon as I was out of the anesthetic, they told me. The uterus was full of fibroids, some of them so deeply embedded in the walls they could not be touched with a curette. And they had no way of knowing whether they were benign or malignant. I would have to have a hysterectomy.

Miss Quinn came out and told me not to worry; they would see to it that Tono was properly cared for. The housekeeper was a good one, and she could stay on. To me it seemed like the end of everything. I knew it would take a long time to recover from such a radical operation, and I was frightened of the operation itself.

So instead of going home I went into surgery. I could take it in stride, except for a few moments while they were waiting for the spinal to take effect. I suddenly had an image of the "field" as I had seen it—the gloved hands, the pulsating organs, the confusion of retractors and clamps. I was swept by the feeling, "NO, NO—not to ME." I looked at the head nurse, who was chatting nearby; her face became grave as she quickly walked over and took my hand. The mask was slipped over my face, and that was all.

I woke up in my room. It was dark, and I was thrashing about while a nurse was trying to get an intravenous needle into my arm.

I had had a complete hysterectomy, leaving one ovary. The fibroids were benign, but they had taken over completely. The doctor said I could not have lived much longer, and he was exasperated that I had not given my condition the necessary attention. "How could you possibly let this get so far along?" he asked. But he promised me that my arthritic symptoms would now all disappear, and that I would have a new vitality.

"Now don't worry about anything," they kept telling me. "Just get well." But it was impossible to keep from worrying. It would be weeks before I could resume any kind of near normal activity, and what was to become of Tono and me during that time? And after I could go back to work, would there be any work for me? Hollywood is not generous with jobs for people who are down; needing work is about the worst way to get it. And I needed it, badly. But the M.P.R.F. knew this difficulty, and they protected us against it. They did not publicize the names of their patients; very few people—almost no one outside of my immediate circle of friends—knew I was there. I finally gave up and decided to stop fretting. I read, and rested, and relaxed. There was a Catholic church near and the priest brought me Communion every day, and my thanksgiving and meditation could be long and undisturbed. I was a bit irritated that my recovery was so slow, but the doctor said it was to be expected because I had been in such very poor condition. They knew I would have no recuperative care at home, so they made me wait until I would be able to take care of my house.

Finally they said I could go. Ed James picked me up and drove me home. What a joy it was to greet my Tono again—and I was sure that he had grown at least a foot. Then I found that the strength I had felt in the hospital was deceptive. I was weaker than I thought, and the house looked enormous as I thought of all the work of running it. But soon it was good to go into the sunshine and hang up a fresh-smelling wash, to be able to wrestle with a vacuum, to drive and to shop. But it was not so good to have to face the problems again—the angry creditors on the phone, the threatening mail, no money except the weekly check from the M.P.R.F. I budgeted the check carefully. A dollar's worth of gasoline at a time, with no driving except to church and the market. Three dollars a day for food.

The weakness and the worry and the loneliness were almost more than I could bear. I couldn't afford liquor, but I discovered that beer helped still the jitters. And somehow one can drink beer in the daytime without feeling decadent. So I began to cut corners on my own needs to buy beer. A quart was thirty-three cents. That was fine for a while, but before long it was two, and then three quarts. That would last me from about eleven in the morning until twelve or so at night.

There was no doubt that I was "through" in Hollywood. I was forty-six. I had been "inactive" for three years. I hadn't even been seen socially. Menifee began to be evasive; there was just no interest. And I became more and more desperate. On Tuesday nights at St. Cyril's there was a Novena to Our Lady of Perpetual Help. I attended it, and prayed for a solution. The day after the ninth evening I received a phone call from Famous Artists Agency. Would I be interested in replacing Shirley Booth for the summer in *The Time of the Cuckoo* on Broadway? For a moment my home, Tono, the comfort of familiar things, held me in a tight grip. I wanted to say "No," but I found myself saying "Yes, I think I would."

For a while I couldn't think clearly. I couldn't do it—there were too many difficulties in the way. Who would take care of Tono and the house? I had no clothes. I had no money even to get to New York, let alone to live on until I had some money coming in. But one by one the difficulties melted away. I called Marylyn and told her what had happened, and I asked her if she and Frank would be willing to move into the house if I got the job. They could live there rent-free, just paying utilities and food for Tono until I was earning something. She said, "Of course we will," and that problem was settled.

Another call came from the agency: I was definitely set for the job. I would get a thousand a week—but I'd have to be in New York to clean up the final details. With the assurance that money would be coming in, I could solve the problem of clothes. I had bought very little in the past few years, so my charge account at Saks Fifth Avenue was clear. It was not an easy thing to do, for I didn't know when they would get paid, but I went in and bought two good suits and two cocktail dresses, and shoes and accessories. I cut it as close as I could—it still came to about three hundred dollars.

That left transportation and a place to live. I wrote a long letter to Bobsy, in Chestertown, Maryland. She replied, "The guesthouse is yours. Come ahead."

The toughest job was to find the money for the trip. I knew nothing about banks—after all, I had rarely deposited any of my own checks, although I had learned how to sign them well enough! I drove in to Hollywood, and went to the Bank of America on Hollywood and Highland, where Tom and I had had our accounts, and where Tom had made loans. It was a rainy day, and I stood in the rain outside the bank wondering how I should go about it. I prayed to Our Lady, asking her to tell me what to say, and I went in. The man I talked to remembered Tom well. I simply told the truth—that I needed money for plane fare to New York, where I was going to do a show. I had a telegram from the company in the East to verify my story. The man was very kind. He shouldn't have given me another penny of credit—but I left the bank with two hundred dollars. I walked up to the Roosevelt Hotel and bought a one-way ticket to Washington, D.C. Bobsy would meet me there.

Thirteen

I think the people most pleased with this new turn of events were the ladies of the Altar Society. They had been helpful but not intrusive or curious when I had trouble; now their greetings were warm and delighted. Marylyn and Jane conspired a combination going-away-birthday party. Banishing me from the kitchen, Marylyn prepared a luncheon and made an elaborate cake, decorated in the form of a theatre entrance, with my name in candy "lights" on the marquee and a "Standing Room Only" sign. And there were beautiful presents—a traveling crucifix, a bracelet rosary, lingerie, gloves, nylons. I was deeply touched, because these were not, for the most part, intimate friends. They were just women who had remembered me in their prayers and now saw their prayers answered.

I was also a little troubled. They were so sure of my success, and success is never a sure thing in the theatre. And I knew I was taking a very long chance with this play; its success thus far had been due mainly to the talent and popularity of Shirley Booth, and I would have two strikes against me, following her. It was by no means the beginning of summer; it was only a break in the weather.

I packed away my personal things and condensed my books to one wall to make room for Marylyn and Frank. And I tried not to think of the long separation. But when the time came to leave, it was almost impossible not to think of it. Determined not to let it show, I put on an act. Ed James drove me to the airport, and Marylyn and Tono came along. I kissed my darlings good-by carefully, laughing, "Don't spoil the make-up!" I walked briskly up the steps to the airliner feeling as though I were walking to the guillotine, and I waved gaily to them from the window. As soon as we were aloft, I went into the lavatory and took two cans of beer out of my case. I drank them off, wishing they were something stronger.

We arrived in Washington that night. Bobsy was waiting for me, and during the two-hour drive to Chestertown we were talking a mile a minute to catch up on all that had happened since we had last seen each other. Carl had retired from practice in New York, so they now lived permanently on the farm.

"Something long and cool will sure taste good," said Bobs as we turned into the driveway. I didn't tell her I had drunk nothing but beer for months (with an odd feeling of guilt because I realized that I *deliberately* was not telling her). The gin and tonics were frosty and delicious; we talked until five in the morning.

I called New York the next day; I told the agency that I was having a lovely time visiting friends on the Eastern Shore, and I hoped they "wouldn't want me too soon." What an act! Star stuff. They mustn't know how desperately I needed work and money. They told me to come in two days later to meet the producer; the director, Harold Clurman; and the author, Arthur Laurents. Bobs drove me into New York, and I was received graciously. Mr. Clurman was nicely embarrassed to ask me if I minded going over to the theatre and reading just one scene with Dino DiLuca, the leading man. He explained that he had never seen me on the stage and wanted to see if I projected the quality I had on the screen. The next day we went to the old Empire Theater, where

I had seen my first play more than thirty years before. I met Mr. DiLuca, who was charming—but unfortunately he could speak only a few words of English—and the play. Holding the manuscript and trying not to shake, I read one scene with him while he gently indicated the moves. Mr. Laurents came up on the stage with a change in reading, a difference in attitude; we went back over it, and halfway through, Laurents shouted, "That's it!" They seemed pleased enough, and I returned to the farm with the contract in my pocket.

There was a dark cloud. They had decided *not* to run the play during the summer. In August, Shirley would take it to Central City, Colorado; I would join the company there, rehearse with them in the daytime, and then take the show on a national tour, opening in Los Angeles in September. And this was only May!

I asked the agency to get me some TV or stock; until something turned up, there was nothing to do but sponge on Bobs. I had no money, and I assured Bobs I would consent to stay only as a working guest. She had only one maid, and did a lot of the housework herself, so I was certain I could earn my keep. And I had a fine time showing off my cooking ability.

After many phone calls and trips to New York, I managed to land a four-week engagement in summer stock, with the freedom to pick any play I wanted. I picked a good one—a good *tough* one —S. N. Behrman's *Biography*. I had seen Ina Claire do it to perfection years ago and did not realize it was not as simple as it looked in her skillful hands. I was to rehearse one week and play for one week in Mountainhome, Pennsylvania, then do one week at the Salt Creek Theater just outside of Chicago, and then play Sacondaga, New York.

I tried to work on the play out in the little guesthouse; I scheduled myself to work two hours in the morning and two in the afternoon. It was rough. The part was much longer than I had realized, and I could not detach myself from the activities of the household and concentrate. Also Bobsy had been away from professional life for long enough to forget the demands it makes and she wanted me to attend "just a few" social activities. Also she had the wonderful idea of sending for Tono to spend his vacation with me on the farm; so, because I was so happy to have him around, my attention wandered even further.

I was worried that memorizing was so difficult. The constant habit had been broken, there were too many interests other than the script—and I was drinking too much in the evenings. Also I had not yet learned how to study a play; I was trying to memorize, to learn by dogged repetition. That is all right in a picture, where the scene is shot before it is forgotten; but in a play it will work only after the scene is completely understood—so that the words one says are the *last* thing that happens.

Bobsy, bless her, put fifty dollars in my pocket to build up my small fund of some thirty-five—all I had left, and I went up to Mountainhome. I worked hard, and received a lot of help from a fine director, John O'Shaughnessy. My main trouble was lack of confidence, and I began to be very glad to have this much of a chance to try my wings before going into the "big time"—the play in the fall which would make much more important demands on me.

At the Salt Creek Theater my confidence went up a few points at the review given me by Claudia Cassidy, "the terror of the *Tribune*." She said, in her article, that she hated summer stock; she had come to see the show on assignment, planning to leave as soon as possible. Instead she had stayed on to the end. "This girl wraps an audience in her arms," she wrote, "she is utterly sincere." ("I do that?" I thought.)

I was pounding along on nerves, however; I was not yet really strong since my operation. One evening I was having my usual five o'clock supper in the dining room of the country club, where I was staying. There was considerable virus around; one of the members of the company had a touch of it, and I had caught it. But I was fighting hard—I had played the last evening's performance with a temperature of around 101 degrees with the weird feeling of not quite feeling the floor under my feet. Suddenly at the dining table I found I could not swallow. A searing pain shot through my shoulder. After a few moments it passed, and I played the show that night. The next morning it was better, but by afternoon it had come on again, and I called the doctor. He was not comforting. "I think this is gall bladder," he said. "It might pass —and again it might not." I wouldn't let him give me any sedation because I needed all my faculties for the show. I got sicker; the pain became, in the medical sense, "exquisite," which simply means unbearable. I called him and he ordered me into the hospital after giving me a hefty shot. The producer said they could put on the company that was rehearsing next week's show and, the inevitable formula, "Don't worry about a thing."

I don't remember the ride to the hospital—just rousing from delirium, being in X-ray rooms, being wrapped in hot wet blankets, more delirium, and still another and another nurse saying, "Now this will sting a little. . . ." Somehow I grasped that my room was like Grand Central Station and that the reason for the activity was that momentarily I might have to go into surgery ("Again! Again!"). There was a stone blocking the sphincter of the gall bladder, which with sufficient relaxation would pass or drop back into the gall bladder. Finally it passed, and so did the threat of another operation. But I was in the hospital for ten days.

Of course the final week of the tour was called off, and I was more discouraged than ever. I don't know what I would have done without the help and encouragement of my good friend Father Dolan of St. Jarlath's. After he had made his tour throughout the hospital he would come and sit with me; he would light up his cigarette and tell me the stories of his unbelievable experiences with some of the famous, tough hoods of long-ago Chicago. One night he came in looking like the cat that had swallowed the canary—he had smuggled in four cans of beer. "Do you good. They don't understand these things in a hospital—with their rules . . ." He was a good friend, and he allayed the desolate feeling of being in a strange city without relatives or friends. We still correspond. He always lets me know when he has seen one of my TV shows, and if I have a Chicago stopover he seems to have nothing better to do than to come to see me when I phone.

My hospitalization was in all the papers. Bobsy phoned, and Marylyn, and Jane. It didn't help much that nobody believed the papers, which, for once, had reported the situation accurately. In essence everyone said, "Yes, we read that in the paper—but what *really* happened?" I had told the doctor I was going on a national tour in *Time of the Cuckoo;* he said the condition might recur, so he gave me a "To whom it may concern" letter describing my symptoms and treatment, which I could give to a doctor. I was mad enough to want to make copies and send them around. I was proud of the fact that drinking had never interfered with my work; but realizing I was being defensive, I cooled off and tucked the letter away in my suitcase.

I spent ten recuperative days back at Chestertown in a daze of near panic. Everything was set except me! A thirty-week national tour with me as the star and all the kinds of responsibilities that incurs.

When I arrived in Colorado, circumstances were not calculated to relieve my tensions. Things began to happen that I didn't understand. I found that I was to rehearse with understudies and the stage manager, and I felt like a stepchild. And this is nothing against understudies as actors or stage managers as stage managers. But the time should have been spent with the people I was going to work with—and a director. The understudies were new to the show also, and also working with the script in their hands; and the stage manager was simply making us imitate readings and moves as they were being played by the active company. In New York the producer, the director, and the author had insisted they didn't want me even to try to "copy" Miss Booth; I was to give the part an entirely different interpretation and approach. But now it was "Now, Shirley does this, Shirley does that." I kept quiet. It was all too terribly important for me to cause any trouble.

I think the people in the company were really just waiting for me to speak up; they knew the theatre better than I, and they knew this was wrong, but I would have to make the move. It was a strange feeling; not understanding it, I couldn't put my finger on it, and I felt friendless and isolated. The only member of the group whom I couldn't even like was a man by the name of Jimmy Ash. Rather good-looking, but there was something odd about him. He was completely withdrawn; he never opened his mouth, except to say his lines. When we took rest periods, relaxing, chattering, he just stood around. As an actor he seemed awful—wooden and monotonous. He kept his eyes glued to the script. I soon worked up an intense dislike for this man, although I kept my judgments to myself. Everyone else seemed to just ignore him.

At the beginning of the second week Arthur Laurents, the author, arrived, and it looked as though I had a friend. He watched a rehearsal, and then came up to the house with me—the comfortable little half of a duplex, with a magnificent view of the Rockies—a view that should have been relaxing. "You've been going through hell, haven't you?" he said, and then I got his story of his personal grievances against Shirley. She wanted her laughs, and she was sacrificing his whole concept of the play in order to get them. She was, he complained, sloughing off the emotional content of the play. Later it turned out Shirley was right. She had very skillfully covered the weak spot of the play, which was that Leona, as written, had no sense of humor whatsoever. There were many laugh "lines," but if Leona was played "emotionally" they wouldn't pay off, as I was to find out.

But that week, still with the understudies, I had a better time, and I felt I was getting somewhere. The third week, Mr. Clurman arrived, and *he* took over, and I was even more confused. Surprisingly enough, we did little rehearsing, mostly listening to his quite excellent lectures on acting.

Finally, the last two days before we left for California, I rehearsed with the active company. And it was bewildering, to them and to me. Tempos were different. I was stiff with a sense of inferiority. It was awful. Laurents stood firmly behind me, however, and in the perfect etiquette of the theatre, as I was the star, they did their best to adapt to me. But they didn't like it. They didn't like what I was doing—I felt they didn't like *me*—and I was chilled with uncertainty.

We opened in Santa Barbara at the old Lobero Theater, of such pleasant memories. It was good to be back in California, to hear the song of the mockingbird again, and see the flaming geraniums and the palm trees. I felt as though I had been away for years. The prospect of the long tour stretching ahead—St. Louis at Christmas time, Toronto for New Year's—depressed me, but I kept reminding myself that I was lucky to have a break like this, with the money at the end of the tour, enough to pay off my debts, and the work that begets work. The play went well enough, but it still didn't "feel" right. I couldn't loosen up; I had to fight through every performance, and I knew (the audience always tells one unmistakably) that I was not doing a consistent job.

On September 28, we opened at the Biltmore Theater in Los Angeles. I had played there in *The Male Animal* and *Tonight at 8:30*, and I knew the theatre well; I knew it was acoustically "dead" in many areas. I told the stage manager to warn the company; we were having enough trouble with the play, and we couldn't afford to be unintelligible to the audience on top of everything else. (Strange—the need of authority; to be right about *something*. What is it called? Compensation for insecurity?)

It was a fine opening night, with all the celebrities turning out to be photographed, and we got fairly good reviews, although the critics differed sharply in their opinion of the play itself. To my satisfaction, Edwin Schallert, in the Los Angeles *Times* Sunday follow-up, complained that the audience could not understand what was being said (See! They didn't listen to me!), and concluded that "the general effect of that first evening was bad, with the possible exception of Mary Astor, who evinced a real capacity to convey what she had to say in plain English. [Is that *all!*] The play with Miss Astor incidentally could have been better than the rendition that was given in New York except for the one element Shirley Booth brought to the show, namely a fine comedy spirit. [So humorless, so serious, so *dull*—I know.] Miss Astor had more emotional force in her portrayal. The second act climax was thus unusually good."

Business was fair, however, and it looked as though we had

nothing to worry about. My own stock was way up; Famous Artists Agency came up with a managerial contract to take effect after the tour was over. But I still had agonizing stage fright every performance. I would stand at the steps off stage, loaded down with my props, waiting for my entrance cue that took me over a little bridge leading to the patio, and I would be shaking, sweating and tense, looking ahead to the next two hours as sheer agony.

I had a room at the Biltmore (I had to live up to my star status even though I couldn't afford such luxury), and it was good simply to get into an elevator, go up to my room, and have three or four drinks of vodka to unwind after a performance. I had no car—I had left the Ford with Frank—so I didn't get out to my home until Saturday night. The little home had changed; it withdrew from me like an offended friend. Furniture was rearranged, and Frank and Marylyn had crowded some of their own things in. With the strain of the play heavy on me I was irritable and edgy. I found myself quarreling mildly with all of them. I felt I had enough to worry me; I couldn't cope with domestic problems too, so I went back into town early Sunday afternoon and slept the clock around.

After such a weekend I felt a certain awkwardness in telling Marylyn and Frank I wanted to bring the company out the following Sunday for a swim and a simple sort of "hot dog and potato salad supper." This was the first trip to California for most of them; they knew no one, and Sunday on tour is a dull day. Marylyn said, "Of course bring them out—it's your house," and I put the invitation up on the call board. They were all delighted; they would rent a couple of station wagons and make two trips with one of them. It could have been a great day, with everyone relaxing around the pool and in the patio. I had bought plenty of liquor and Frank was tending bar.

Jimmy Ash, our one company problem, was on the very best behavior. He was sitting, silently as usual, in the patio watching the swimming.

"Don't you want to swim, Jimmy?" I asked him, and I teased him about being so quiet.

He smiled rather weakly and said, "I have to be quiet. I was ill all last year."

Of course I felt remorseful, and embarrassed that I had been so lacking in understanding—that I had been so irritated with him. After all, he wasn't such a bad sort, especially now that I didn't have to try to act with him. "Let's go in and have a drink," I said, and he replied, "I'd like that, Mary." No one in the company, except Dino, Lydia St. Clair, and the company manager called me Mary. The etiquette of the theatre again—but it always made me feel shut out. So for a short while, I suppose just because he called me "Mary," there seemed to be a bond of companionship between Jimmy and me, but by the end of the afternoon we had drifted back to our usual impersonality.

After the party there was a warmer attitude of the company toward me. They complimented me on my home, my lovely children, and my adorable granddaughter. I began to hope that I might yet break down the barrier that seemed to cut me off from them.

The three weeks in Los Angeles ended, and we were off to San Francisco and the Alcazar Theater. I had been looking forward to this. San Franciscans are an appreciative and responsive audience, and they had always been wonderful to me when I played there before. The opening went well, and the number of curtain calls was gratifying. But the next day the reviews were devastating. They tore the play to pieces and they tore me to pieces. The spirit of the company plummeted; many of them questioned the wisdom of staying out the three-week engagement. And the ax fell. With only a fair take in Los Angeles, and now this—the management said, "Close it." And our two weeks' notice went up on the board.

Close it. Close it. It shattered me. No tour. The debts loomed large again. I tried to tell myself that the reviews had grown out of a local grudge, perhaps against our public relations man; they were too much alike, too unfair—as though they had ganged up and said, "Let's blast 'em." But billowing up to overwhelm all my attempts to justify myself was the deadening thought that I had let the company down, that I had crushed all their hopes and expectations, along with mine.

The future looked even more dismal after I talked to my new agent over the phone, who said, "Well, we'll do our best, but of course—a flop . . ." I decided then and there to go back to New York, where one is not judged solely by his "flops." In the theatre flops are expected; there are more of them than there are successes, and they don't reflect on the actor's ability in any way. (Thus I rationalized—without admitting that "New York" also has an ability to perceive a bad performance.) In the meantime I had twenty-three more performances of this play—I was tired, so tired I couldn't face the thought of the future beyond that. I'd go home and rest. ("I'm a flop.") Something might break. ("I'm a flop.") Thirty thousand dollars had just flown out the window. And I'd let the company down. ("I'm a real great flop.")

I was in my room—the papers strewn around the floor, two days old now—thinking and trying not to think when a visiting committee from the cast came in—Jimmy, Lydia St. Clair, and Lois Holmes. They had come to cheer me up. Nobody, they insisted, felt it was my fault. They knew it was a great shock to me—of course, for the rest of them it was mostly a financial setback. (Like everyone else, they thought I must have plenty of money —that home, and a swimming pool!) "Try to take it philosophically," they said. "Tell yourself 'That's show business!'" But I knew better. I knew they all felt, and rightly so, that if it had been "their Shirley" the show would have run. And I knew they hated me.

After they left, I wandered around the rooms of my lovely— expensive—suite at the Huntington. I wanted to let go and cry, but with that dull despair eating away at me I couldn't. I had a couple of drinks and a warm shower, and got into bed, to fall asleep immediately. Four full hours later I awoke, and all the ache poured in on my mind again. Well, no matter how I felt, it was time to eat something and get down to the theatre. But I felt very odd. The ends of my fingers and toes tingled as though they had been rubbed with sandpaper, and I couldn't get enough breath. I kept sighing, deep, gasping sighs that I couldn't control. While I was dressing I could hardly keep awake; I would lean against the wall, and the desire to sleep almost overcame me. But I couldn't call the stage manager and tell him simply that I wanted to go back to bed. And I was afraid to take a drink—it was past my deadline before curtain time. Somehow I got to the theatre. My maid took a look at me and said, "You're sick. You're white as a sheet." I told her not to tell anyone, and I began to put on my make-up. But the awful sleepiness kept washing over me like a heavy wet fog. "Maybe you'd better tell somebody," I said to the girl.

The parade, the frantic, anxious parade into my dressing room, began. "You'll be all right. We've sent for a doctor," someone said. But I kept slipping off, and they had more and more difficulty arousing me. I have experienced "pass-outs" in my life, but I have never before or after had this particular strange symptom. The doctor came in and gave me a shot; it was emotional exhaustion, he said, and something about over-oxygenation, and that I shouldn't try to go ahead with the show that night, and what about my understudy? There was more confusion—about the audience already being in the house, no announcement, the girl was too weak in the part, etc. Lydia tried scolding, which of course was the last thing that would bring me out of anything. Actually, everything was just over my head, and I couldn't have cared less —I was slipping into a world that was quite safe, and painless.

Then there was no one in the room but Jimmy Ash, and the door was closed. He sat down beside me, where I was lying on the dressing-room couch, and put an arm under my shoulders. In a very quiet, low voice he said to me, "I want you to listen to me, very carefully. I have something to say that may help you— or if you don't want to listen, you can throw me out. Are you listening? I have loved you all my life. You are the only woman I have ever loved. I know everything about you that has ever been printed or shown on the screen—and a great deal more, because I have always been so close to you. . . . I took this job only so I could be near you. . . . You have been with me all my life."

I was shocked into attention—which is what he had intended —and ready to believe. He went on, "If you want me to, I will help you get through the play tonight. I will be at every entrance and exit. I will give you my strength; the strength of my belief in you."

He disappeared for a few minutes. My maid came in and dressed me quickly. He was waiting for me outside the door; he put an arm around me and we walked into the wings onstage. Everything was set to go. I heard as in a dream the familiar chant between the stage manager and the electrician: "House to half —house to half"; "And out—house is out"; "Curtain." I gave a long shudder as he helped me with my props—the camera over my shoulder, the bag; check on post cards, pen, and cigarettes; the dictionary, the two wrapped packages. He kept talking very quietly as the show started. "Remember now, even though it's a tough fight I'm in your corner. Now, think a minute . . . Where have you been?"

I looked at him blankly.

"*Where has Leona been?*" he repeated.

I said, "Oh . . . I've been shopping . . . I bought a beautiful antique goblet."

"Did you have a good time? And don't you want to tell these people you are staying with about it? Don't you feel kind of 'bubbly' with anticipation?"

I was at the top of the bridge. I heard the usual applause, and as it faded Lydia's voice came up to me, strong and encouraging: "*Buena sera . . . Come sta . . . ? Come sta?*"

"Not so *bene* . . . I fell in a canal." Laugh—and the play was on.

I don't remember much except the game we played, and it was Jimmy who kept the ball in the air. He caught me at every hurried exit. Mostly I was afraid I would miss my entrance cues because voices kept fading in and out, starting up panic; but he would hold me by the shoulders in front of him, talking, not giving me lines or telling me what to do, but making me think about what *Leona* would be thinking. "Maybe you can get past those two

—they seem to be asleep. You'd just as soon they didn't see you —they made some lousy cracks last night——" And then a gentle shove.

By the time for the party scene in the second act I was tiring badly. "You don't have to worry about being steady now," he said. "You're tight—you're high and happy and in love . . . Listen to the music—and float, girl—float."

The curtain calls were over, and everyone in the company embraced me with "God bless you" and "You're a real trouper."

All I could do was to shake my head and gasp out, "Thank Jimmy. He gave the show."

He took me back to the Huntington. Physically I felt better, but I was wound up as tight as a dollar watch.

"Get your make-up off," he said, "I'll fix a drink."

I came back wrapped in a robe, and he sat me down and began rubbing my feet.

"How did you know they hurt?" I asked.

"I've watched you," he said. "You walk about five miles on that stage every night, and when you come off you limp."

Suddenly he said, "Mary, can I have a kiss?" and his arms were hard around me. "I've been waiting for that for more than twenty years. Good night now. I'll be back for breakfast, about eleven-thirty."

My confidence in myself, even my own volition, my self-esteem, my individuality, had completely rotted away. I could live only by drawing strength and will and approval from outside myself.

Jimmy persuaded me "just to try" a few different things each performance. First came the most rewarding—the laughs; he explained why I wasn't getting them, why they were only titters where Shirley had moved the audience to explode. He explained the mechanics of laughter, how it has to be "set up," like a bowling pin. He showed me the construction in the script—they were all there, but the preparation had to be clear and right. To humor him, not really believing in these theories, I did it "his way" just once, and I was almost thrown off balance by the laughter that came like the crack of a whip. I was fascinated by the fact that

this man had an ear like a musician. After three performances I
had—we had—every laugh that was in the play, and the whole
company began to sparkle and come to life.

We worked on the second act, tearing it apart and putting it
back together. I would play it, and after the show we would work
on it some more. The other people in the cast, all more experienced than I, were on their toes and responded magnificently,
playing to my changes, no matter how subtle. One night Jimmy
started me up over the bridge with the key word, "Bubble!" but
instead of being at the exits when I came off, to keep "at" me, to
keep me on pitch, he was over talking casually to the stage manager. I knew, and felt proud—he had turned me loose. "We" had
been getting a wonderful applause at the close of the second-act
scene. I sailed into it, the curtain fell, there wasn't a sound from
the audience. As it hit the apron, I looked quickly over to Jimmy
with a "What did I do wrong?" feeling. He put his finger to his lips
and a second later the applause came, full and rich. After the
show I found him and asked, "What happened? What on earth
was that?"

"That, my dear girl, was the greatest compliment an audience
can pay an actress. They were still *thinking*—they were still up on
the stage with you when the curtain came down."

The play ended—and on closing night the company did me the
honor of stepping back and applauding me themselves at the final
curtain call. I know that it is customary, but they didn't *have*
to do it, and under the circumstances I would not have blamed
them for omitting it.

Jimmy went back to New York. Where people knew him—where
he could get work. He said I would be okay now as long as I
prized my sobriety above all else. "Remember—one day at a time."

I had many things to attend to. I moved from the Knicker-
bocker to the Westwood Manor; I needed a better address—a
better "front." I had lunch with a representative from Famous
Artists, and I was disgusted—he gave me a lot of Hollywood talk
about how sexy I still was, and not to worry, getting a job would

take a little time, you know. Well, I was fresh out of time, and soon I would be fresh out of money.

My divorce was filed, but I could not get on the calendar for several months. I sold the Ford to get the money I needed to live on. When the play had been running in Los Angeles, my first week's salary was attached and I had to get a lawyer to handle it for me. Frank thought it would be a good idea for him to handle all the money difficulties; it needed a lawyer to keep the creditors quiet when I got another job. I had a meeting with the lawyer to discuss how he was going to handle the whole thing fairly. He would talk to all of them, and when I had money I would send him over and above what I needed to live on until they were paid off. He would also give a check to Frank every month to help pay Tono's expenses. The lawyer said the house would have to be put up for sale, too.

A call came from New York offering a week's engagement in winter stock for Don Swann, in York, Pennsylvania, playing *The Time of the Cuckoo*. I grabbed it and I was on my way. It was a meaningless engagement in a blizzard that paralyzed traffic and killed the box office, but it was a thousand dollars minus agent fee, taxes, expenses—minus, minus, minus.

The week was soon over and I went to New York, and there I met a fascinating actor named Ferris Hall and fell in love with him on sight. He was a Greenwich Village type with blond hair and blue eyes, and although he was several years older than I was he looked surprisingly young. I soon realized he wasn't much of an actor, but I was in desperate need of a man to lean on.

I found an apartment, an old, once lovely apartment, now shabby and run-down. I signed a two-year lease. It had recently been "redecorated"—at least it was fairly clean, with the odor of fresh paint and new, cheap covers on the furniture. And I could unpack my trunk after—was it only six months?—living out of a suitcase. I could stock the kitchen and not have to eat at restaurants. And the Church of Our Lady of the Sea was only a block and a half away.

Ferris helped me get settled, and came around every day, and

I soon realized that he had a drinking problem, too. A few nights after I moved in I was preparing dinner, waiting for Ferris, who had made the rounds of offices during the day. I answered the door to his buzz, and he walked in, weaving, staggering, not saying a word. He was almost at the pass-out stage. He put his head on my shoulder, and all he said was "I came home, didn't I?"

I fixed a bed for him on the living-room couch. And then I sat at the window and tried to find the stars above the building, and thought and thought.

The next day, I went shopping at the supermarket at the end of the block. There was a liquor store next to it, and I purchased a bottle of dark rum. At the apartment I had drunk about half of it when the full meaning of what I had done burst upon me. I had not even planned it—I just went into a liquor store and bought a bottle of rum as I would have bought a pack of cigarettes. I was drinking—I was drinking! In a panic I called Ferris' apartment.

"Slipped? Of course you slipped," he said.

I saw I could expect no help from him so I remembered, and called the Fellowship. As luck would have it, two of their members lived right in the apartment building. They came up and talked to me, and I thought, "Same old line." There was not much for them to do, they couldn't get through to me because I was far from sober, but they did stay until I went to sleep and saw to it that I did not go out again. Ferris came in, but he saw the Fellowship members, turned on his heel, and left in a hurry. And that was the last I saw of him for several days.

I went drearily to some Fellowship meetings. They conveyed nothing to me. I was willing to admit to Ferris that I was an alcoholic—I was willing to say anything to him—but I could not admit it to anyone else, including myself.

A few days later the first break came. I got a call from Charles Wilson's office to see them about a play that was going into rehearsal immediately—and would I consider co-starring with Eva Le Gallienne? That's the difference in New York—flop or no, I had *starred* in *Time of the Cuckoo*, and therefore that was my status. I went down to the office to meet Mr. Wilson, who would direct the play, and we discussed the script. He phoned Miss Le Gallienne, and she told him to ask me if she could come over to the apartment and see me that evening after I had read over the play. About ten that night, she came in—a little, almost plain woman, with a powerfully attractive personality, perceptive and sensitive. I was thrilled to be working with her; to me she was Mrs. Theatre. She said she had wanted me for the part—she knew I had been on the road and had had bad luck (as simple as that!) —but she had no idea I was in town until that day, when Mr. Wilson had happened to run into my agent at Sardi's. We talked about an hour, got acquainted, and liked each other very much.

We went into rehearsal the following week. Ferris read the script and agreed that it was a wonderful break for me. He said he wished he could have a small part, but unfortunately someone else had already been cast. "Well," said Ferris, "he's got a better 'name' than I have." But he told me he would be right with me all the time; after we finished the preliminaries he would get permission to sit in on rehearsals. This worried me a little because, except very rarely, it just "isn't done." But I needn't have worried. After he had called for me at the theatre a few times after rehearsals, he disappeared. The old agony, I'm sure, of being around the atmosphere and not being a part of it.

I was happy about the play, even though we all knew it would never be any kind of a smash hit—it had some elements of worth and might have a good run. I worked hard and happily. Wilson was a good director, but Miss Le G., as soon as I told her I would like it, helped me more. Out of her great experience she taught me many things—and I felt I was growing as an actress.

Worriedly I was fighting a bad cold. The weather was cold and rainy, and my California blood was "thin." I was taking aspirin and drinking lots of water, but the relief it brought me was only temporary. About ten days before we were to open in Philadelphia I was running quite a bit of temperature. In the late afternoon, while they were working on a scene in which I didn't appear, I went into one of the dressing rooms and rested my head on the table. One of the women came in and asked if I was ill, but I protested quickly ("I mustn't get ill—I am not frightened of the work any more—I'm sober—I mustn't miss this great chance!")—I said I was all right, just feeling a little lousy with my cold. But in a few minutes Eva was there feeling my forehead. She immediately called a cab and took me home; then she phoned her doctor. He came out, examined me, and informed me I had lobar pneumonia.

I had to tell him about my non-existent bank account, that I couldn't afford a hospital and I couldn't afford a nurse. (Actually I had been skimping on food—with forty dollars in my purse and no money in sight until the play began its run.)

The doctor said it would be all right for me to stay at the apartment, and he would come by as often as he could. It would be okay *if* I could dig up somebody to give me medication every four hours; I couldn't take it myself, because it would keep me pretty groggy. Ferris was unavailable—I knew he was drinking. The only people I could think of were my Fellowship acquaintances, and with wonderful willingness they arranged to send people in on shifts; and they took good care of me. The next evening after rehearsal Eva came up, with encouraging words, a thermos of soup, and an envelope with $250 cash. I had been getting sicker, wondering how I was to pay for the expensive drugs from the pharmacy. "You've got a great doctor," Eva told me, "and he says he's using everything in the book to get you back on your feet in a hurry. You'll make the show—don't worry about it."

And he did have me back on my somewhat shaky feet in about five days. By the time the show opened I was feeling fine.

We played at the old Walnut Theater in Philadelphia, where ten long years ago I had done *Many Happy Returns* with Henry Hull and Rex O'Malley. I thought of something Rex had said about that miserable play: "This is not *Theatre*, Mary." Well, *this* was. A good though not great play, a wonderful company of fine actors. Our reviews were excellent. Eva and I hugged each other, and she said, "I wish we were doing something really great together. I don't give this one three months."

Ferris came to Philadelphia the first weekend. He didn't have much to say, even though he managed to convey to me that I was doing no very great job—and a hurt "It's all right, you just keep listening to Eva—she's got you eating out of her hand. And," he warned, "she'll 'take it away' from you on opening night in New York."

He wasn't feeling very well and he lay down on one of the twin beds and fell asleep. I went out and had a steak sandwich at the bar with some of the people from the company; when I returned to the room, Ferris was feverish. I got out the thermometer I had brought along to keep a check on myself and found he was running a temperature of 103. He had a room over at the Ben Franklin, but it would be suicide for him to go out in the heavy snow, and we couldn't risk calling a doctor. Then I remembered a strange story someone had told me, how, many years ago, before there were any wonder drugs, he had been on a trip to Europe with Eva and some other friends. They were in an out-of-the-way place and he had very little medicines with him. Eva had run a flash high temperature and he had simply given her massive doses of aspirin. So I prepared myself for an all-night vigil and gave Ferris three aspirins every half hour, with as much water as he would take. When his temperature crawled up to 105, I was at the point of calling a doctor, and to heck with what people might think. But then he broke into a sweat and the temperature slid back steadily. He got on his feet by midafternoon and took the bus back to New York.

During the night, while I was sitting over Ferris, I had nothing to do but think. My thoughts were not pleasant ones. I was compromising with my religion. I had been away from the Sacraments for many weeks—it had even, I realized, stretched into months. I had been afraid of confession; afraid to disclose the fact of my drinking; afraid that I would have to give Ferris up; and afraid of what might happen to me without him. I was compromising with my resolution that *nothing* would ever become more important to me than the Church.

St. John's was just a few blocks from the hotel. For a few days

I tried to decide what to do. Then one day, between matinee and evening performances, I dropped in to the church. I thought—just to make a visit. I remembered that this was the church Rex had brought me to when he had guided me back to Mass during my long estrangement from God. I went in, and the Sacrament was exposed. The altar was a blaze of candles and reflected the flickering of the banks of votary lights. The church was full—they seem always to be full in the East—and every confessional light was on. I sat down and felt the tremendous pull of that attractive Presence. There was just nothing else I could do—I couldn't walk out on It. I went into one of the confessionals, and with my first stumbling words the priest knew I had a bad problem, and he helped me get it all out. He was gentle—firm and uncompromising. Finally it was all over and I came out of the little booth with a lighter heart than I had known for a long dreary while. As I left the church I turned for a last look at the Sacrament. "Please," I whispered, "stick with me."

We closed in Philadelphia on January 9, 1954. It was a happy and boisterous company in the club car of the train to New York that night. Everyone felt strained but pleasant anticipation of "Broadway." They had all been through it many times before, and knew how chancy it was. Almost everyone was drinking a little—but I was pleased to find that I was happy with a Coke.

We had a dress rehearsal at the Royale on Monday, and an invitation preview on Tuesday, with a packed house. Eva had taught me many valuable things: one of them was that an actor has to "pace" himself—like a runner. Tomorrow was the night when the all-important critics would be present, so tonight—just 90 per cent.

After the preview Eva said, "I'm worried, Mary. I think they gave their show tonight. Tomorrow will be like a second night!

And it was. They were let down—trying too hard—the first act took a whole five minutes longer than usual and Eva came off looking a little tight-lipped. I always had to "sweat out" the first act since I didn't go on until the second. When I made my first entrance and Eva, her back to the audience, greeted me with her full vitality, her eyes shining and her voice vibrant—I felt confidence right to the tips of my fingers. At the curtain calls we got our "bravos!" separately and together.

The reviews were mixed. The acting honors were well distributed. (I still keep a faded clipping of John McLain's, whose lead was "Take a Bow, Mary Astor!" Thank you, Johnny.) As to the play, the consensus of opinion was "slow," "talky." Eva called and said she was disappointed that it wasn't better, but the show ought to have a chance at word-of-mouth success if the Shuberts would keep us open for a few weeks.

At about three o'clock I received the following telegram:

THE STARCROSS STORY CLOSED AFTER THE PERFORMANCE WEDNESDAY JANUARY 13 SO PLEASE DO NOT REPORT TO THEATRE TONIGHT. SALARIES WILL BE PAID AT ROOM FOUR SHUBERT THEATRE BUILDING AFTER FOUR P.M. FRIDAY. EDWARD WOODS, MANAGER.

My telephone began to ring itself off the hook. Everyone had received the identical telegram—the brusque dismissal without a word of explanation. At the very worst they should have kept open until after the Saturday night show; it was a mystery, because there was enough advance to cover more than that. It was not until a few weeks later that we read in the paper that a plagiarism suit had been slapped on the management the opening night—and there were other rumors of a tax nature. But they didn't help anybody.

So now I had two flops in a row—and nothing to do but say, with as much courage as possible, "Well, what's next?"

I did a TV show. I was able to get Ferris into it, and while we were rehearsing I made a disturbing discovery. I had been right about Ferris, he was a lousy actor! The director was almost out of his mind because he needed to spend so much time with him. Line by tedious line. He was wooden, he couldn't learn his part —even on the air he made some serious "flubs." I couldn't understand how a person with such a fine ear could be so deaf to himself. He thought he'd been great. I knew his own opinion of his acting; I had heard many long stories how when he had done some stock he "took it away" from someone, or "stole the show" with a small part. I could say nothing to wound him, but I felt I was in a bad spot. We had planned to develop as a team—acting together or as director-actress.

Before we started the show we had an offer from Dallas to play a light little comedy that we thought might be good for summer stock—and the week in Dallas would familiarize us with it. I had already committed myself to do it—with Ferris; the contract was signed for him to play the lead. When we got to Dallas to begin rehearsals we found there had been an embarrassing mistake. There are two leads: the "Freddy" character, and the "Hank" role. "Freddy" is a good comedy part, and better written than "Hank." "Hank" is technically the lead—longer; but the character is stuffy and humorless—the victim of the comedy. (And psychologically wrong for Ferris, who could not bear to be laughed *at*.) Ferris assumed he was to play "Freddy," but it had been given to a man from the local company. Ferris was politely pleasant about switching to the "Hank" part—but as rehearsals proceeded it became obvious that the man playing Freddy was going to get the honors. Ferris went back into his shell, off in a corner, sullen and uncommunicative. He made me feel that as the star I should have insisted that he retain the role he came out to play. And perhaps I should—if it hadn't been for the TV show. His very woodenness was apt for Hank!

After the run I longed to go to Los Angeles just for a day or two to see my kids and have a last look at my home, which was about to be sold. I knew it would all be too painful so I decided it was a foolish, sentimental waste of money. (Run from pain—get back to New York. Later to learn that pain and geography have nothing in common.)

A strange, intimate bond had developed between Ferris and me. We were like people who had been married for twenty years, but without so much as a gesture of affection, and without any sexual attraction at all. There was not even the casual affection of theatre people who embrace and call each other "darling" meaninglessly. We had the security of familiarity; we could safely express ourselves to each other, saying what we felt and thought —knowing it would go no further. We were both highly anti-social, and this tie cemented us together against a hostile, jungle world. It was actually Ferris' world, and hearing more about it and seeing it through his eyes, it became more and more frightening to me. I felt that I could find safety from it only in him. I knew I was easy, gullible, vulnerable; he reinforced this feeling, and the feeling that with him I was very well protected.

Back in New York we waited for work, and none came. A dreary month went by. I knitted. We talked shop and watched TV. Finally I did what was always most difficult for me—to call an agent and say, "How about some work?" Gloria Safier, who had handled so much Eastern work for me when she was with the Jaffee agency, now had her own agency and was considered tops. I called her first. "Well," she said, "I wondered when you would be coming home." Of course she would handle me, and on an exclusive deal. (Later, when I emerged from all my troubles, I found many such friends—people who had been standing by watching hopelessly while I got myself into one mess after another and being unable to do anything about it.)

Immediately Gloria got me a TV job with Chester Morris on "Studio One," and the bank account was temporarily revived. Then about the first of May, Rex O'Malley called from Florida— would I be interested in coming down and doing Noel Coward's *Private Lives* with him for two weeks? He had both directed and acted in it before and he could make it very easy for me. Gloria handled the contract—very profitably. I flew down to Miami on the third of May—my birthday.

Rex met me and took me to the nice little apartment that was all prepared for me, complete with silly little birthday presents and a tiny cake with candles. I spent three happy, relaxed weeks there. The strain of being with Ferris was lifted—although I could not have admitted to myself that Ferris' absence was a part of my pleasure. (You keep a crutch in a corner *in case* you might not be able to walk without it.)

Rex was a joy to work with—a master comedian, a great craftsman—and a crackling wit of his own. We couldn't have had more
trouble with the show, or more fun about the trouble. Scenery,
lighting, furniture, everything went wrong before it went right.
But it was something to be worked at with a light touch—it had
no world-shaking import that grew beards on our faces. The wonderful thing to me was that I had gained great vitality; I felt like
the "new woman" they had promised me I would be so long ago
in the M.P.R.F. Hospital. After the famous knock-down, drag-
out athletics of the second act I thought wonderingly of the
difference from the listless old woman I had been only a year
ago.

Rex and I went to Mass together, and one Sunday he asked
me if I was going to receive. I said I wasn't.

"I'm sure you could," Rex said.

I hesitated. "Yes—but it's a problem I can't get straightened
out just yet."

True—there were no illicit relations between Ferris and me,
but I had to admit to myself that he was living in my apartment
most of the time. It was not "giving scandal," for in that apartment we saw nobody and nobody saw us. But I knew that any
priest would say quite simply that the situation was impossible
and would have to be changed. I didn't know how to change it.
I couldn't stand the thought of being alone.

Michael Ellis, who ran a summer stock company in Pennsylvania, sent me a new play to read, perhaps to try out for Broadway
in the fall. It was a good comedy, but as I read into it I became
more shocked and surprised. The whole theme was about a
woman who had written a diary! That such a play should be sent
to me filled me with righteous indignation. I gave it to Ferris
without telling him what I felt—and he thought it was just great.
We had a battle about it, but he finally convinced me that the
psychology was perfect; the diary had been haunting me for
years, and now I could laugh at myself, then say to the world,
"See—I realize how foolish I was." But I was far from ready for

that yet. I thought it was in rather bad taste, but I agreed to talk about it after we got back to New York.

And for two weeks in New York we did nothing *but* talk about the play. *So Much Velvet*, it was called. Frankly, while I love the theatre, it is not my whole life; I am not the great artist who can give his life and every thought to nothing but theatre. And there are certainly many other things I like to talk about. The play was on—and off—and finally the people who said they had wanted to put up the money for it called it off. They truly hadn't realized, they said, how close it was to my case. Ferris was annoyed with me. There was a good part in the play that he had been anxious to get.

I had a physical checkup, and the doctor said I was in remarkably good condition: "You must be made of steel." Ferris went for his own yearly physical examination. He came back very low. He told me that his heart was in bad shape, probably caused by the strain of the tour. Of course, all my irritation with him left— I felt truly miserable, and sympathetic. We talked most of the night, or rather I let him talk while I listened.

I racked my brains to think of something that would help him. On a few occasions we had discussed a managerial arrangement of a personal sort and now this thought came again into my mind. I knew that a position of authority would revive him. And I felt that he had done certain things for me, such as keeping my books. He might as well get paid for what he was doing. So I suggested that I give him 10 per cent of my earnings, and put the whole thing on a business basis. I had another thought in the back of my head. I felt I could relax and express my pleasure when I was offered a good salary, instead of feeling that such an announcement was just rubbing salt into his wounds. Now, he too would have reason to rejoice, for he would be profiting from it. Real sensible thinking!

It didn't have quite the salubrious effect I had hoped for. He continued to wear me down with either his miserable monologues or his heavy silences. I was still frightened of his heart condition and the possibility that I might lose him. I was weary and tired and depressed. The weather added its bit of misery—it was a dreadful heat spell. Things were piling up, tensions, pressures, piling up.

Late one steaming afternoon Ferris said, quite casually, like any normal person, "Let's have a drink." I think I waited no more than half a second before I said, "All right, let's."

Ferris went down to the corner and came back with vodka, tonic, and limes, and nothing ever tasted so good. Troubles vanished. The world wasn't such a bad place after all. For nearly a week we lived in a happy alcoholic mist. And of course we remembered that we loved each other . . . How foolish that such a thing had escaped us . . . Well, it hadn't, had it! Of course it hadn't.

From the stage of loving we progressed to the stage of hating, and as the week progressed, the arguments became hotter and emptier. By the end of the week we were making no sense at all; I had just enough self-possession left to realize that I had to do something about it.

The next day, Ferris and I slowed down a bit. He was feeling remorseful and went out in the afternoon while I slept some more. I was getting dinner when I heard the unmistakable "Wow!" of a Siamese cat. Thinking someone down the hall had brought one in, I ran to the door, but it was Ferris with a somewhat frightened Siamese lady on his shoulder. "You've been needing this," he said, grinning and happy. I could have wept with pleasure. She was seven months old, with the pedigree name of "Isis Ali Si." The s's became just plain "Missy," and Missy at once became the focus of all the love and affection I could bestow nowhere else.

In spite of the shakes and a shattering headache I stayed sober Sunday and Monday. Monday night was unbearably hot again, and in the icebox were bottles of beer—pale, cold, and inviting. And another week of increasing drinking began. Ferris was gone most of the time, visiting bars around the town—I stuck to my privacy and four safe walls. By the end of the week I was ill.

Ferris came home one afternoon and found me running a high temperature and vomiting blood. Even he was frightened. He phoned a doctor, and I was at once taken into Lenox Hill Hospital under the name of "Mrs. Wheelock."

There in the dark room I lay in a lethargic despair and listened to Hurricane Edna scream her way into the city.

Fourteen

I didn't like *me*. I hated *me*. And there was no escape from *me*, the person. I would have liked death, on my own terms—a nice, quiet release from the life I did not know how to live. Not knowing that living is an art, a skill, a learned technique—I could do nothing but rebel at living. I hated my traitorous body that fought for survival and yet demanded the baffling anesthetic of alcohol to endure that survival. And more than anything else I feared pain, and the painful, horrible death of the alcoholic that Ferris had described to me; that he knew about and had seen. At least that fear accomplished what nothing else seemed able to; after my release from the hospital I stopped drinking—for a while. I did not yet know that I had a real recognized disease, the disease of alcoholism, which is now known to be as insidious and fatal as cancer or tuberculosis, and no more shameful, and just as "arrestable."

Sources of pressure and depression were still everywhere about me. The show had closed on August 20, and for many weeks afterward I had no work. It is a slow time in the profession at that time of year, with TV showing mostly repeats and the theatre planning shows for the fall. It is the time to have a backlog of money so as to be able to "sit tight." But in early November I was down to $165, and Gloria sensed it, and said, "Need some help, girl?" And loaned me five hundred dollars.

Marylyn had called from California to tell me that Tono had to have surgery to remove a piece of glass that had been left in the flesh of his arm when a cut had been sewed up. And I grieved over her news that my friend Jane James was in the hospital after an operation and was not expected to live. I needed work, for money, for activity, to change my emotional climate.

And the upswing came, as it usually does in show business— the old saw, "a feast or a famine." Gloria got me a live half-hour TV show "just for the money"—a popular thriller called "Danger." The day following that show I went into rehearsal for the "Producers' Showcase" production of *The Philadelphia Story.* Less than a week after that had gone on the air, I began a "Philco" show, and the day after that I started rehearsal of *The Thief* for U. S. Steel—and the following day began on *The Hickory Limb* for Pond's. A few days later I started three weeks' rehearsal on NBC's big color production of *The Women,* where I got into money—three thousand dollars. I was what is known in the business as "hot." Gloria happily turned down other offers because of conflicting dates.

This was not at all conducive to peace in the apartment. Ferris got no work at all, and he was bitter with resentful jealousy.

When I got home after the show he would be drinking in the apartment—having made a tape recording of the telecast, pointing out how lousy I was because I didn't listen to him any more. It was during rehearsals for an "Elgin Hour" that I finally figured out (it shouldn't have been so difficult) why I'd had such an unreasonable case of nerves the day before the show. I checked back on my calendar, and about every three weeks I found I had made a small notation: "F. drinking." The dates coincided almost exactly with the last days of rehearsal, just before a show. Instead of keeping fit by resting and relaxing, quietly thinking over the show, I was torn to shreds, listening to Ferris talk about his hard luck and worrying about him.

In March the flood of TV engagements slowed down and stopped. The season was almost over—and I was also what is known as "overexposed"—seen too often. A script was sent from the Coast for me to read; it was not good, and Gloria turned it down for me. But it set me to thinking that perhaps I better get back to the Coast.

The more I thought of it, the more enthusiastic I became. I could stand a bit of California. And I wanted to see my kids. There was one thing I was not sure of—my professional standing on the Coast. It is strange how insular New York and Holly-wood are; even well-informed people are not interested in what is happening on the opposite coast (unless it is sensational). In New York I had become a star in the theatre, and a star on TV— though I had never had star rating in the movies. Also I had been away from movies—and if and when I made a movie it would be called a "comeback"! Gloria sent Famous Artists an accurate account of what I had done in New York so that they could at least be informed that I had been "active." And she said, "Don't worry. You can always get a play in New York any time you want one."

We left New York on April 15, 1955. We loaded the station wagon, installed Missy in her traveling box on top of a trunk, and set off across the country. The countryside was glorious— the changing beauty, new things to look at, to feel about, to think about, made all the crises and chaotic living in New York a distant thing.

And Missy was a joy as a traveling companion. She had never been out of the apartment, except for a trip to the vet's, and her first feel of earth and grass and the bark of a tree was something to watch. Soon she could be trusted out of her box, and would sleep contentedly between us on the front seat, waking at gas stations and scaring the wits out of the attendant by her Satchmo-voiced greetings.

We went through Missouri, among the lovely Ozark lakes.

Kansas and real horizons—no steel walls to stub the toe of vision. Oklahoma, a bit of Texas, New Mexico. Tumbleweed and dust storms. And finally California. It looked so beautiful to me, entering it from the great desert, through the little towns, and the slowed-down tempo—women shoppers in bright sunsuits, with brown legs. The slower, rounder speech. I had been wandering for two years—I must have been very homesick indeed.

For a minute anyway I could catch my breath before I took on the "pressures" again. I could sit in the window of the apartment I had taken in Brentwood and see eucalyptus and lemon trees. Even the bells of the Good Humor man sounded sweet and familiar. I saw my children. Tono was tall and strange and wonderful to me. Marylyn was pregnant with her second child, due in July. She hadn't told me, she said, because she wanted to surprise me.

Within ten days things began to look good for me, and I was very much encouraged. I went to Warner's to see about doing Jane Wyman's mother in *Miracle in the Rain*. (I didn't get the part, and Ferris was indignant: "What's she got against you!" I calmed him, saying, "You just don't get every part you're up for!")

I talked seriously with Ferris about drinking in Hollywood. Perhaps you can get away with drinking in New York, where your business is more your own. But Hollywood, despite its area, is a small town where everyone knows everyone else's business. You have to be a valuable star indeed to get away with constant drinking. If you have a hang-over, perhaps the cameraman will be the first to notice it—and then the assistant knows it, because you are a little late, etc. Nobody cares much, but movie making is an expensive operation and a person who looks bad—or costs the company money by being late or consuming time because lines are not learned well—just probably will not be called again. I told him he must be very circumspect and build a reputation for being reliable. These are the things that breed jobs as much as talent. But I was just whistling into the wind. For Ferris had his own dream world. If the producers rolled out the red carpet for him, and let him know they thought he was the greatest thing that had ever happened to movies, he probably would not drink. But the moment the going got tough, it would be the old story.

We looked all over town for a place I could live. Everything seemed so expensive, or landlords would not accept pets or wanted a long lease. Ferris had found an apartment for himself that was convenient and cheap. While I was still looking, my lawyer sent me a paper that I had to sign. I phoned, asked him to come out, and told him of my housing problem. He knew "just the place" for me—in the apartment house near where he was living. Only eighty dollars a month, convenient, pleasant, clean.

It sounded fine, but it turned out to be pretty dismal. A corner room with a wall bed, a kitchen, bath, and dressing room. The furniture was something left over from a Sears' sale in the twenties. But it was cheap, and there was a roof where I could take Missy to stretch her legs once in a while.

I got a good script from CBS—an adaptation of *Dinner at Eight* which was to air on June 1. And a week's work in a picture at Twentieth Century-Fox; a trashy story, and no part at all, but the three thousand dollars looked wonderful. I was engrossed in studying for the "Climax" show.

Meanwhile Ferris was getting calls for interviews at studios; something was bound to bear fruit, between the agent and the door I had opened for him. But if he kept drinking heavily he would be throwing away all his opportunities, and I was angry with him and told him so.

In my need to "talk" to someone—someone who could discuss something besides petty everyday events, the kind of talk that is akin to nervous drumming on a table, I went out to the Valley to call on Father O'Dea. He was pleased to see me, warm and friendly. I told him how tired I was of working toward nothing. He made a suggestion that I work toward a pleasant retirement; think about some quiet spot in a foreign country—work hard for a while, saving every penny, and then settle in Italy or Spain, perhaps, where I could get along on very little. Of course, this had strong appeal: it would provide the ultimate escape. The trouble was that I didn't know what I was escaping from—and I know now that a geographical change would not have helped me to escape from myself.

Ferris got a job, hurray, hurray. A part in one of the better Westerns. He would have to do some riding and he worried that he had been on a horse only a very few times—when he was drunk. "Learn to ride," I told him. "Don't underestimate Westerns; there's a lot of money in them." (Prophetically.) So he found a riding academy, got some blue jeans, and took a daily riding lesson. With sun and air and exercise he began to look better.

The skies were clearing. Ferris' chances looked good, and I had jobs lined up that would provide a good start toward my dreams of retiring far from all the breathless rush and worry that I had known so long.

I got a quick call to fly to Tucson for locations on the picture for Twentieth. Only two days of work were scheduled for me on the exterior of a big estate, but they were my first days of work in pictures for five years. I expected exciting changes—the wide screens, offering a chance to play long uninterrupted scenes—cause and effect seen at once—manipulating the attention of the audience by attraction instead of by the film cutter. But making movies was just the same as it had always been. Rush, rush, rush. Get it in the can before the sun goes down—if you say all the words in the script—if the cameraman and the sound man say they "got" everything—print it. Wardrobe lady, make-up man, hairdresser buzzing around like gnats right up to the second the camera turns. No moment of collecting myself, of a thought of "Who am I?" as the character. "What am I going to say—why am I saying it?" "Rehearse" a scene while everyone is talking—quiet only when the cameras are rolling.

I had asked Ferris to stay at the apartment to take care of Missy; it was too short a time to put her through the business of being boarded out. I returned from Tucson on the plane about midnight, twelve hours earlier than I had planned. I telephoned the apartment from the airport, but there was no answer. I didn't know what I was going to do: I had given Ferris my key, and the apartment lobby door was locked at nine in the evening. I got a cab and rode into Hollywood, and made another call when I got to La Brea and Sunset Boulevard. Ferris answered, sleepily and very drunk. "Can you make it downstairs and just open the door for me?" I asked. In a few minutes I was there and Ferris was in the lobby, grinning, his shirttail hanging out of partially fastened pants and Missy in his arms with her tail blown up in fright. A couple of people came in at the same time as we went up in the elevator. They talked about the "pretty kitty," but I knew they had recognized me (there is a "look" that is unmistakable) and were enjoying the general picture. I was burning mad. As the door of the apartment closed behind me, I threw my things down and rescued Missy, who was fighting to get away from his heavy embrace; I tossed Ferris a blanket and said, "Don't try to go home the way you are. You'll never make it. Get some sleep on the couch."

I was so tired that I slept heavily and didn't hear him the next morning. I had the movie script to study for the next sequences and the "Climax" script to start thinking over. We were scheduled to do the interiors of the picture during the next few days, and TV rehearsals would start immediately afterward. About four o'clock Ferris came in. He had been riding and he had been drinking. His manner was so unusual, it seemed as if he were playing a part. He was smoking a cigar, leaning back in the big chair in a kind of sneering arrogance. And he was loaded with "cracks" with "subtle" insults. He bated me into an anger that was explosive. Feeling the danger, I said as steadily as I could, "Ferris, I don't want you around when you're drunk. It's too hard on me. I've put you to bed and nursed you and dried you out for the last time. Now get out."

The next day, I went into rehearsal at CBS, and as usual, the work of TV was so all-absorbing and concentrated that what happened last week might have happened last year. It was a great escape for me. Ferris came around a few days later in a better humor. He wanted my help, for he had worked three days on the Western and I gathered it had not gone too well.

He said he was having trouble memorizing his lines. I worked with him one morning, cueing him, drilling him on something that should have taken no more than an hour. He didn't retain a word. "It's trash," he said, "it's bad writing. That's why I can't remember it." The artistic nature, of course. For a fee anyone can memorize a few pages in the telephone book or *real* bad writing.

The rehearsal was called for that afternoon. About seven he phoned me: "Come and pick me up. I'm all through." I knew what he meant—not just "through for the day." He had been fired. I went out after him, and all the way back he didn't talk at all. He sat in the car, not looking at anything—stunned. As he got out at the apartment he said, very seriously, "I want you to remember . . . I was not drinking." It was not the time to suggest to him that, sober or not, a ten-day bout previously is not conducive to an alert brain.

It didn't help Ferris' ego when a few days later I was handed a plum. Shaw's *Don Juan in Hell* had been a very great success as Charles Laughton had directed and played in it. It was a unique experience in the theatre. On a simple stage with only a backdrop and four lecterns with a microphone beside each, four people entered, dressed in evening clothes and carrying large leatherbound scripts. They sat on high stools or stood and apparently "read" the play. Audiences everywhere had been captivated. Now another tour was being planned, and a new company formed, with Agnes Moorehead, from the original company, directing and the four parts played by Reginald Denny, Ricardo Montalban, Edward Arnold, and myself. I hated the thought of "hitting the road" again, but this was an opportunity, both artistic and monetary, too great to miss. I was engaged at a thousand dollars a week, plus 5 per cent over the net earnings.

At the apartment alone, when I *was* alone, I did a lot of daydreaming. If I really made some money from the *Don Juan* tour I could get away from Ferris and find another life. I dreamed about a little place in Portofino maybe—just me, and lots of cats, and the seas and beauty around me—and blessed quiet. It was a lovely daydream—but it was a distant bubble filled with rainbow colors. A closer one, larger, less fragile, took its place.

Ferris came in late one evening, fairly drunk, but struggling for coherence.

"I've just spent two hours with your friend the monsignor," he said.

I hadn't heard right.

He went on, "You seem to have something that keeps you going. I don't know what it is, but I see you trotting off to Mass come hell or high water. In New York, or on the road, and now here; I don't know what it is. But I want to find out. I want some of it, too."

I could only sit and listen. I had sent up many a prayer for this, but still I couldn't believe it. Even when he said he was going for his first instructions the following Friday night. There was a clean sweep of resentment, all bitterness, all anger out of my mind. There seemed to have been a real reason for my having stuck with him now. People *can* change.

On Thursday, Ferris was still drinking. "But I'm going to knock it off tomorrow," he said. "I'm going to start being the guy I'm supposed to be." He seemed truly humble. And on him it had great charm. We went out to dinner that night and he talked a great deal about how it seemed to him that he had just had the wrong angle about everything. "I seem to be bucking the stream instead of going along with it." We were sitting in a candlelit booth and coincidentally the music was the familiar entr'acte music they had used in *Time of the Cuckoo*. It was fatal. Ferris said, with great sincerity, that we should be married. We had been through so much together, and in spite of everything somehow we had stuck. We knew each other. We contained no surprises.

"Let me hear you say that again when you're sober," I told him.

"I'm not so drunk," he smiled.

Friday, Ferris was sober, shaved and shining, and he went for his instructions. My divorce from Tommy would be coming through any day now and I was seriously considering Ferris' proposal.

Rehearsals began on *Don Juan*. I liked Agnes Moorehead— "Aggie," as we called her. A fine actress, now she proved to be an excellent director. Having been with the play with Charles Laughton and Paul Gregory at its inception, and having played it in London and New York and on the road, she knew all its values. There was much work to be done, but we had a four-week rehearsal schedule, so there was no sense of rush or pressure. *Don Juan* is different—and difficult because there is no imaginary "fourth wall." Each character speaks not only to the other characters, but to the audience as well, bringing them directly into the discourses on Heaven and Hell and the foibles of Man. Aggie stressed the importance of playing it like a quartette, with great precision of movement, with harmony. It is all memorized, contrary to the general impression, and the pages are turned for emphasis, or "punctuation." Each character stands or sits on a definite word cue, so there is no inharmonious popping up and down.

Then it became evident that Eddie Arnold would have to be replaced as the Devil—the illness that was to take his life had begun. Kurt Kasznar, a brilliant actor, said he would take the job.

The heat and smog were heavy and oppressive over the city that September, and to escape from it Ferris and I drove to the beach several Sundays. I was beginning to tune up like the strings on a banjo in anticipation of the tour, already living the tensions and discomforts in that wasteful expenditure of energy known as crossing bridges before—before they are even in sight. The cool air from the sea was soothing, easing the insecure thoughts of geographical changes.

The show felt good. It had style. Every detail had been meticulously worked out. Kurt showed his craftsmanship in his quick comprehension of the part of the Devil. He had power and variety. He could be reasonable, charming—sulking pettily like a child—strong in his contempt. Ricardo was splendid as the cynical, passionate Juan; and Reggie had the stuffy, amusing "Statue" right in his pocket. We worked with the smoothness of a team.

Our producer was more businessman than theatrical producer. He was very slow in giving us our itinerary, but he constantly assured us that we would have one-week and split-week stops only, with the exception of a few one-night stands at the universities. The night before we left for San Francisco we got the itinerary. After the week in San Francisco the first one-week stop was in St. Louis, not until mid-October. We were worried. This was to be no de luxe tour, as had been described. But from there on Mr. Goldberg assured us that he would book nothing but full-week stands, and held up the promise of Carnegie Hall in New York. Nice promises.

Ferris and I drove up to San Francisco on Saturday, September 17. We opened the following Monday in the Geary Theater. And what a great evening it was! The old theatre rocked with applause and laughter, between the long periods of intense stillness and concentration. We were a very high, happy company. Ferris spoiled my pleasure by drinking too much; only I knew why, and in spite of my irritation my heart went out to him. Dressed impeccably in dinner jacket, he came weaving back-stage after the performance, forcing his way through the people crowded in my dressing room. With maudlin tears on his face he wrapped his arms around me, kissing me wetly, saying, "Now—now you are an actress . . . God bless you!"

The next day, Ferris kept saying, "You were perfect, just perfect! I've never seen you 'work' an audience like that!" He was still a little drunk; he kissed me good-by and he never did that when he was sober. As he was leaving he turned at the door and said, "How I *resent* your being one of the greats!"

There is no point in going into the details of that tour, which was a fiasco, illy planned by a non-professional. We rattled from town to town, with no advance publicity—and no money. It was as though it had been set up as something to be deducted from a rich man's income tax. Our comfort was non-existent, and our morale lowered after each huge auditorium echoed with emptiness. We played twenty-eight one-night stands in a row, throughout the Northwest and Canada, before we had a night off, flying six- and seven-hour trips during the day. For over two weeks no one got more than four hours' sleep at night, and sometimes that had to be snatched in the lobby of a hotel—one time in the cocktail lounge of an airport in Montana we snatched fitful catnaps on the hard benches by the wall, with the radio blaring that the Dodgers were winning the pennant.

I kept in touch with Ferris by phone—he was staying at the apartment, receiving my mail, taking care of Missy—holding the fort. One day he reported that he would have to leave the apartment; the cat had ripped the upholstery badly, and the landlord was complaining. He would have to get the furniture repaired, and would send Missy to a good boarding place in the Valley, then get another apartment for himself.

When we got to Appleton, Wisconsin, we had our first days off—two of them in a row! I caught up on some sleep, and felt that I could think things out more clearly. And I told the company I was going to hand in my notice. I resented a little having to be the one to do it; I felt that each of us had been trying to outwait the other, which was just plain silly. At heart we all wanted to go home and be done with it. We played a split week in Minneapolis and St. Paul, and the two-week notice was posted in St. Louis, where we arrived seedy and tired and discouraged.

Everyone had been sick. Reggie had some flu, Ricky got laryngitis, and Kurt had picked up some food poisoning. In St. Louis it was bitter-cold and my chest became painfully congested. The local doctor gave me some penicillin, and then asked casually, "What do you take for your heart condition?" I had been aware that my heart was behaving rather strangely; I noticed that it would "stutter" frequently, and sometimes it seemed to stop for a couple of beats and then rush on. But I hadn't minded it, I had thought it was just fatigue and nervous tension. Now I was thoroughly alarmed; I told him I had not been "taking" anything. He said that I should have a thorough checkup when I returned home—and I had better not wait too long.

After the panic I could not control had worn off, I felt tired—

and for the first time—old. All this foolish rushing around, making plane schedules, shivering in the corner of some draughty building, putting on stage make-up with nothing but my compact mirror—I was too old for "roughing it." I wrote Ferris a long letter about what the doctor had said, and that I knew I would have to slow down. I tried to keep it light. "So," I wrote him, "please find me a little place to live—and obviously now a lease is okay—and have a chicken in the icebox and my cat to welcome me."

With a kind of relief that I had to make no decision, that now the choice was beyond me, I began to do some daydreaming which I thought was "thinking." Perhaps, I thought, Ferris' constant jealousy of me might diminish now. I would have to give up my "career"; I would simply try to make enough to get along on. Perhaps I could do some recordings, readings, for an income, do a little radio work. Ferris would no longer have to feel that he was "competing" with me; he would have greater peace of mind. We were "used" to each other. We had had our arguments and our battles, but perhaps now we could settle down—and get married. If he had to take care of me—me, not Mary Astor, the actress—he might feel better; it would be good for his pride. I didn't know quite how I felt about him emotionally. I had put up with a lot, I knew—maybe that was love. Real love, and not just romance.

There were still a few more stops to complete the tour: Teachers' College at Cedar Falls, Iowa, State University at Iowa City; Lincoln, Nebraska; Denver, Colorado; and one night in Colorado Springs, and then back to finish out the week in Denver. We got caught in a terrible snowstorm in the mountains, getting to the theatre just in time to throw on a make-up and get on stage.

My dreams of a domestic life with only one actor in the family had grown rosier by the day. My emotions were building, and I could hardly wait to be with Ferris again. The last time I had talked to him, he had sounded so happy—and I felt an excitement in his voice that I was coming home after the long weeks. We had so much to talk about. I had given him my arrival time and he would meet me.

My heart began its unrhythmic thumping as the plane circled and landed. And suddenly he was there on the ramp, looking well—so very well. He was grinning as he hugged me. "Looks like you need a rest, girl . . ." While the luggage was being unloaded, he said, "Let's go into the bar and have a beer." And he told me enthusiastically all about the place he had found for me to live; how he had found it, just by chance—the rent, the convenience, the wonderful view.

"You look so well, I can't get over it—what have you been doing?" I said happily.

And he said, "I got married, three weeks ago."

Steady now, Mary. Find some words. Don't scream.

"Well, what do you know! How wonderful! Anybody I know?"

"No, she's an English girl—name's Mildred. It's funny how I met her—I was . . ."

But the fog had closed in . . . I heard very little—my training came to my rescue and I was doing an excellent impression of an interested friend.

"You look awfully tired, Mary. Are you sure you're all right?"

"I'm exhausted, that's all."

He was chattering now, as though he were relieved that I hadn't been troublesome.

I heard him say, "Milly's the kind of girl that when I say, 'Go over and sit down and stay there,' she *stays* there, and loves it."

There was a beat in which my mind said, "Sure, boss man." But what came out was "Yes, the English women really know how to be wonderful wives."

"I told her that you were still 'in the picture' and I'll have to see you any time you want me."

"We're all going to be friends—is that the way it's going to be?"

"That's the way it's going to be."

We drove on to my new apartment. My landlady was extremely pleasant, apologizing for the unfinished state of the place. Ferris had talked her into renting to me before she had put it up on the lists. There was much to be done. She had converted what had been a large "rumpus room" into a living room, bedroom, and bath—with the living room divided off by a cabinet for a combination stove and refrigerator section. The bedroom had a wonderful double bed in it, into which I wanted to sink and sleep —one night after another in the same bed—no more horrible hotels that looked out over the Main Streets of the land.

Ferris took me out to dinner, and then we drove to the Valley to get Missy. We stopped at several bars on the way. The drinks revived my fatigue, but otherwise seemed to have no effect. I was putting time in, letting time happen; piling up hours between me and shock. My mind was like a radio with several stations overlapping; my emotions twisted the dial, and first one would come through and then another. "I'm free, free, free. I would have *married* him. I've escaped!" "I'm glad for him. I hope he's really in love with her. Maybe love will keep him more sober than I could." But the strongest signal to come in was the most persistent: "What am I going to do without him? I have no one. No one in this whole world."

After Ferris had left me at my new home and we parted with pleasantries: "Good night; see you . . ." "Glad you're back . . ." "Glad to be back," I tried to sleep. I woke and walked around. I finally cried. I drank. I got noisy. My landlady came down, concerned and kind. She knew the demands of show business—and she had also had a little trouble with men in her time. My heart was performing all the tricks it had learned during the tour, and I was hoping it would do one big nip-up and get it over with. I knew I was in a flat spin and couldn't pull out. I called my doctor, and when he asked me to describe exactly how I felt I said, "I'm drinking—and I can't stop." "Well, maybe you'd better come in and tell me about it," he said.

That evening I went into Sierra Madre Lodge, over near Pasadena. I stayed there ten days. In a few days, when I felt better, the doctor talked to me. "You've really been in a spin," he said. "The peculiar part of it is that the alcoholic content in your blood was not very high. I think it was secondary to physical depletion.

The only way I can explain it non-technically is that you are sort of consuming your own tissues."

Of course one's life just isn't like a novel or a play; it just doesn't come to a satisfying or dramatic climax and then quit. It doesn't ride off into the sunset.

Mentally I was at a point where I couldn't figure anything out; I knew I had to be decisive, and I made some strange decisions. I had areas of disorientation, of conflicts that I couldn't reconcile. I had to learn to live alone, I supposed. Living alone meant to me something horrible, like inhaling one's own breath. It meant that I could not ask for help: that was my definition of independence. I knew, deeply, that I was lucky to be free of Ferris, but on nights during the winter when the pine tree outside my window sighed in the rain, and a little dog in the house down the hill howled because someone had left him, the self-pity would consume me, and I would shiver and pile more blankets onto my bed, feeling something protective in their warmth and weight.

Gradually I began spiraling down into lonely depression. There was enough work. A "Lux" show—then to New York for "Star Stage." Back to Hollywood, then New York again—a "Matinee," a "Climax," a picture for Metro . . . I was nervous with the discipline of drinking, of trying not to drink. From the tension and complete lack of enthusiasm or appreciation of the fact that I was so very lucky to be "wanted" for work. I would sit on the steps outside my door in the sunshine in utter emptiness. Absorbed in my own nothingness. Unable to contact people except in the most superficial fashion. Withdrawing, withdrawing; drinking to ease the unnamed pain.

Fifteen

And so I come back to the point where I began this story.

I don't pretend to have all the answers, but I believe I have enough material with which to make living in this world a little pleasanter for myself and, it must follow, for others.

Most people come by this material gradually, over a lifetime of good, common sense, everyday living; without the aid of any kind of therapy except that which nature and God supply in abundance. But I had to condense my learning, my growing up in a very short time. And I had to learn in order to live.

I was fortunate enough to have an inherent vitality; the deepest need, survival, was very strong. This quality Father Ciklic must have perceived very quickly, like a surgeon who knows that his patient has a strong heart and can endure radical surgery.

I knew this was my last chance. I could only place my trust implicitly, follow instructions to the letter, co-operate to the fullest. Even then it might not work. But I had nothing to lose because I had nothing—I was bankrupt, emotionally and mentally. I was carrying a load of guilt too great to be borne, and in my depression and near despair I probably would have furnished one more miserable headline and that would be that.

The first step was the hardest, the hardest for any human being —to admit defeat. To honestly ask for help, without reservation, without one part of the mind hoping for reassurance, without desiring to be taught how to do things "my way." Even my prayers had somehow been all wrong. I could not even promise God I would not drink any more—I could not "amend my life." I was saying "Thy will be done" and then taking the bit in my teeth and doing things my way. I finally put it simply: "I give up— help me—let me do things Your way for a change."

I gave in to the small scheduling of my days—and I hate schedules! Daily Mass, breakfast, housework, etc. Then at one o'clock I would sit down at the typewriter, freshly showered, wearing a cool pair of shorts and a shirt, the telephone muffled with a pillow —and I would work at writing about my life.

My sessions with Father were looked forward to with a confusion of feelings; a little of the dread of going into surgery, a little of the feeling of going to school, which was heightened by the atmosphere of the campus, but mostly a feeling of pleasure at seeing an understanding friend.

The answer to my knock and question, "Father?" would be a warm "Come in, come in, how are you, Mary?" It was amazing how much he could put into asking how one was. He always smiled as if it were a very big and important joke, just between us. With a command of a dozen languages and an English vocabulary large enough to fill a dictionary, Father still has an accent and some pronunciations that get him into trouble. Usually the conversation would open normally with some remarks about the weather. One very hot day he said, "It is a good day for the beaches——" I laughed and said, "Watch those vowels, Father!" He paused, frowning, reviewing his sentence. Then his eyes flashed in merriment and he said, "Well—it would be good for *them* too!"

And so perhaps the conversation would drift easily into talk of languages, and without realizing it I was directed into talking about my dad, of his absorbing interest in speech and teaching language, how he taught Europeans the difficult peculiarity of our speech, the sound of "th," which exists in no other language but a Spanish dialect. And gradually we would be discussing my work of the previous week.

As priest and psychologist, Father was shockproof; there would be no raised eyebrows or words of condemnation. I knew this, and yet my self-disgust and remorse often made the sweat start out in beads. Father, glancing at my twisting fingers, would smile and say, "If you were a moron, none of this would bother you, you would be quite happy—be glad that you are intelligent and sensitive, for you can learn."

"Don't you think it's a little late?" I wondered.

"Never. Living *is* change. Your past will always be part of you —it is in your mind, your memory—but with understanding and education it need not affect what you are today, or what you will be in the future."

There was no dramatic discovery of a hidden single trauma. There was no couch—only the big chair placed in front of his desk, behind which he sat with an almost contagious quality of quiet calm, his expressive fingers clasped on the desk or curled around a pipe. There was no need for "deep analysis," apparently. I had not slipped into the realm where there is no contact with reality, thank God. Although my whole technique of adjustment had been escape, I had not yet "escaped" from communication. But without a doubt that is where I had been headed.

As an occasional check Father would use the "word associa- tion" technique. He had asked me to keep a tablet beside my bed and make notes of my dreams as quickly as I could recall them. They were many, vivid and nightmarish, as the censor would fight to stop my self-revelations. Father would ask me to put out my cigarette, to lean back in the chair and relax, and then he would use the words or phrases of the dreams by them- selves: "door," "shouting," "the roof," and I would try to respond with the first word or phrase that would come into my mind. This was very hard to do; it filled me with embarrassment and squirming; my mind would shy away like a startled animal; and often I would try to avoid even the most harmless-sounding associations. I often felt trapped and nervous. I was trapped into seeing things as they are. I was taken mentally by the shoulders and asked, with great kindness, but firmly, *"Can you see . . . ?"*

The "free association" was pleasanter. He would start me off with "Just start talking—perhaps about the little girl in the checkered dress you were telling me about," and I would let the images flow in my mind, picking up all sorts of strange fragments, from wondering about the color of my nail polish—to the color of the Gulf Stream in the Caribbean Sea, and pebbles rattling on a beach, the words of a poem: "That Voice is round me like a bursting sea: 'and is thy earth so marred, shattered in shard on shard?' " and red anthurium, and——

"Good—good. That is fine—come back, Mary." And it would seem as though I had been asleep and dreaming aloud, and I would hate to "come back." He would not permit me to "escape" for long. "You have a tremendous longing for beauty—for what is right, what is good." All very fine, but back we would go into my writing—teacher and student now.

"Can you see . . . ?" Sometimes I did not *see*, and he would explain, patiently, until I did. In my relationship with my parents I had to see the separation between what I knew—that they had been well-intentioned, that never did they believe that what they were doing for me was not "the right thing"—and the fact that they did not love me. Father explained, "When you love someone you cannot help showing it—it will be there in all ways. A scolding from a parent is received with howls perhaps, but without deep injury if the child *knows* he is loved. If you obey an authority who loves you, there is pleasure in the obedience."

I began to see. A human being needs love for growth as much as he needs food. There is an imbalance if it is not met. All nature is constantly moving, "adjusting," or "compensating," for balance or lack of it. It is all around us, in music, architecture—in the active and passive sections of living. Rhythm and dancing satisfy by their constant achievements of balance. We are "shocked" when something is "left up in the air"—we don't like a piece of music that sounds "unfinished," a story that doesn't have "an ending."

We cannot stand too much shock. Without realizing it I was under the constant shock of not being loved, for, as Father explained, "When you love someone you want what is the right thing, the good thing for *him*. To exploit a child, to use him as an expression of one's own frustrations of ambition, is to show there is no love—only selfishness."

"Well then," I offered, "since my parents rejected me, I can blame them for my load of troubles. That seems too easy a way out."

"Blame is the wrong word, Mary," he replied. "Childhood rejection causes many things according to the nature of the individual—hostility, withdrawal, aggressiveness, or escape. But you *cannot blame* your parents. Either the love was there or it was not there. Maybe they were incapable of loving. You do not know their problems, and they must have been tremendous, full of suffering and bewilderment."

There was so much to learn. When I was on the way home from my "lessons," relaxed, with the clean air in my lungs, the smell of the sea wind that sweeps the grassy campus grounds, my mind would feel as though it had been put through some ballet exercises. I would begin to see myself objectively. I could clarify the two elements, the combination of forces which had affected my patterns of behavior. The combination of not being loved and overprotection. I could remember my temporary relief each time when I found someone who would "take care of me." How I thought I loved him, leaned on him, happy for someone else to make decisions. And then how I would look at the results with shock and fright, wondering how it had happened, blaming myself for not judging people properly, and again starting on the heartbreaking search for someone else to *lean* on. I thought of Father's word, "exhausting" myself. How any decisions I made were done with a kind of desperate effort—always with my emotions, and never with my mind.

I had to break from solving problems emotionally; rarely had I acted without "feeling strongly" about the situation at hand, and realizing that these strong feelings were as witless as those of a mouse in a laboratory maze, running through the same labyrinth to get the same miserable bit of cheese. Hardly a picture conducive to self-esteem! My only treatment for my wounded ego, as mistake piled upon mistake, was self-lectures couched in slick cocktail-party descriptive prose that begins with "Really, darling . . . !" In passing I find it interesting to observe what a devilish little phrase that is; I have had people say that to me thousands of times, and have never found it therapeutic. It simply says what one knows already—it is a bit of salt rubbed into the wound.

A big step was made one day when the real meaning of self-esteem finally penetrated. It reminds me of the story of Helen Keller and her teacher, who spelled the word "water" over and over into the blind child's hand. Over and over, with the other hand held under a spout of a well; and again when she would take a drink, and the great joy when she grasped that the symbol and what she drank and what she felt were all the same.

I had said to Father, when he had told me of the importance of a sense of worth, "What in the world do I have to be proud of? Certainly not of my life or what I have done with it." I had always lived with mistrust of myself, afraid that no matter what I would do it would be another mistake. Mistrusting even my accomplishments. Underrating myself. Somewhere in my reading about my religion I had found a good excuse: pride was a sin; therefore it was all right for me to be miserable and not be proud of myself. Of course I had missed the point, that pride is "an inordinate love of one's own excellence," the sign of the rebel against God. So I was a little astonished when Father—a priest!—said, "You must be proud of yourself." I told him how I felt, and he gave me something to chew on: "Did it ever occur to you that pride can be a source of humility? If you are proud that God loves you, that He has given you great gifts, then you are acknowledging His existence and dependence on Him—and that is humility. You can be proud of being an American, of being a Catholic, of being an actress, of being a woman, et cetera—and this is not a 'sin,' but a virtue."

I began to *choose* not to feel miserable. I had been accepting many things which I could change, accepting them in a kind of irritable melancholy; sensitive, vulnerable to the slightest disappointment. Thanksgiving Day at this period became a small danger point.

My place on Sycamore was completely inadequate for cooking or serving a meal for more than two people; except for the pony tail and jeans set, who would find it "gay" to serve spaghetti on paper plates on the floor. I didn't want to barge in on anyone else's celebration, and I had not yet reached the point where I could casually call up an acquaintance and say, "What are you doing for dinner?" I felt the downward pull of self-pity, of hurt, loneliness. Little beginning danger signs. It was a good place to say, "The hell with it," and blot out Thanksgiving Day, and country girl memories of the succulent bird, and families gathered in warmth and love and prayer—nostalgia for non-existent events—tenth-rate thinking leading inevitably to 100 proof vodka.

The first swing in the opposite direction was way off. *Service to Others*—italicized and capitalized. I would call up some organization and find out if they could use me to serve Thanksgiving dinner at one of the charity centers; those other unfortunates who didn't have a family or a home. I could visualize myself sweating happily over heaping platters, and the smiles of gratitude—oh, let's go the whole way—*tears* of gratitude on the faces of the poor. Real big shot-itis. It broke me up, and in my laughter I found the first high reward of self-conquest.

The big balloon of self had been punctured—the whole situation became very unimportant. Nevertheless, to occupy myself I got busy; I went to the market and bought a little frozen Cornish rock hen, a small box of wild rice, some cranberry jelly, a lovely bunch of asparagus, and an extra half pound of butter. The preparation of the meal was fun, and I even satisfied my need to dramatize the situation by putting a candle on the minute coffee table. I wouldn't take a million dollars for the memory of that dinner, because I had turned a big corner. And around that corner was the beginning of the relief of not having to meet the same old me, tomorrow and tomorrow and tomorrow, simply getting older, more unhappy and no wiser.

The time I spent with Father, I can see now, was just a beginning. As near as I can remember, I think I imagined that the results might be a further justification, a kind of rationalization of my life; and that afterward everything would be just gingerpeachy; that with a kind of magic wand, and no effort at all, I would be heavily insulated against pain and sorrow, that I would be able to move around in the world without having the world or life touch me at all.

The past was finally past. Written down, examined, and discussed—and discharged, deprived of energy. With great skill, patience, and caution, like a member of a demolition squad, Father had removed the detonator, the pin, the key to my self-destruction, which was ignorance. I could look back over my life and see it as bizarre, fantastically foolish and unnecessarily miserable. I could feel and know with blessed certainty that I could never again act under the dynamics, the forces of old habits, the caprice of infantile drives, the reactions to former conditioning. Interesting enough, but what now? I had evaluated my past life, and it had been painful of course; but I began to realize at an accelerating and exciting pace that that is not the only purpose of psychotherapy. It is also *re*-education.

We demand that "things" in our life function properly: we must have good roads to travel on, we like precision and beauty in almost everything from a faucet to an office building. We have demanded education, research, and improvement in bodily health, but still many of us live and put up with misery and unhappiness within ourselves; weeds choking the garden of our minds. We go to the dentist twice a year, we have physical checkups, but we minister to our inner needs with a rabbit's foot—we read books, articles, and pamphlets on personal charm and how to "influence" other people. To be "mentally ill" is unfortunate, but we often wait too long to get expert help. We have a *right* to be as whole a person as possible, physically, emotionally, and mentally.

I know how long Father Ciklic waited before telling me that I should take the material I had written for him and "make a book out of it." The reasons he gave me at the time were reasons enough to satisfy me. I knew that what I had written and told him was held in a sacred trust; this man had too much dignity, too much sincerity to suggest that I write my story simply to let the public "in" on my life, or to set the record straight for my own satisfaction and "explain" things. Nor could anyone learn anything from *my* mistakes, because no one else was *me*. But I could take his phrase, "Can you see . . . ?" and use it: "Can *you* see?"

Suddenly all the "sick, sick, sick" jokes seem puerile; the couch and the notebook as a symbol of self-indulgence for the wealthy, the mental hospitals only for those of weak wills who have "flipped." All the ignorantly used psychiatric terms, the tampering of fakes, the lack of understanding seem like a kind of nervous giggling at something odd and strange and therefore frightening. These attitudes will someday disappear like jokes about the automobile. Anyplace along the line in my life, if it had been interrupted with sound teaching and sound learning, things that followed would not have happened. Normal behavior and abnormal behavior are quantitative rather than qualitative.

There was no pause, no vacuum, no "Well, that's that," after Father dismissed me from regular therapy. I began to look around me, I began "hearing" some of the practical things that Father had been suggesting to me. It would be "fun" to have a home of my own again. I had lived in the Sycamore apartment for a year and a half, afraid to budge, afraid that every job might be my last one. But now I could depend on myself, and oddly enough, on the one thing in my life that I had not pursued and clung to, my profession. It had always been there, I realized, always ready to take me back on my own terms. I was part of it and it was part of me. I could depend on it, like a friend.

I had very little money, but at least I could make some inquiries, find out how much a down payment would be—figure out the difference in living expense. I looked at furniture ads, and they began to suggest exciting—if long-range—possibilities. It would be good to have "things" around me that I liked: a fireplace, books —what about this hi-fi business? Why, just the most beautiful way of listening to music—a whole opera on only *two* records? Where had I been!

Interest, interest—it began to vitalize me. I got a script of the old, wonderful movie that Gloria Swanson had made, *Sunset Boulevard*, as a TV show for Robert Montgomery. I took it to Father and said, "Would you mind reading this—tell me a little how this kind of person acts—why does she behave in such and such a manner?" Would he! He wrote a full diagnosis and analysis. I showed it to my director in New York, we worked and studied together, and when the show went on the air I was no longer a bundle of nerves waiting for it all to be over with.

Back in Hollywood a "Playhouse 90" with a wonderful group of people and a beautiful script called *The Ninth Day* had me looking forward to rehearsals.

Then there was another "Matinee Theater," another "Climax," a "Zane Grey Theater," "Lux," a picture for Paramount. And I could go house-hunting and, when I found something I liked, say, "It's a deal!"

The deadly alcoholic problem also had been faced. Right in its bloodshot eye. During my work with Father he rarely dwelt on my drinking problem, but he had told me in no uncertain terms that it is a fact that if one is an alcoholic there is no "cure." One can never go back to "social" drinking, not even an ounce. But he carefully refrained from telling me outright that I was an alcoholic. This I had to find out for myself. I could "discipline" myself, as usual. For a while I would have a drink now and then, and I would tell him about it. But he seemed unconcerned. Occasionally I would drink more than I intended—and I wouldn't tell him about it. By this time I had undergone quite a course in how not to kid myself, and I knew well this odd area of insanity, this complusion that will rationalize and produce a fifth of whiskey from a top shelf, where it stands "in case someone drops in." The bewilderment when the bottle is empty, and there is a desire for more and yet not more. I located some old friends who belonged to the Fellowship and who understood. They said, "Welcome back, Mary—we've been waiting for you."

I had some compunction about telling Father—and this is part of that former thinking!—I was "afraid" he might think that I felt his therapy had been inadequate. When I called him to tell him, he said quite simply, "That's wonderful—I'm sorry I couldn't hurry matters for you. I knew you would see it; I'm so relieved."

And so was I. The fights, the struggles, the time-wasting preoccupation with how to drink and not get into trouble were over. I had to learn and to accept that once one has passed over the line to compulsive drinking there is no return. The tolerance has become nil, and remains that way. The only remedy is total abstinence. But with my friends and with group therapy, regularly, the frightful, boring sound of "total abstinence" becomes the life-giving attitude of "total sobriety." The whole problem is considered and worked on the three levels, physical, emotional, and mental or spiritual. Self-pity, resentments, childish attitudes are to be carefully, constantly guarded against; and if they are, there is never any trouble about not taking a drink, because there is no necessity for one. Alcoholism is something that happens to someone else—it is more difficult to admit to oneself than to admit to the most horrible disease; because somehow the word is still associated with "weakness" and "lack of will power." When one learns that one is not guilty, that there is a still unsolved combination of organic and psychic factors in the make-up of some individuals which make them helpless against the insanity and destructiveness of alcohol—there is tremendous relief. And relief is vitalizing. The body, the mind, and the heart respond with a bounding lift that seems miraculous. One's self-esteem returns, and with that solidly in place there is no constant need to turn within oneself on constant repair jobs.

On the southwestern rim of the basin that contains the fabulous, spreading, urgently growing city of Los Angeles is a real estate development that is advertised as an "island in the sky." Numerous dead-end little streets wind and switch back to an elevation which looks over the broad plateau to the Santa Monica Mountains. The homes are neat, in well-styled contemporary architecture. There is a suburban air—station wagons, good-looking children, friendly neighbors. It is suburbia in the city, for, look north and east, there is City Hall; sewn together with stitchings of lights, moving and stationary, patterned with the snaking freeways, are Hollywood, West Los Angeles, Brentwood. Snugly tucked into the hills that overlook this fantasy is my home. My home, where I live quietly, comfortably, at peace with myself.

My classes at Loyola University in psychology and further talks with Father Ciklic are part of my continuous education. And the application of what I learn is a daily, fascinating job. The rewards spill over into everything I do, in a kind of astonishing joy.

Of course, I don't mean any kind of euphoric, Pollyanna attitude. Problems, troubles, annoyances are part of life. But what I do about them is the important thing. I know that I must avoid "escapes"—that I must not wander off and daydream in my childhood surroundings, where I learned to avoid pain. Playing with fantasy is a softer, easier way of solving problems.

Deliberate escape is necessary and fine and healthy, but habitual escape is simply a bad bargain because we are up to our necks in reality. And the key word is *habitual*.

It was interesting to me to learn that all of our personality traits and behavior are acquired—and that no one is doomed from birth to be neurotic or psychotic. Ten people, for instance, undergo a variety of traumatic experiences, a parental rejection, the shock of loss of loved ones, financial disaster, accidents, hurricanes, illness, or a crack on the head. Five of them will face the situation and see it as it is and bounce back, and these are "whole" persons. Three of them will resort to "escapes" for a time and discard them as useless—two will continue to use the escapes habitually and eventually deteriorate completely. Therefore it is not the experiences one has had, it is not that "I" have suffered more than "you"—it is how one has reacted to them. I am not speaking of the feeble-minded, or the intelligent sociopath, but the legion of the "normal" which lies between.

I know I will carry many scars, as most of us do, but they don't concern me any more. I know that all my habits of thinking are not going to disappear like *that*, but I recognize them, and beat their ears back when they appear. I know that solving problems emotionally is not solving them—I wait till the emotion dies down before acting. The textbooks call it acting upon a "reality principle." It doesn't dilute enjoyment to postpone it a minute—instead of grabbing at it like an infant.

When I first moved to my new home I was eager to furnish and decorate it "all at once." Naturally, I couldn't afford it. I could have groused and grumbled and pitied myself with thoughts of "if only I had the money that I had at such and such a time." But that doesn't get a house furnished! Instead I got the necessities, the refrigerator and stove—shopping around for the best values (I don't know arithmetic, I can't count—you buy it for me—spend a few dollars more so I will be saved the embarrassment of having to subtract. . . .). I bought a mattress and springs and put them on the wall opposite the TV set and next to the fireplace. Some books stacked on the floor. I bought a vacuum cleaner. And stocked the kitchen. I was *living*. My neighbors gave me a "welcome to our street" party—and I was able to surrender my "perfectionist" ideas and say, "Come to my house —as it is—accept it, and me, as I am." Work seemed to appear from all directions, and with each check I would decide how much I could spend out of it and buy myself a "big" present. A sectional couch and coffee table. A lovely Drexel desk with a leather top. A blond wood Danish-designed table and chairs for the dining area. Each item a little project—a little "reward" to savor. I reveled in the big shower—a whole tankful of water just for me! Missy and Slippers (acquired the year before) were "home" putting on their own floor show in the room-to-room dimensions of the living room and long hall, and zipping out of their own foot-square swinging door into the patio—up over the cement wall and clambering up the sun-warm hill.

I know I am a "nest-builder," a home lover. But this home I am making is not to crawl into and hide and wish to not have to work, to wish to be "taken care of"—to hope for death. To be lonely and grieve that I have made a hash of marriage, that my children have grown and "left the nest." This is simply "home base." Privacy and "aloneness," yes. Because I loved to read I have discovered that I enjoy writing, and that takes quiet, disciplined hours. But it is a place to go *out* of also. The telephone rings. I don't "jump" and wonder suspiciously "Who wants what of me now!" It's a friend with something to share—a bit of news, a joke, or some troubles. Or it's Marylyn to talk about the new baby—the third little girl, Gabrielle Marie.

I am able now to accept my children as grown human beings. I saw Tono graduate from high school in the ceremony at St. Monica's Church, where he—and I!—were baptized. Tall, good-looking, a very practical person, he is now in college, falling in and out of love, taking cars apart and putting them together again; working at jobs in the summertime—going to be whatever *he* wants to be.

Marylyn, the busy homemaker with three little girls . . . We are as close as two generations can be—we are *friends*—in a very real sense of the word. We have an unspoken sense of each other's attitude toward life and work. We consent, each to the other, the fact that we are as we are, accepted and made room for, appreciated in each other's life.

Naturally, I have many moments of lost "momism"—of wishing that I might have been "closer" to my children. But is it, after all, only a wish that I might have been of more "influence"?

When I am not working I like to go to friends' homes for dinner—or to have them in, and I'm glad I learned to cook beautifully, and I purr louder than Missy to have people enjoy my cooking. I have a lovely life and I don't take one minute of it for granted. It is no one's fault but mine if I don't work at it to *make* it a lovely life. I thank God in everything I do, I try to do His will as nearly as I can know without fretting about it. I get goose-pimples when I think of the miracle of my narrow escape, but I must not stop and sentimentalize and wonder at it too long. He has willed the path, but I must do the walking. Now, this minute, today. Yesterday is gone, tomorrow never comes.

I find that living on a "today" basis is the real trick. To look ahead too far is too great a burden. What "might" happen next week or next year can be disturbing, the panic of losing, or the unreal unexperienced joy of gaining. Anticipating to a certain extent is prudent, and pleasant, *if* I know it will never happen completely as anticipated.

For instance: "today" I am sober. I enjoy it—I feel alert—on the beam. I feel happy that I don't "need" a drink. I personally do not need a drink, to work better, to relax, to enjoy things more. I taste the flavor of food, I sleep better. All my senses are more acute—I smell the air from the sea, and I'm glad when there's no smog! Articles that I touch seem drawn to my hands as though they were magnetized—they don't slip away and fall or break as though they had a mind of their own. "Trigger" situations may come along; fatigue, upsets, disappointments. If I prepare for them, soberly, saying each and every day as it comes along—with the help of God I will not drink *today*—I am building up insurance, a different kind of habit pattern. I know I cannot live and drink; but I am not facing the rest of my life without drinking. Only today.

It's a great beauty treatment too, and that part of it is a lot of fun. No cosmetic in the world gives a clearer skin. An "alcohol-free diet" is a figure toner. My eyes look clear and sparkly, my hands are warm and dry. And people say, "You look wonderful!" And that never hurt anybody's ego!

Sometimes I feel as though I were living in another dimension. I wish I had thought of the phrase someone used: "wearing life like a loose garment." I go to work in a picture, and of course I still have to get up at five-thirty. But it's easy—I can eat a good breakfast, for one thing; and my mind is not on the fact that it would have been pleasanter to stay in bed. As I get into the car there's a bright star still shining in the sky and a pinkish-bluish tinge to the horizon. The street lights are off and the houses look closed and hushed. I feel a kind of tingly energy and I laugh at Missy waving good-by with her tail, perched on the roof of the garage. There is a sequence in the picture to do today that promises to be interesting, and I'm off on a plan of thinking about the character, what is *she* thinking about, why is *she* saying what she says, etc. If it is just a routine day, with nothing much to concentrate on, maybe I'll have somebody out for lunch—or write some letter in my dressing room, or read a light book.

If I'm doing a TV show I realize I'm not waiting for the "last red light on the last camera" to go off. I'm having a *ball!* For one thing, by show time I'm thoroughly prepared—each day has been spent with nothing else cluttering my mind, and I have worked hard and it is all *there*. As show time nears and the excitement rises, all the glands start pouring out that extra something that lifts the performance on a little higher level of behavior and my feet never touch the ground. And of course I've called everybody I know to watch, and as soon as I get home the phone starts ringing, and that's even more fun. I never knew before the pleasure in my work that I am having now. I "hated" it, and I didn't know why I hated it. Father C. pointed out to me that it was a rebellious feeling against being *made* to do something. Then later it was an escape from the home surrounding and Daddy, of course. And later still, a financial necessity. It is still a "financial necessity"—everybody has to work in some way in order to live. And how lucky I am that, in spite of myself, I had skills and techniques developing that I can turn to and use with all the pleasure of a good craftsman.

I don't feel that this "today" method excludes ambitions and reasonable goals. And it's fun to daydream of something wonderful—*if* it is something that is attainable by doing something about it. I do feel that the "if I were only——" "if things were different ——" "if I could just——" type of daydreams are strictly out of bounds. I have found enjoyment in writing this book; it's fun to plan to write a novel, but it would be senseless to dream of writing *the* great novel of the year, with critical acclaim already sounding in my ears. I know I have to learn to write, to work at writing, and that is far enough—it is a pleasant, attainable goal. I think each day should have its "little goal," even if it's no more than having done the best I can with whatever I had to do. Then I can go to bed and say, "Thank you, God," and sleep like a top.

But the most wonderful thing of all to me is that I am discovering people. I am finding out that they knew me and liked me a whole lot better than I ever knew myself, and certainly better than I ever liked myself! In all the turmoil and effort it took to live life as it was *not*, I had no time, no ability to find out about people. I was busy molding and building the "Mary Astor" mask so that "I" would be protected—from the hurts, the wisecracks, the flattery. Poor little battered ego! I bury it daily and say to it, "Be still." I have stopped estimating people in relation to myself: "What do they think of me . . . ?" "How do they think I should be—or think or act or react . . . ?" I see people as people. To me, of course, every human being in the world has an immortal soul, and so these are the immortals with whom I talk about the weather. What they are, "important" or "unimportant"; what they do, if they run a country or a grocery store; their fame, their fortune, their position—it is historically obvious that these things are as ephemeral as the dust on a butterfly's wing. I am not saying they are not important and are to be disregarded. I am sure that the dust on a butterfly's wing is a "must" for the butterfly.

What does matter is that I am a person, a human being. I need people, and people need me. We are a kind, a being, one body. A "wonderful, mystical, magical miracle." And if we deny that fact, and make the world a lousy place to live in, it is our fault. I know that we make it difficult for ourselves to get along with each other, that our precious little egos are touchy and flammable, and all I can do about that is simply to accept myself as I am and people as they are. To know that first and foremost, I must be honest with myself. That is not as easy as it sounds, but if I am not I war against myself. The mind rests in truth, and it is turbulent and muddy and unproductive if truth is avoided. I can not always find "reasons" for what I do or say or think or feel, but if I can't I must say so, I must say "I don't know," and not dream up a lot of excuses. Everyone feels "depressed" at times. Just for no reason, or for a number of reasons that are unimportant: a change in the weather, not enough rest, improper food, etc. But I must not find release from my depression by saying it is caused by something that I know has nothing to do with it, or by somebody. This is only further aggravation, and possible injury to someone else—and I have no right either to injure myself or someone else. Also it is silly to employ Pollyanna techniques and deny it, and go about saying, "Heigh ho, I feel great, life is lovely." No—*I feel depressed*—at this moment. Shift down to a lower gear and operate at that level—gently. Being just as kind to myself as I would be to someone else who felt the same way. It will go away, and much sooner, for being recognized. What if circumstances prevent such solicitous nursing? Even better. The very action of having to work, to keep an appointment, is fuel to burn up the mood.

If I am honest with myself I will not try to run other people's lives. I avoid the phrase "The trouble with you is——" like poison. How do I know what their troubles are? I can see a great deal of their problems, but it is only the small section of the iceberg that shows above the water. I will listen to them if they want to talk about it, because talking is good, it ventilates, it lets a person hear himself. But to advise, no. Suggest, possibly. Even if solicited, "I want your advice," I prefer to simply throw out some suggestions, because the phrase "I want your advice" so often means "I want you to tell me that what I am doing is right." If I give advice I may simply be trying to make a person into something he is not, telling him to do something that is impossible for him, making him "nearer to *my* heart's desire."

I see people differently than I used to. I used to slip on my mask quickly, and from behind it judge them, evaluate them, come to quick decisions as to whether I liked them or not. Poking them into little pigeonholes of being "wonderful" or "phony" or "interesting" or "dull." Liking them if they seemed to like me, hating them if they didn't or, worse, squirming in misery if someone looked too keenly at me, understanding me. Now I have relaxed, my mask does not conceal me. It is worn as clothing or adornment. I do not fuss with it, fight to keep it in place any more than I fuss with my clothes after I am dressed. I have time to see people, to listen to them, to find that they are just what they are, other human beings. Someone who likes a book I read or who doesn't like a book I read. Who makes a funny joke or a bad joke. Who has an inner life which none but God knows about, just as I have. Who has his troubles, his fears, his strange personal place of inner loneliness, just as I have. But we are in communication, and that is a kind of loving. And—watch it!—not necessarily *liking*. But it is easy to love someone when you accept him just as he is, as simply as one accepts the fact that the ocean is *there*, that it is what it is, and nothing more. All the little complexities of what a person says or doesn't say, whether it is stimulating or offensive or silly, are incidentals. If someone helps me, does something nice for me, I am grateful to the bottom of my heart. If someone hurts me, or my precious ego, accidentally or deliberately, or does something simply to *obtain* favors, I figure as closely as I can why: perhaps he needs to hurt in order to put himself "above" me, perhaps there is jealousy or envy, or any number of unhappy problems I can know nothing about. The little arrows bounce off, I say yea and nay and let it pass. If I can really help someone, do something that makes him feel better, if I can help him to help himself, I am twelve feet tall. I am the one who has received.

Not long ago at Universal Studios, I remember I was walking quickly into one of the big sound stages, made up, wearing one of the make-up department smocks, my hair still in pin curls, heading for my portable dressing room on the set, where I would dress and have my hair combed out. It was about eight forty-five in the morning, and there was rain in the air. A group of technicians were standing by the door, and we exchanged "good mornings," and one of them said, "Hold on there a minute—what are you so all-fired cheerful about at this time of the day?" I stopped and said, "Do I seem—cheerful?" And he replied, "Well, you sure are wearing a loud smile!"